Sheltered from
the Swastika

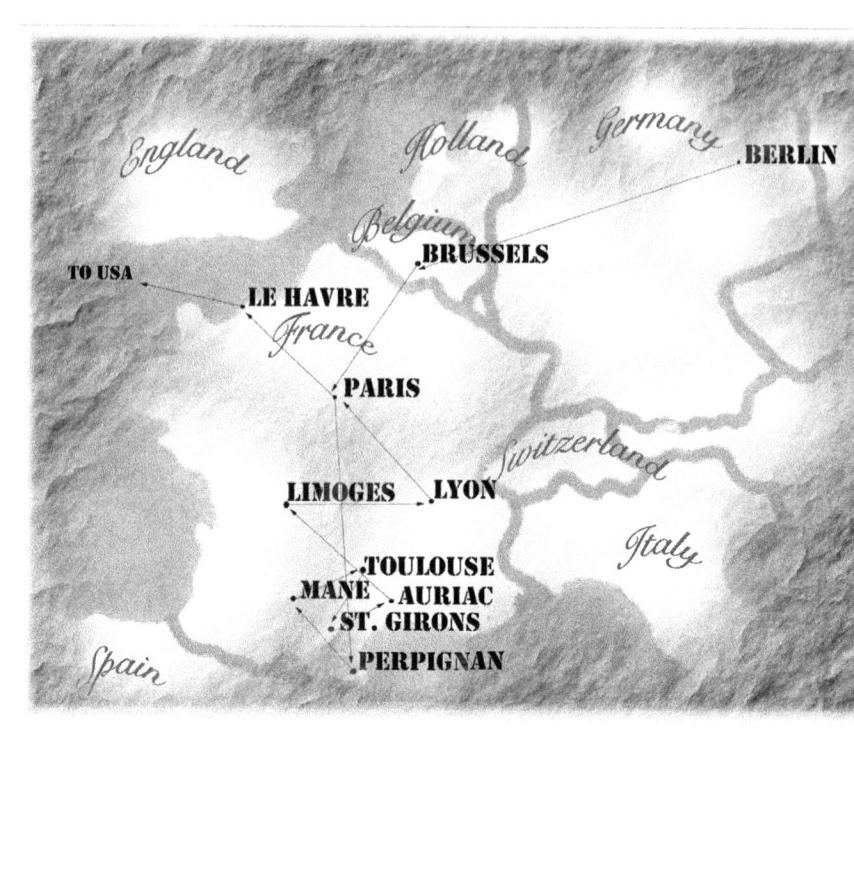

Sheltered from the Swastika

Memoir of a Jewish Boy's Survival amid Horror in World War II

PETER KORY

McFarland & Company, Inc., Publishers
Jefferson, North Carolina, and London

Frontispiece: *Map of Europe showing the author's journey from 1938 to 1948.*

Library of Congress Cataloguing-in-Publication Data

Kory, Peter, 1931–
    Sheltered from the swastika : memoir of a Jewish boy's survival amid horror in World War II / Peter Kory.
        p.   cm.
    Includes bibliographical references and index.

    ISBN 978-0-7864-7045-7
    softcover : acid free paper ∞

    1. Kory, Peter, 1931– — Childhood and youth. 2. World War, 1939–1945 — Personal narratives, Jewish. 3. Jewish children in the Holocaust — Biography. 4. Jewish refugees — Europe — Biography. 5. Escapes — Europe — History — 20th century. 6. Berlin (Germany) — Biography. 7. Brussels (Belgium) — Biography. 8. France — Biography. 9. World War, 1939–1945 — Underground movements — France. 10. Immigrants — United States — Biography. I. Title.
    DS134.42.K67A3 2012   940.53'18092 — dc23   [B]   2012010112

British Library cataloguing data are available

© 2012 Peter Kory. All rights reserved

No part of this book may be reproduced or transmitted in any form or by any means, electronic or mechanical, including photocopying or recording, or by any information storage and retrieval system, without permission in writing from the publisher.

Front cover: Passport photo of Peter Kory used for immigration to the United States; background © 2012 Shutterstock

Manufactured in the United States of America

McFarland & Company, Inc., Publishers
  Box 611, Jefferson, North Carolina 28640
    www.mcfarlandpub.com

To Joyce, my wife of nearly 20 years. As a Baby Boomer, she did not experience the Second World War. But, having lived with me while I wrote this memoir, and having been forced into indentured servitude as the editor of my prose, she feels that she has fought the war, albeit vicariously, and suffered the trials and tribulations of all the events related in this book.

Joyce has been more than a partner in this undertaking. As my soul mate, she is part of my inspiration and motivation to produce a work that would bridge the generations and yet remain relevant to both my generation, which is memory-based, and hers, which is anchored in the realities of today. As I am probably anachronistically challenged, she has emerged as the indispensable guardian of the book's flow of events, its consistency with the facts and the logic of the circumstances. Without her contribution, the text would emerge as an incomprehensible maze of events without cohesion and continuity. In many respects, she is really a co-author and has earned that credit.

In the process of correcting errors and inconsistencies, we spent hours and oftentimes days discussing the events that flesh out the book. When the final product emerged and we read it through from the beginning, Joyce was moved to tears by the emotional content in many of the passages. This made me realize how profoundly the book affected her, and why it is really hers as much as mine.

Table of Contents

Acknowledgments ix
Preface 1

Chapter 1	5	Chapter 11	95
Chapter 2	15	Chapter 12	106
Chapter 3	28	Chapter 13	117
Chapter 4	39	Chapter 14	126
Chapter 5	49	Chapter 15	137
Chapter 6	60	Chapter 16	150
Chapter 7	64	Chapter 17	158
Chapter 8	69	Chapter 18	165
Chapter 9	82	Chapter 19	179
Chapter 10	89	Chapter 20	188

Epilogue 195
Bibliography 217
Index 219

Acknowledgments

This book would not have been possible without the help, encouragement and historical knowledge of family members, friends — both those from my past and the more recent ones — and very special organizations like the American Red Cross which was so nobly dedicated to helping Holocaust victims and their families.

Beginning with the latter, I want to thank the French and the American Red Cross "Holocaust and War Victim Tracing and Information Service" for confirming the death of my parents at Auschwitz, and for providing me with copies of the original transport manifest and related documents identifying the train on which my parents were taken away, and other information regarding their deportation.

I also want to thank my wonderful children, Erich and Lisa, and my grandchildren, Dana, Avery, Ari and Ross, for their patience in awaiting the completion of this work. I hope it will help provide them with a broader insight into the life their grandpa led so long ago.

Further acknowledging members of my family, I want to mention my cousin Aviva Schmelzinger. She is the undisputed doyenne of my family in matters of recollection. When Joyce and I visited her in 2009 in Jerusalem, where she has been living for many years, she filled a huge void in my knowledge of my family's history. Almost 90 years old at that time, she met us in the King David hotel with photos, stories and recollections that have significantly and uniquely enriched the substance of this book. Aviva's existence came to light after Michal Lublin Frostig, a second cousin who moved to the U.S. from Israel, did online research until she located me. She, together with her sister Ronit Lublin Glassberg, set out to educate me about my family, contributing immeasurably to the book. They not only reviewed text involving the history of my family, but also expanded it considerably by elaborating on facts about the family I knew nothing about.

Acknowledgments

In 1942, when I was hiding in the little village of Mane, southwest of Toulouse, I had an intimate friend named Robert Soula. We lost touch over the gulf of time and distance. It wasn't until after the turn of the millennium that we found each other again. I want to thank him for making it possible for me to more accurately recount the details of the period when I last lived with my parents. I suppose I should also thank him for reminding me of some of the more embarrassing events that could only have happened to 11-year-old boys determined to find some joy in their lives during a terrifying war.

This is also the place where I must acknowledge, posthumously in all too many cases, the many to whom I owe my life. First and foremost, there is the de Bonnefoy family. As a group and as individuals, they are the heroes of my existence, as are the many others who, at their own peril, assured my safety during the Nazi occupation.

Shifting to the here and now, I want to give thanks to those who reviewed the manuscript. We asked several friends who had expressed an interest in reading it to make suggestions for improvements. While I won't attempt to meticulously reflect all the comments received as a result of this review, I do want to express my gratitude to everyone who participated in this effort. I would like to single out a few who I feel went above and beyond.

First, a very special thanks to our wonderful friend Nancy Denison, not only because of her talent for picking out syntax, punctuation and capitalization flaws, but for her remarkable perception. She identified a fatal flaw early on in the writing of the manuscript, commenting that the story lacked emotion. I had told the story in a matter-of-fact style, keeping my feelings and emotions to myself, in the same way I had managed to survive all my life. But clearly, this was no way to write a memoir, or to live out the rest of my days. She triggered a rewrite of the manuscript, one replete with details that humanized the events.

Next, our friends Tom and Becky Matkov — Becky, with her schoolteacher precision, found the typos; Tom, a West Pointer and former Army ranger who is now a successful real estate lawyer, was remarkably thorough in his reading. I never appreciated the depth of his interest and knowledge in history, but I am grateful for it, as he challenged me to do additional research on several aspects of the war.

Another history buff, our dear South African friend, Stan Berger (an accountant with a large firm in Johannesburg), encouraged me to include more historical references. He also triggered many discussions about the meaning of being Jewish during our visits with him. Well, we did not settle the matter, but I want to thank Stan for forcing me to tackle the subject with far greater sensitivity than I might have otherwise.

Joyce and Danny Klein offered very interesting comments, as did my old friend Malcolm Miller Jones and his wife, Ruth Ann, who tortured their minds over the significance of the word "kismet," thus engendering hours of discussion about the meaning of the book. Sergio Cardenas and I debated the importance of Albertine, the cook at the Auriac Château, as a character in the book. I argued that life there was the ultimate proof that, no matter how dire the circumstances, there is always a deep cushion of good will and warmth in the midst of adversity. Life in the château had amply demonstrated that to me, and I am indebted to Sergio for making me appreciate this.

And how can I ever express my gratitude to Carol and Bill Crowe? They not only read the manuscript, they showed up at my door with a Lionel electric train set for my 80th birthday! At long last, I have that train set I lusted for since I was a kid!

Finally, an immense debt of gratitude is owed to those who made the publishing of this book a reality. Early in the writing of this book, our cherished friends, Marsha and Malcolm Witt, mentioned that they had a friend whose books are published by a company specializing in non-fiction, and thought we should meet him. One chilly fall evening, they introduced us to John Stewart. In addition to being one of the more memorable characters I've ever met, John is a prolific and accomplished author. To Marsha, Malcom and John, know that Joyce and I are forever in your debt for helping make my dream become a reality.

Preface

While I live in the reality of today,
I will always hear the echoes of my past.

My name is Peter Kory. In the short span of 17 years — the first 17 years of my life — I was also known as Peter Korytowski, Pierre Engglenger and Pierre Boivin, depending on who was hunting me at the time. This is the tale of those 17 years, which encompass that mid–20th century calamity known as the Second World War. It is the story of my fate, my fortune ... my kismet.

As I finish writing about these long ago war years, I have just passed my 80th birthday and 2011 is well underway. I retired some years ago, after a long career in architecture, city planning, urban development and real estate entrepreneurial adventures. I enjoyed these careers in Cincinnati, New York City, New York State and about a dozen other communities scattered around the Northeastern United States. In the process, I've gained some official honors as well as recognition from distinguished peers and colleagues. I also had the opportunity to learn the mechanics and behavior of both the private and public sectors of our culture; in fact, I became an expert in maneuvering inside the far more subtle and complex universe of the quasi-public sector. This is where public benefits must be achieved within the constraints of legal, legislative, financial, political and economic realities ... but that's a subject better saved for another book.

I now enjoy a very secure, peaceful and comfortable lifestyle on a small island paradise called Key Biscayne, a mere seven miles away from downtown Miami. The latter has become a gigantic Latino-influenced, multicultural gateway city. It is effectively a Latin-American capital and a mecca for visitors from all over the world. The once-prominent English language has been joined, if not overwhelmed, by a wealth of dialects and tongues from every corner of our planet. The proximity of the Caribbean, Mexico, and Central and South America make for a wonderful mix of Latin cultures. Many consider the city the defacto cultural center of the Americas. Evidence of this can be seen in the permanent additions to Miami's previously mostly transient winter population. People from all over the world have moved here to enjoy our climate and, in the process, they enrich our culture. This is especially true in our variety of foods and cuisines.

I live here with my wife, Joyce, a former high-powered banker who retired young enough to enjoy life and our many travel adventures to the fullest, after having achieved great success. She has been my love and constant companion for more than 18 years now, after my second wife, Ruth Batchelor, succumbed to multiple myeloma, a particularly nasty bone marrow–destroying cancer. Ruth had enjoyed a brilliant career as a journalist and songwriter. She wrote several songs for Elvis Presley, among others, and headed the influential Los Angeles Film Critics Association for some years. She certainly had a way with words. I will always remember how she used her rapier-like sense of humor to place serious situations into their proper perspective. An unforgettable example of this talent was evidenced in a sardonic pun that came out of her mouth just a few days before she died when, at a small party of intimate friends, she announced, "While I may be here today, I'll be gone to marrow!"

I have two children, both from my first marriage: Erich, named after my father, and Lisa, named after my mother. Lisa has four fabulous children and this, magically, makes me "Grandpa"! My first wife, Marianne, became a lawyer after she raised Erich and Lisa. We both graduated from CCNY at roughly the same time but, unlike me, with my predilection for bad scholarship, she graduated magna cum laude and was honored as the first woman in City College to be inducted into Phi Beta Kappa.

Writing this book has made me realize just how much influence my culture and my ancestry have had on my life, the way I've lived it and what I've become. What occurred during those first 17 years of my life has given shape to who I am and has influenced my beliefs. I find it natural to link most things in my current life to my background and experiences. The fears and deprivations of the war, for example, have filled me with a huge, albeit unhealthy, respect for food. I consider it a deadly sin to leave anything on my plate or to throw out food or leftovers, something I simply could never bring myself to do. Joyce has had some luck in curing me of this predilection

Preface

by referring to anything I leave in the refrigerator too long as one of my "science projects," particularly when they start to sprout mold or "long green hair."

My European education had a profound effect on the seriousness with which I approached my years in college and the intensity with which I focused on my career. I tend to be conservative, though not in a partisan political sense, and I am obsessively methodical in the way I try to address technical problems. I am generally uninvolved in organized sports and other activities I consider trivial, while nevertheless using games and experiments with unorthodox solutions when solving problems. Although I have joined clubs and fraternities, I am usually a wallflower when it comes to dancing or participating in group activities which include loud sounds and reveling. But I am certainly no misanthrope, as I thoroughly enjoy conviviality and entertaining. It's just that I prefer serious conversation.

Similarly, the decisions made by my parents, and their parents before them, tended to be influenced by the history and political climate of the time in which they lived. As such, they have provided a context for my story. That is why I have spent what some people might consider too much time detailing their lives and the history of their time. To me, to omit this part of the story would be inconceivable for three very important reasons. First, there is so little left of my family that every effort must be made to preserve anything — photos, writings, mementos — that can help recreate the past. I hope this book will serve as a tangible contribution to this effort. Second, without a description of my family, my experiences could not be explained, nor could I show how they fit into the matrix of events of those confusing times. Finally, this memoir is an invitation to those who read it to add to, correct or edit its content so that it can endure as a living document that can be updated to more perfectly serve its purpose.

Having said all that, the intent of this book is to focus on what life was like during the German occupation of France and how I found my way through the turmoil and the uncertainties which, many decades and two wars later, Robert McNamara so eloquently described as "the fog of war" in his book of the same name. This memoir was not written as a plea for redemption or atonement to assuage my survivor's guilt, but merely as yet another contribution to a time capsule, which reminds us of the world-shattering event known as the Second World War.

While my story parallels those of all too many others who were in similar circumstances, it differs in one important respect. Many memoirs tend to arouse sympathy, evoke pity, outrage and remorse, and wallow in the pain, suffering and misery of the war. Because I have always had an optimistic, almost naïve and, sometimes, even a humorous outlook on the events I encountered, I saw my experiences as adventures rather than ordeals, perhaps because I knew no other life for comparison. Taken together, these events make up a story similar to Voltaire's 1759 novel, *Candide*. Voltaire, a giant of French literature famous for his biting satires and his profound cynicism about society, wrote of the adventures of Candide, who believed that his world was the best of all possible worlds, one where everything that occurred was for the best. Voltaire's sinister satire was the realization that this was not true, and that to believe it would unfailingly lead to disaster.

Unlike Voltaire, I was not accompanied by cynicism through the war. Rather, like Candide, I have always managed to find a very personal niche of comfort from which to face adversity. In fact, I have always considered myself an extraordinarily lucky individual, even while surviving some fairly cruel turns of events. And, fortunately for me, my story has a better ending. The dominant theme of my life has always been *survival*—often in the midst of very confusing and dire circumstances. As such, my story describes one life among so many with similar experiences and, in the process, adds to the treasury of memories ofS the Second World War.

My tale is bracketed by two events in my life that I find unforgettable. The earlier took place in 1932. I was less than two years old when I experienced what I can only describe as a prescient encounter with Berlin's Brandenburg Gate. My tale ends in 1948 when the S.S. *Mauretania*, having brought me from the port of Le Havre in France to New York, sailed past the Statue of Liberty in New York Harbor, signaling the start of a new life on a new continent. While the encounter with the Gate filled me with undefined and unexplained fear and dread, the statue in the harbor overwhelmed me with hope and expectations. The time in between is what this book is all about—flight from the evolving persecution in Germany, escape from the Stukas and *Blitzkrieg* in Belgium, the search for my imprisoned father, changing identities, flight from discovery, escape gone wrong, a new life and a new family in a château in France, coming face to face with Hitler's dreaded SS, being kidnapped for religious reasons by well-meaning Zionist zealots, deprivations in postwar orphanages, the court battle over my future ... and through it all, kismet has been both my guardian and my nemesis.

Chapter 1

"The Jews here [bei uns] will be annihilated [vernichtet]"
(Adolf Hitler, January 21, 1939).

And thus, I was sentenced to death before my eighth birthday. My parents may have understood it at the time, but I wouldn't comprehend its meaning until much later. Under that death sentence, in the span of a few years, my family would be diminished to virtual extinction and scattered in a postwar world like lost and scattered pieces of a tragic jigsaw puzzle.

The adventure started for me seven years before Hitler's pronouncement, with a mindless moment of inexplicable terror. Hitler was assuming the chancellorship of Germany, but I was barely aware of life around me. Nonetheless, on that particular day, I experienced what would become my first indelible memory, and it would haunt me all of my life. It was in Berlin, circa 1932. I was more than a year old, but not quite two. My mother was wheeling me in my baby carriage as we passed under one of the imposing arches of the Brandenburg Gate, Berlin's last remaining city gate. The gate has always been one of the main symbols of Berlin and Germany, both in peacetime and in war. It occupies a strategic location at the entry point of the Unter den Linden Boulevard and the Pariser Platz. At one time, Pariser Platz led to the city palace of the Prussian monarchy. The gate consists of 12 Doric columns forming five passageways. On top of the gate is the quadriga, the chariot drawn by four horses driven by Victoria, the Roman goddess of victory. But beyond its classic baroque and neo–Palladian architecture, beyond the grandiose scale of the monument, the Brandenburg Gate is really a mass of contradictions.

On the one hand, in the late 18th century, King Frederick II of Prussia commissioned it as a symbol of peace. With the rise of nationalism, peace

Peter Kory at Brandenburg Gate (circa 1932).

was clearly not a passion for Kaiser Wilhelm II and his martial propensities, so the perception of the gate as a symbol of peace morphed into one designed to inspire heroic fervor and national pride. The ultimate blow to any idea that the gate might be a symbol of peace occurred when the Nazis claimed it as their unifying symbol.

When I encountered the gate on that day in 1932, I was struck by an irrational panic. I was crying with the unconscious desperation of the helpless. I was gripped by a horrible dread that transcended reason or emotion. I realize now that I was never aware of my existence until that moment. Then suddenly, I was not only aware of my existence, but of how fragile it was! The famous philosophical statement thought to have been originated by Plato, Aristotle or the mathematician René Descartes, who is most often identified with it, "Cogito ergo sum" ("I think, therefore I am") best reflects what I feel when I recall this first memory of dread and panic at the gate. It has stayed with me all these years, welded to my being as a prescient yet unarticulated message of how it would affect my life.

When I think about the earthshaking events that followed — the upheavals in Germany, the terror regime that killed six million Jews, the scattering of so many families to the far corners of the earth — I can't help but reflect on the fact that, no matter what effect these events had on the

Chapter 1

Brandenburg Gate.

world, they did not change the Brandenburg Gate. It has not budged and, to this day, continues to stand as a silent witness to events around it. It remains a stone sentinel, affirming the stirrings of the nations that surround it with blithe detachment. I suppose that is traditionally what monuments do; they are magnificent calls to glory. But, in the end, they turn a stony heart to all who act out the spirit of their symbolism. It would be years after my encounter with the gate before its real significance in my life would dawn on me. The gate was not Germany extending a welcome mat of peace. Quite the opposite, it was an invitation for us and so many others to get out ... and to do so forever!

It wasn't the irrational panic attack I experienced under the pillars of the gate that propelled my family into the exodus from Germany. Rather, my parents had already felt the drumbeat of the events that would follow. Indeed, it was the Nazification of Germany and the approaching perfect storm — a heavy dose of brutal anti–Semitism and a national economy devastated by the First World War blended in a single cauldron — that yanked my parents from the fatherland.

My family had lived in Berlin in relatively innocent serenity since the turn of the 20th century. They watched as Germany adapted to its new constitution, established at Weimar on July 31, 1919. In the process, Germany made epic efforts to manage the fledgling new government known as the Weimar Republic. The diplomatic dances of the nations and the pressure cooker of geo-political tensions had exploded into the First World War apocalypse. A begrudging peace treaty was finally sanctified in Versailles, while Germany obsessively groped for the proper constitutionally established form of democracy. As the country reeled under the hardships of the First World War, the German people, embittered by the humiliating terms of the Versailles Treaty, staggered under the draconian financial burden imposed by reparation payments. This provided the basis for the German military and industrial establishments to undermine the fragile Weimar Republic, using it as a scapegoat for the many postwar problems and hardships that had to be faced and endured. And then, of course, to complete this plethora of political miseries, gargantuan inflation gripped the country.

The causes of the inflation were complex. One trigger, according to Isaac Asimov's *History of the World*, emanated from a post–Versailles side treaty between Italy and Germany that raised fears that Germany might breach the weaponry limits imposed by Versailles. France expressed serious security concerns over this and proceeded to occupy the Ruhr Valley. The Germans retaliated with work stoppages and other job actions. This labor strife was reputedly tolerated, and perhaps aided, by the Weimar Republic. Printing a seemingly unrestrained flow of currency without regard to economic impact, the German Treasury directly supplied the money for these activities. As a consequence, this became one, but by no means the only, factor that set off the inflation, which soon spiraled out of sight. By the end of 1923, one American dollar was worth four trillion German marks! My parents often spoke of situations where prices could double or triple in the time that it took to enter and leave a store. Banknotes took more space than the goods they purchased, and no respite seemed to be in sight. The inflation ruined and impoverished Germany's middle class, thus adding fuel to the public anger and frustrations that prevailed in the fatherland. These circumstances left Germany ripe for the emergence of Hitler, Mussolini and Fascism. By 1925, Hitler had finished the jail sentence he had earned in the wake of the 1923 Munich Beer Hall Putsch. While serving his term, he wrote *Mein Kampf,* the manifesto, which, by 1930, was destined to infect Germans in plague-like proportions. The book was the bible of Nazi doctrine and inspired much of the nation to espouse its precepts. It was a time when the aged General von Hindenberg became Germany's president of the Republic; a time when Erich Maria Remarque wrote his anti-war novel *All Quiet on the Western Front;* and a time when the most popular show in town was Kurt Weil's depression-inspired musical, *Three Penny Opera.* It was a time of swirling tensions, when the last war was far from forgotten and the prelude to the next one was in motion. The doves and the hawks, the new order and the old, the right and the left elements of the German culture, the pacifists and the militarists, all had irreconcilable differences. All these conflicting socio-political crosscurrents had to be reconciled in the middle of monumental economic agonies.

By 1930, the economic and political upheavals that Germany experienced in the 1920s coalesced into a singularity. They had created irresistible pressures for a new order, and that would eventually lock the country in the iron grip of National Socialism, the National Socialist German Worker's Party's totalitarian ideology more commonly known as Nazism, which was embraced by Adolf Hitler. The movement had captured the hearts and souls of Germans everywhere. Throughout all the economic and political turmoil, my parents had ignored the ever-darkening clouds of anti–Semitism that were gathering momentum. Towards the end of the 1920s, however, the ideology of the Third Reich, inspired by the philosophies that Friedrich Nietzsche promulgated in the 1880s (or, more accurately, through their interpretation by his Nazi sister during the 20th century), became maliciously popular.

Understanding the relationship between the Third Reich and Nietzsche will challenge one's intellectual capacities. While Nietzsche considered Christianity to be "the one great curse," thundered against democracy and parliaments, preached the will to power, praised war and proclaimed the coming of the master race and the superman, he hated anti–Semitism and wrote that the Germans "have no conception how vile they are" ... not exactly proclaiming them to be the master race. Nevertheless, I always recall him as being identified with the foundations used sometime later to rationalize National Socialism and the Nazi culture.

Ben Macintyre, a British author and journalist, provides an interesting insight into how the philosophies of Nietzsche were intertwined with the moods of the times. He is probably best known for the novel *The Man Who Would Be King*. He wrote an article entitled "Nietzsche and His Nazi Sister," which was published in *The Times* on March 28, 2008. The following is an excerpt from that article:

> Two gravestones stand side by side in the churchyard of the little village of Röcken, south of Leipzig: one belongs to Friedrich Nietzsche, one of the greatest and most misunderstood philosophers; the other marks the grave of his sister Elisabeth, a lifelong anti–Semite who hijacked her brother's writings after his death and used them to serve the cause of Nazism, leaving a stain on his philosophy that has never been fully erased.

Prophetically, before insanity struck Nietzsche down in 1889 at the age of 44, he lived in fear of being misunderstood. "Above all," Nietzsche wrote in *Ecce Homo*, "do not mistake me for someone else." Macintyre describes Nietzsche as "a conservative, an elitist, and an aphorist of brilliance championing individual greatness in the midst of mediocrity. His writing is explosive and apocalyptic, dense and complex, and often shocking in its violence." But, as Macintyre stresses, "Nietzsche was no Nazi. He vigorously opposed German Nationalism, as he rejected all mass movements; he had no time for ideologues, mocked the notion of a Teutonic master race and loathed anti–Semitism in all its forms." Nietzsche believed that his sister was "morally bloated" and "a vengeful anti–Semitic goose." Further, Macintyre declares, "Nietzsche's sister, by contrast, was thus an enthusiastic Fascist," concluding that she "set about transforming her brother, now irretrievably insane, into a symbol of her own twisted philosophy." She edited his works, wrote her own prejudiced versions of his life, and gathered his rejected jottings and published them as if they were real books, most notably *Will to Power*, which would be adopted as a sort of totalitarian bible.

These were far from easy times for my parents, yet they were preoccupied with an even more significant matter. My mother, who was 33 years old, was pregnant. Although they had wanted a child for a while, everybody agreed that it was really not a good time. No indeed, this was not the ideal time for me to be born — between two world wars, some 12 years after the Treaty of Versailles was signed. I was introduced into a

Chapter 1

world that was quite different from that which had greeted my parents at the end of the Victorian era. Nevertheless, on July 29, 1931, I came into this world in a Berlin hospital, 18 months before Adolf Hitler's assumption of the German chancellorship.

It was, to say the least, a difficult and perilous birth. I evidently gave my mother such a hard time that, after the delivery was painfully completed, it was determined that I would never be burdened with brothers or sisters. In reality, my mother had a heart condition and this, coupled with the difficult birth, was the cause of my hallowed only child status. While it stands to reason that it was my mother's health, not my birth, that made the event so difficult, I have always carried an undefined sense of guilt, wondering if it might have been that I, through my abominable womb behavior, caused the heart condition, but we shall never know.

My status as an only child stands at the root of some entirely predictable, but less than endearing, characteristics that have stayed with me all my life. At least, I'd like to think this was the cause. The fact is, as an only child, I grew up never having to share anything. I was spoiled rotten and, as to being the center of my parents' universe, well, *C'est Moi*, after all, I was irreplaceable! While I earnestly tried to act against these innately selfish instincts in order to comply with the pressures that polite society exerted on me, they would always prevail. And, like a stubborn rubber band, no matter how I might try, I would always snap back, making it possible for me to resume my exalted position at the center of the universe. As a child, I felt that I was the most important commodity around. I, and only I, mattered. I guess this is what is known as a strong survival instinct, an instinct that no doubt saved my young life on many occasions as I navigated through a Nazi-infested France with the ever-present feeling that collaborators lurked at every corner.

Knowing that this outrageous sense of self is clearly not a virtue, I have tried to mitigate or, at the very least, disguise the problem. Ultimately, however, the real me, the ego, always managed to emerge. Sometimes this occurred with unanticipated results. One such instance, much, much later in life, was the political advice given to me by one of my professional *consiglieri*—to always use the word "we" instead of "I." Alas, much as I tried, it wasn't long before my "we" was interpreted as the "Royal we," and this made things even worse.

For my mother, the consequence of the enormous amount of parental doting required by my standing as an only child translated into a fierce protective instinct. Justified or not, I found this passion to assure my survival so intrusive that it was smothering. It affected virtually every living moment of life with my parents as we moved from Germany to Belgium and later to France. It was not until many years later, after much wear and tear and a well-rounded 40-plus years of a professional and entrepreneurial career filled with exhilarating successes and sobering failures, that I acquired a respectable amount of humility. Later, when I retired, I found that I was even able to enjoy the subordination of my ego to my wife's brilliant banking career.

Shortly after I was born, the political and philosophical foundations of the Third Reich had acquired such popularity in the homes of the mainstream population as well as in the streets and public places that a peaceful life for a Jewish family was no longer possible — not only in Berlin, but throughout Germany. Life there had reached the point where financial survival was impossible. No one would hire or deal with Jews. More importantly, the streets were no longer safe for Jews, where the civil authorities aided and abetted increasingly open brutality.

The Great Depression, felt throughout the world, struck Germany most harshly. There were over six million people unemployed. These increasingly difficult times led to the strengthening of the extremists, particularly Hitler's Nazi party. Bands of louts and delinquents, who made common cause with the party and its philosophy, found it especially easy to blame everything on the Jews and the Versailles Treaty. More broadly, the political balance as a whole had shifted. In 1928, there had been only 12 Nazis out of a total membership of 491 in the Reichstag, which served as Germany's popular assembly. By 1930, with the Great Depression in full swing, there were 107 Nazi members. By the 1932 election, votes for the Nazi party had climbed from 800,000 out of about 30 million cast, to 6.5 million. By that time, the Nazis held 230 seats in the Reichstag — nearly 50 percent. The 85-year-old President Hindenburg, unable to garner a reliable majority in the Reichstag, suffered three quick, successive resignations of chancellors — Heinrich Bruening, Franz von Papen and Kurt von Schleicher. With all the economic and political turmoil as well as the wide-ranging level of public dissatisfaction, Hindenburg asked Adolf

Hitler to assume the chancellorship. Hitler's acceptance triggered the beginning of a reign of terror that led to the Third Reich.

The term Reich evokes, and may have found its roots in, the historical reference to the First Reich, the Holy Roman Empire of the Middle Ages, and the Second Reich, another form of empire under the reign of Kaiser Wilhelm and Bismarck which fostered the titanic German unification undertaking, spanning the years from 1871 to 1918. The Third Reich took roots amid a suspension of all civil liberties, control of the streets by Nazi storm troopers and extreme oratorical violence.

In his books, *The Rise and Fall of the Third Reich* and *The Nightmare Years*, William L. Shirer tells of the collapse of civil society in the Reich's early years. Hundreds of thousands of *Sturmabteilungen* (uniformed rowdies and thugs), also referred to as SA, storm troopers and brown shirts, took to the streets. Sadistic and brutal, these storm troopers in their jackboots and shabby brown uniforms ruled under specific instructions from Hitler. Shirer writes: "Hitler had insisted the storm troopers were to be a political and not a military force. They were to furnish the physical violence, the terror by which the party could bludgeon its way to political power."

The storm troopers roamed the streets in gangs, on foot or in trucks, attacking and sometimes arresting citizens who were taken to SA dungeons for torture. These were Hitler's original street-brawlers and their venality fell heavily on Jews. They painted the Star of David on shops and businesses with great strokes of yellow paint in order to warn "good" Aryan Germans not to go there. These were the streets of German cities in the early 1930s and the tactics worked to destroy opposition to Hitler. Ultimately, these circumstances induced the Reichstag to grant Hitler dictatorial powers that tossed Germany into a nightmare world of paranoia and legalized brutality. This fell heaviest on the Jews, who were subject to systematic harassment, theft, violence, imprisonment, torture and death. The atmosphere for Jews was perversely toxic and increasingly menacing.

Once the brown shirts' terror tactics had accomplished his goals, Hitler set about destroying his creation. The SA had acquired such power that it threatened its own creator and had to be destroyed. Shirer points out, "He did not need it ... it was a raucous rabble that only embarrassed him." Hitler had a more efficient replacement, an elite unit of superior young men who were controlled, dedicated and fiercely loyal to the *Führer*.

No more rabble, no shabby brown shirts, but a menacing jackbooted brutal replacement, the SS, or *Schutzstaffel*. The black-coated SS storm troopers' aims were more heinous than their predecessors'.

With the rise of National Socialism, the ideology of the Nazi party and the unraveling of the Weimar Republic, our family, like many other Jewish families, split into many pieces, leaving Berlin and Germany to join the exodus for foreign havens deemed safer and more comfortable for Jews than the fatherland. Palestine, Holland, Belgium, France, Romania and, of course, America would give safe haven to various members of my family over the course of the next decade. When the war was over and it was finally possible to try to bring the pieces together again, not much of my family remained. Many simply had disappeared without a trace, some had died from natural causes and others had perished in concentration camps. Various search efforts by well-motivated organizations proved futile. Time and events had taken their toll.

My parents abandoned or, to express it more accurately, escaped from their home in Berlin to start a new life in Brussels. As we left the Berlin station, our senses were numbed by the repetitious sounds of cast-iron wheels on steel rails and by the kaleidoscope of views that were unrolling past the window of the train compartment in which we were sitting. It was not long before my mother sank into a contemplative mood and she was drawn away from the anxieties and dangers of the escape and into thoughts of the events that had led to our current situation.

Chapter 2

My parents died in Auschwitz, but I'm getting ahead of myself....

Her name was Lily, and she was short, pretty and prematurely gray. She was not given to heroic projects and dramatic accomplishments. In a country where cleanliness and sanitation were inherent and obsessive national traits, my mother dedicated her professional life to health work and childcare. She thus represented a double threat to anything that interfered with the German mania for order and cleanliness. Naturally, this made her the undisputed guardian of the family's sanitation protocol. Hands had to be constantly washed, public toilets were anathema to good health and should be avoided, and food had to be scrubbed, then scrubbed again. In fact, cooking in general was a surgical enterprise. I had to be particularly careful about touching anything in public places, which had been adjudicated as dirty and full of God knows what sort of microbes, germs, bacteria and the like. Handrails were prime suspects, and one could never be safe from the mysterious ailments they harbored. But there was a lot more to

My mother, Lily Neustadt Korytowski (circa 1929).

my mother than her obsession with cleanliness. I will always think of her as the "boss of the family." She was always the reasonable counterpoise to my father's flights of fantasy and his propensity for involvements in outlandish plans that reflected his adventurous spirit and ambitions. Once they were together, they became two halves of the whole.

A year or so younger than my father, she was born in 1898, as the 19th century was turning into the 20th. These were the waning days of the peace and stability known as the Victorian era. In the context of world history, it was a time when complex alliances were being hammered out, balances of power were weighed and national defense and security activities were being institutionalized. The murky shadows of a major war began to appear and anxieties over this started to intrude on life in Germany. Despite this malaise, my parents and their families witnessed an era of remarkable enlightenment. To cite a few examples, the Curies brought X-ray technology, Zeppelin built his dirigible airship, Diesel developed his engine, Behring developed a vaccine against tetanus and Max Planck created quantum theory, which signaled the arrival of modern physics and which was subsequently enthusiastically embraced by Einstein. Also not to be forgotten was Freud, with his genius making its way into our dreams and sexual proclivities.

The latter part of the 19th century saw a scientific revolution comparable to the one set off by Copernicus. It will also be remembered as an era of massive public works and major public enterprise. Water transport, whether by canal, river or across the seas, impacted all the major populations and industries. Empires with trading colonies and partners lay thousands of nautical miles apart on distant continents. Ships needed months to round Africa or South America to deliver or collect their goods. Anything that shortened those voyages made transport quicker and safer, as many routes traversed turbulent waters. Among other accomplishments, the Kiel Canal, started in 1887 and opened in 1895, shortened critical German canal traffic as well as eliminated the trip around Denmark for ships sailing from Baltic ports. A proposed rail line was started from Berlin to Baghdad in the Ottoman Empire. The world, and especially the British Empire, welcomed the completion of the Suez Canal, which cut the travel time from Europe to India and the Far East. In the American hemispheres, the digging of the Panama Canal promised to cut ship travel from the East

Coast of the United States to the western shores by more than half, eliminating the strenuous voyage around the southern tip of South America. With these achievements, the world shrank decidedly and competition between nations increased.

On the political front, England's Queen Victoria's 29-year-old grandson, Wilhelm II, ascended the German throne in 1888, becoming the Emperor Kaiser Wilhelm II and the king of Prussia, as Germany had not yet been unified into a single state. Contemporaneously, Britain proudly proclaimed, "The sun never sets over the British Empire." Peace became increasingly fragile throughout Europe. Yachting, once considered a gentlemanly, almost chivalrous kind of maritime sport, became a national rivalry between Britain and Germany. Pursued passionately by the Royals on both sides of the Channel, these avid yachtsmen were quite oblivious to the fact that their activities would ultimately grow into an arms race. As brilliantly described in Robert K. Massey's definitive tome on the subject, *Dreadnaught*, this rivalry between the Royals and their respective domains became part of the prelude to what would eventually blossom into the First World War.

Meanwhile, Germany's chancellor, Otto von Bismarck, was trying to unify the German states and create a new continental superpower. He preferred territorial supremacy to sea power, and eschewed the colonial ambitions of Britain, France and many other European nations. Instead, in the hallowed name of national security and defense, he created a pattern of alliances that included Austria-Hungary, Russia and Italy. But Kaiser Wilhelm, who by that time was better known as *"Der Kaiser,"* allowed these arrangements to lapse in 1890. France and Russia were by then acting together, Wilhelm II had alienated much of Europe with his imperious dreams of world power, or *Weltmacht*, and the British were diffident in dealing with Germany and the Kaiser. Germany was isolated and clearly vulnerable to the possibility of a two-front war. This was more than enough reason for this genetically bellicose nation to begin growing an industrial capacity to make war.

Perhaps there were no terrorists in those days, but there were anarchists and nihilists who, having turned violent, engendered their own brand of terrorism. The increasingly popular and martially inspiring music of Richard Wilhelm Wagner's operas about larger-than-life Germanic heroes like Siegfried and the glorious Valkyries on their galloping horses further added (probably without malicious intentions against the Jews) to the mix of nationalistic fervor that eased Germany into fertile territory for the spawning of anti–Semitism.

Long before the horrors of the Third Reich, anti–Semitism was already rampant throughout Europe. The infamous Dreyfus Affair, for example, sent a strong message. It involved a captain in the French army who happened to be a Jew. In 1894, he was assigned to the war ministry where a disreputable character, Ferdinand Esterhazy, was acting as a German spy. There was a leak in the ministry and Esterhazy forged a document that seemed to place the blame on Dreyfus. After an extensively publicized and notoriously unfair trial, Dreyfus, as a Jew, made a good scapegoat. He was found guilty and was condemned to life imprisonment on Devils Island off the coast of French Guiana. The verdict was very popular, and mobs gathered to howl against the Jews. Ultimately, justice prevailed. There was a retrial, Esterhazy was found guilty and Dreyfus was found guilty with extenuating circumstances. In the end, he was completely exonerated, with his honor fully restored.

Meanwhile, in 1897, Theodore Herzl organized the first Zionist congress in Basel, which later would evolve into the Knesset, the legislative branch of today's Israeli government. Part of the reason for its creation, beyond the urge for a Jewish homeland, was the rise in anti–Semitism. Volumes have been written on the subject, and it is not my purpose to document this trend here. There were many excuses given for the vilification of Jews in Germany at the end of the 19th century. To cite one example, there were some notorious financial scandals such as those related to the Panama Company fiasco. It reportedly involved Jewish bankers who, along with other money handlers, had lost some 1.5 billion francs that had been raised through a stock purchase lottery, with the proceeds earmarked for canal construction. The money was frittered away by mismanagement, cover-up bribes and misappropriations by scoundrels. In the end, the funds disappeared and were never found.

During the first decade of the 20th century, as my parents grew towards adulthood, war was not a dominant concern in Berlin, nor was it a matter of urgent concern in the rest of Europe. Nevertheless, tensions between the European nations increased, partly caused by the ambitions, paranoia and machinations of the leaders of the larger powers of that period. They seemed to be involved in an endless dance around green, felt-covered conference tables, where the nations took turns in bluffing and acting out brinksmanship scenarios while testing the issues of the day. Their behavior was portrayed sometime later in Kurt Jooss's famous 1932 anti-war ballet *The Green Table*. Jooss had it exactly right, except that this piece of hindsight was not performed until well after the end of the First World War!

By the summer of 1914, the tinderbox that had been smoldering in Europe eventually erupted into an uncontrollable conflagration of gargantuan proportions, when a Serbian assassin murdered the heir to the throne of Austria, the Archduke Francis Ferdinand. Austria-Hungary declared war on Serbia a month later, in July of 1914, and the cataclysmically disastrous chain reaction of human events reached its climax. The First World War began.

My mother's reveries on the train were suddenly interrupted by the sounds of a nearby commotion. Whistles were blowing; brakes were squealing; metal on metal, the train slowed and ultimately came to a full stop. We had reached the border out of Germany! When we joined in the exodus along with so many others in like circumstances, I was still in diapers. My parents had hoped that, in addition to their traditional function, my diapers would prove to be an effective way of hiding our jewelry and money from the border authorities, who did their best to search everything the emigrants had with them. We had to be ingenious if we were to avoid the confiscation of our worldly goods. And, indeed, my diapers provided the ideal way to do this. It was relatively easy and sufficiently disgusting to hide the family jewels in my well-soiled diapers, and the agents allowed us to pass without a major inspection. We had been extremely lucky; we were able to transport enough jewelry and money to set up housekeeping in Brussels. In just a few years' time, as Hitler and the Third Reich closed their death grip on Europe, this sort of smuggling would become impossible.

If my mother was the boss of the family, then my father was its guardian. Once the immediate border dangers receded in time and distance, my father could finally relax. His family would now be safe.

His name was Erich and he was dominated by artistic and creative passions. He was a large and very handsome man, exuding strength and bravery. He was fiercely protective of my mother. As a matter of fact, the only time I recall him losing his temper was on a train, when someone who seemed to be looking for an argument threatened my mother. Roaring like a lion, he jumped up, terrifying everybody. It was a side of him I never knew existed.

My father was capable of great deeds and accomplishments. He was also hopelessly gullible and tended to overpromise, lest someone's feelings might be hurt — traits that always got him in trouble with my mother, who would launch into endless tirades expounding her beliefs that, in the final analysis, the true character of human nature could not be trusted. But it was his hands that really spoke volumes about who he was. He was endowed with unusually long, sensitive fingers that seemed genetically evolved to dance on the keyboard of a piano. In fact, he was first, foremost and in the end, a musician with great talent.

My father had no interest in political activities. It is no surprise, therefore, that as a young man he eschewed the infamous academic pastime of fencing, called *Mensur* or *Pauker*, typically advocated by the more militant elements in the universities. *Mensur* was neither a duel nor a sport, but it does illustrate the sadistic nature of the Teutonic mentality of that time. It was a traditional way of training and imbuing character and personality. In a *Mensur* bout, there was no winner or loser. A chain mail shirt and gauntlets and padding on the throat and right arm protected fencers' bodies. However, little protected the head, only steel goggles with a nose guard. Fencing at arm's length, participants stood more or less in one place while trying to strike unprotected areas of their opponent's face and head. Flinching or dodging was not allowed, the goal being less to avoid injury than to stoically endure pain. The scar resulting from a hit was called a *Schmiss*, German for a mite, which was seen as a badge of honor. Hollywood certainly capitalized on this by endowing German villains with at least one facial scar. I am delighted to report that my father did not sport a *Schmiss*, and that he never felt that proof of his manhood depended on his performance in a *Mensur* ritual. He had a very different focus. When very young, he emerged as a piano virtuoso, preparing for a professional career in the field of music, like several members of his family. The most famous was my father's distant cousin, Joseph Schmidt.

Schmidt was a tenor of incredible fame throughout Germany. Because of his short stature, he was known as "The Tiny Man with the Great Voice" as well as "The Pocket Caruso." After a concert in May 1933, the press wrote: "...The voice of Joseph Schmidt is recorded in its full clarity and natural warmth ... the audience was delirious ... even Goebbels applauded enthusiastically."

Later articles reported that Goebbels was going to have him declared an "Honorary Aryan." Apparently, Goebbels had other, more pressing business, as Cousin Joseph died in 1938 of a heart attack in Switzerland, after fleeing from the Nazis and toiling in a Swiss labor camp. Although my father was Joseph Schmidt's contemporary, fate would intervene, assuring that he would never share the level of fame enjoyed by the "Pocket Caruso."

My parents' families could not avoid a cocoon-like outlook on a world that

My father, Erich Korytowski (circa 1929).

revolved almost entirely around a cosmopolitan life in Berlin. They did not stray far beyond home, family and friends. This reinforced a sense of security and a natural reluctance to abandon much of what they had always cherished. As such, they remained quintessentially German, living in blithesome unawareness of the progress, speed and ferocity of the oncoming upheaval. The anxiety and unease of war talk gave substance to the vague shadow of that war which they had felt during their earlier childhood. Remote and hardly noticeable events were occurring, and even a modern-day Nostradamus would not have discerned the broader patterns that were emerging in Europe. Nobody was, to put it in post 9/11 parlance, connecting the dots.

During this unsettled period, my parents grew from childhood to adolescence enjoying the comforts of the Berlin middle class, living near one another in their family nests. They shared the same values and friends, participating together in the same kinds of games and activities that intimate cultural relationships have a way of engendering. My parents, and indeed most of their family, considered their Jewish ancestry purely a matter of personal religious choice, not one of Divine intervention. They did not consider themselves Chosen People, endowed with special privileges handed down by biblical fiat since the dawn of civilization. Assimilation was the way my family got along in society.

They were a fairly cohesive family — all in one place, reasonably well to do, productive, with a clear sense of purpose, identity and belonging. Since organized religion played no part in their life, they did not say grace, observe special High Holidays, follow any dietary rules and were generally oblivious to any kind of religious orthodoxy. At the same time, they didn't reject the concept of God or the mysticisms that the subject engenders, nor did they dismiss the importance of maintaining a good conscience and in following the commandments ordained by so many of the world's religions. Indeed, it wasn't religion, political philosophy or an organized system of ethics that held them together. Their rituals transcended all that. The common bond that ultimately held them together was music. Many in the family enjoyed singing, and most were active in choirs and musical groups. Music somehow was always within ear range. It represented the soul and the metaphysical life of the family. As such, music and the enjoyment of it became their equivalent of religion.

My parents had met before my father was mobilized in the First World War, and they quickly became an inseparable couple. They enjoyed their early years together to the fullest, working and playing in a cosmopolitan Berlin. They were surrounded by an abundance of close friends who, despite the fact that they later pursued differing career paths, were a monolithic bunch determined to take on the challenges of adulthood with zeal and zest. They attended the same schools and shared pastoral outings, picnics and innocent games in the many parks and forests that still surround Berlin. If it is true that opposites attract, then it is not difficult to understand how my parents discovered each other within such a circle of friends, and eventually married.

My father was the dreamer and my mother, always the practical one. She always looked for security and safety. Caution was her mantra. My father tended to throw caution to the wind, acting on impulse and leaving the task of repairing any damage that might ensue for my mother to sort out. She always needed exhaustive proof before consenting to anything; in contrast, my father trusted everything and everyone implicitly. My mother wanted to prevent and heal; my father, to invent and build. Yet, it was through these dissimilarities that they complemented each other. In reality, they had a lot in common. They shared similar cultural roots, a passion for the arts, music in particular, but most importantly, they shared common social, political and religious values. Like the rest of their family, they shied away from politics. As such, they eschewed street demonstrations, parades, and other public displays of patriotic fervor by which the Germans liked to express their seemingly inborn nationalistic and militaristic instincts.

My parents, Lily Neustadt Korytowski and Erich Korytowski (Germany, circa 1925).

My father was on his way to a great musical career, performing in recitals more and more frequently, in front of more important audiences each time. He had just turned 17 at the start of the First World War. He had no idea that all of his professional aspirations as a concert pianist would soon be shattered. Nonetheless, a few short years later, he was drafted into the kaiser's army. Although he was an educated professional and considered officer material, according to the customs of the times he was forced to serve in the same way as all those mobilized through the draft — in the infamous infantry. And so, he found himself fighting in the mud and the trenches of a hideous war. His prospects for a music career would be brutally shattered and he would have to trade his dreams of artistic glory for a different and considerably less enjoyable kind.

During those sweet moments when I was allowed to cuddle in my parents' bed, my father related what trench warfare was like. He described what he had felt, when adrenaline overwhelmed his senses beyond all rational thought during the course of night assaults. His vivid narration of being herded toward the enemy's trenches was unforgettable. His vision was blurred by poisoned gas; the gas mask he had to wear blinded him further. The noise of flying debris, the blinding dance of searchlights, the merciless staccato of machine gun fire, and the whistling explosions of mortar shells and artillery panicked him. The mud on the battlefield was more than knee-deep, and hindered his relentless progress and that of his companions toward a destination that they hoped never to reach — the French trenches. Barbed wire was everywhere. Shell craters and other unknown obstacles pockmarked the landscape. The real horrors were the fallen soldiers, both German and French. My father stumbled over dead bodies, heard the screams of the dying and saw the wounded wallowing in a sea of toxic mud and poison gas. The way he described it, Dante's Inferno seemed like a walk in the park!

On other nights, he would tell me of his most heroic deed, the one that earned him the Iron Cross. His entire unit was trapped under fire inside a trench complex in an indefensible position. They were facing inevitable annihilation. However, because my father knew enough French to communicate with the enemy, he managed to negotiate surrender for the unit, thereby saving the lives of its members. For this act of heroism, he was awarded the Iron Cross by Germany. However, the surrender meant capture, and he spent the rest of the war in a French prison camp. There, the physical hardships and harsh living conditions, as well as the grueling labor, robbed his fingers of their earlier dexterity and flexibility. What he lost was that small margin of skill and sensitivity that distinguishes concert wizardry from mere artistic proficiency. He still played with furious passion, but the spark of greatness was irretrievably lost. I still feel a thrill each time I look at an old photograph of him standing in his field uniform with a gas mask around his neck and a steel helmet on his head — the kind now so popular with the super-macho, leather jacket-clad "Hog" riders on their noisy motorcycles. In this photo, he is sporting the usual ammunition bandolier around his middle. He looks so young. The date on the back of the photo is 1917, which indicates that he was only 20 years old when the picture was taken. His demeanor seems to lack expression and, upon closer observation, I am not sure whether his look is that of a proud conquering hero standing at attention or that of a victim of tragic circumstances.

Upon returning from the First World War, my father had to shift his career from music to something new. He chose architecture. The piano was relegated to a form of therapy, and it remained a source of psychological comfort. He no longer dreamt of virtuoso public performances, but instead would play his music at home every night for the sheer pleasure of translating the essence of his moods into the sounds of the music he was producing.

My father's change in careers occurred during the same era as the founding of the Bauhaus School of Architecture in 1919 in the city of Weimar, Germany, headed by Walter Gropius. The Bauhaus was probably the Weimar Republic's greatest contribution to an explosive and inspiring revolution in the fields of art, architecture and design, making its presence felt in all aspects of the home, the workplace, and the arts. The Bauhaus profoundly affected how buildings were built and how they were finished, how stage sets for the performing arts were designed and how products were manufactured. The school was, in large measure, responsible for evolving modern culture from an essentially Victorian and decorative

My father, Erich Korytowski, in his World War I field uniform in service to the Kaiser (circa 1917). "The First War explains the second and, in fact, caused it" (*A.J.P. Taylor,* **Origins of the Second World War**).

aesthetic to one where form follows function, where, in the words of the great Mies Van Der Rohe, "Less is more," and where the principles of design geared for machine-made mass production were the paramount criteria for success.

Indeed, my father's work was strongly influenced by the Bauhaus. He specialized in what was known as interior architecture. This is not to be confused with interior design, and certainly not interior decorating — the science or art that Frank Lloyd Wright liked to call "inferior desecration." Interior designers and decorators typically accept the architecture of the structure, as delivered by the architect and the contractor, as a given. As such, they achieve their end product with a minimum of structural and electro-mechanical alterations, focusing essentially on finishes, including floor and wall surfaces, such as rugs, tiles, carpeting, paint, color schemes, furniture, decorative objects, fabrics, fixtures, lighting, hardware and the like. In contrast, the interior architect was a licensed architect qualified to deal with the building as a whole, including changes to its structural and electro-mechanical systems as well as its permanent decorative elements. An unflattering comparison might be that of a beautician versus a plastic surgeon. In other words, my father's work encompassed all aspects of a building necessary to accomplish the full range of design objectives.

My mother had been diligently pursuing her career in public health and children's well-being. In the 1920s, vaccination was a popular topic, but the treatment of communicable diseases, inspired by the accomplishments of Louis Pasteur, was really in the forefront of medical progress. The global Influenza Epidemic of 1918 and the ongoing ravages of tuberculosis combined to add further incentives to address these diseases. As their treatment relied extensively on patient isolation, fresh air and new kinds of specialized care, the design of hospitals and the corresponding impact on the nursing practices and the management of patients was deeply affected. The new treatment approaches involved the construction of large sanitariums in the countryside and a new configuration for hospitals that relied on separated pavilions replacing monolithic structures to minimize infectious contacts. My mother was understandably interested in this effort, and participated in the evolution of this branch of wellness medicine.

My father, on the other hand, was interested in the essence of the sanitarium as a building form. It was the translation of medical science into functional design and architecture that mattered to him. As an interior architect, he participated in translating the principles embodied in sanitary isolation and the separation of buildings with a large amount of air flowing between them, into structures with wings that later became known as pavilions. This style dominated the design of hospitals worldwide until the middle of the 20th century, when the emphasis on surgery and the need for clustering and centralizing procedures, imaging technology and sophisticated medical specialties contributed to the conclusion that the pavilion configuration for hospitals had become inefficient at best, and unworkable at worst.

It was probably a melding of my mother's obsession with sanitation with my father's passion with buildings that produced their shared interest in hospitals, both as a building form and as a functional concern over their purpose. They spent a lot of time on the subject and, ironically, so did I some four decades later when, as part of my city planning and urban development activities, I was called upon to deal with the jumble of Cincinnati's Pill Hill, a huge concentration of five major hospitals in the middle of a deteriorating residential neighborhood.

Chapter 3

Brussels

When we arrived in Belgium, my parents chose to live in Brussels, or *Bruxelles,* as the Belgians call their capital city. On the plus side, Belgium was an enlightened country, which had signed neutrality agreements with its neighbors. Anti-Semitism was not prevalent in this constitutional monarchy governed by Leopold III, a king more loved than feared. There was freedom of speech and, unlike the toxic climate which prevailed in Germany at that time, no one feared expressing views about the government, the politics or the policies that influenced the mood of the country. On the negative side, my parents had to adapt to a new country, learn new customs and master at least one new language. While French was prevalent in about one third of the country, other languages, including Dutch, German and Flemish, the language of Flanders, reflected the multinational origins of the country as well as its immediate neighbors, the Netherlands (Holland) and Luxembourg. All three shared a history, and were known as the "Low Country"; they became known collectively as the Benelux countries after World War II.

Peter with his father (Brussels, circa 1937).

Chapter 3

I have always considered my life in Brussels to be my real childhood. During the next seven years, I would grow from a babe in swaddling to a nine-year-old ready to take on the world. Initially, we lived on the fourth floor of a modern building on Avenue Paul Deschanel, a wide, formal, well-treed and meticulously-groomed residential thoroughfare of upper-middle income apartment buildings with balconies, landscaped medians and wide sidewalks. One day, my father forgot his keys and called up to my mother from the sidewalk, asking her to toss them to him from our balcony. She was only too happy to oblige, and as gravity propelled the keys toward the sidewalk, my father looked up and gave my mother his most radiant smile of gratitude along with a gallant bow. Unfortunately, the keys landed squarely on his mouth, knocking out enough upper teeth to force the poor man into the world of denture-wearers forever! Perhaps that was one of the reasons that, some two or three years later, we settled for lower altitudes, and my parents bought a three-story row house at 323 Rue Des Coteaux, around the corner in the same neighborhood.

Actually, our move had more to do with the joys of property ownership and the existence of a private yard at the new location. The address also meant a more intimate and totally residential street. The only intrusion into the residential character of our new neighborhood was a café located directly across the street from our new home. This commercial intrusion into the residential inner sanctum was only possible because the concept of complex, lawyer-driven zoning laws and the institutionalization of citizen activism and all-powerful neighborhood organizations had not yet arrived on the urban scene. That would not evolve for at least another half a century. And so, the residents of Rue Des Coteaux were punished for this violation of modern planning and zoning principles by being shaken out of their slumber once or twice a week by a beer delivery truck that made an enormous racket as they replaced empty barrels with full ones, resupplying the little café with the product that was their trade.

The house at 323 Rue Des Coteaux was where my recollections began to acquire specificity and clarity. This was where I started school, where I had my first encounter with surgery, where I had my first sexual experience, where I formed my first social relationships and where toys acquired special importance beyond a mere test of my dexterity. It was also where I experienced different means of transportation and where awareness of my parents evolved from a subliminal sense of presence to full consciousness.

Life in Brussels became almost tediously normal. As a fiercely neutral country, and a kingdom at that, we were like a small island of calm, floating in a sea of horrendous geopolitical turbulence.

I certainly was not precocious. In fact, I really did not learn to speak properly until I was three or four years old. By that time, we were well established in Brussels. In our home, my parents spoke mainly French, and I have always considered French to be my first language, despite my German origins. When they did not want me to hear or understand what they were saying, my parents lapsed into German. Naturally, it was this restraint in communication that induced me to pick up a little German. Amazingly, I was able to parrot what little I absorbed and could express myself in perfect *Hoch Deutsch*, or standard German, fluently and without a foreign or regional accent!

School was always unpleasant for me. Each day, I walked for what seemed like a very long distance, wearing a beret, very short pants, knee-length socks and a wool poncho (also known as a cape). In the winter, when frostbite and soaked clothes were normal fare, this daily trek was particularly uncomfortable. Sore feet, usually caused by my congenitally protruding big toe joint, served to round out what clearly was not my favorite activity. But then again, there is always a silver lining. Let me, for a moment, shed my inhibitions and explain that the extensive hiking produced, quite accidentally, my first orgasm thanks to those very short and extremely tight pants I had to wear. They kept rubbing against my crotch and the friction inevitably resulted in something I can only describe as an incredibly pleasant strangeness that I subsequently tried to duplicate without success at first, but eventually, I managed to succeed. However, I did not understand what this was all about until years later, under vastly different and far more titillating circumstances!

From all reports, I must have been a difficult child and a horrible student. I fought a lot, and I didn't study enough. My abysmally low grades reflected my performance, or lack thereof. This was further confirmed by a stream of notes from my teachers, always full of condescending advice on how to best handle cases like me. On more than one occasion, I managed to intercept such writings and I became a very adept censor, limiting the flow of communication. (This skill would later prove essential to survival during my years in hiding from the Nazis.)

We were required to study Flemish, a language I found ugly, crude

Chapter 3

and guttural and one that I simply refused to learn. Flemish dates back to the ancient history of the area and the invasion of the Germanic Franks into the Gallo Roman lands in the fourth and fifth centuries. I simply could not understand why I had to learn such a useless language. In fact, I thought that the bilingualism which prevailed throughout Belgium was an unnecessary imposition on my limited learning capacities, and one that I felt to be without any benefit toward the welding together of Belgium's historically diverse cultures.

I did, however, excel in art. That was my most coveted subject and, much as I was chastised over my performance in Flemish, math and French, I was considered a prodigy in drawing and *aquarelle* (watercolor). My father, however, had different ideas. He insisted that I take music and piano lessons. Predictably, I did abominably and quit so early in the process that my entire repertoire never got past "Frère Jacques," the French equivalent of "Chop Sticks." More advanced beginner pieces like "Für Elise," which required two hands, were not even on the radar screen. (It would seem that my battle with the ivory keys has transcended the eons since my infancy; I am notoriously inept at bonding with either the almighty computer or, even worse, the iPhone, both so dominant in our key-driven culture today.)

Much as I hated school, the institution did bring order to my life. Thus, Sundays fortified me for Mondays; Tuesdays got me into the swing of things; and on Wednesday I was able to look forward to Thursday, which was a day off for many children, to allow them to catch up on religious matters. Catholic students in particular had to dedicate that day of the week to religious education. Friday was the day I always dreaded. It was the day for quizzes, the day when students got called upon to recite the classics, which had to be memorized, and the day when "chalk and talk" work had to be performed on the blackboard in front of the class. Generally, it was the day for "show and tell," which felt more like "truth or consequences" to me. Half of Saturday was also a school day, usually reserved for physical training and organized sports, but also used to clear up unfinished business from Friday. The concept of weekends simply did not exist at that time in Belgium.

Like so many children, and despite my mother's epic crusade against dirt, I contracted the normal collection of childhood diseases like chicken pox, measles, roseola, strep throat, colds and fevers. In every case, my mother morphed into the professional nurse she was, and pampered me to the ultimate. In fact, the pampering was so extreme that I actually felt cheated when I was one of the few kids who didn't catch the mumps. My mother's tender love and care was so compelling that it became an inducement for faking illnesses and thereby succumbing to hypochondria. When I had my tonsils out, the operation was performed at home, where I was asked to sit on the lap of the "nice man who came to visit." I still recall the bewildering multicolor, psychedelic, chloroform or ether-induced state that was thrust upon me. I had no idea what was happening until, on a more pleasant note, I was forced to consume tons of ice cream to recover from the surgery. The experience could have been traumatic, but it turned out to be a comforting reaffirmation of the extent to which I was precious to my parents.

Life at home was cozy. My father spent a lot of time, mostly late in the evenings, playing the piano. Our meals were always *en-famille*, and dinner conversation usually revolved around world affairs in which we, quite naturally, had an acute, and excruciatingly vital, interest. That is not to say that other subjects were not discussed, but what was happening in Europe at that time had everybody mesmerized and focused on what the future would bring, relegating virtually all other matters to the category of the trivial and mundane.

I do not recall any kind of social life outside of our immediate family. If we had visitors, or my father entertained a business acquaintance, they were few and far between. It's not that my parents were not gregarious; it's more that there was safety in keeping one's privacy. Being Jewish was not a potential death sentence in Belgium, nor even a cause for harassment, but having already tasted the vitriolic mood that forced them out of Germany in 1932, this was clearly not a time to indulge in an active social life. Of course, we were not misanthropes. We were friendly with our neighbors, the neighborhood merchants and public service people. But there were no deep and lasting friendships that I can recall. We were, after all, German immigrants, something considered not quite right among the well-established French and Benelux population of the region. We did not frequent restaurants and I was perfectly happy eating my mother's essentially German cooking, which always came off to the passionate sounds of my father's piano therapy. Our family life was as close-knit and insulated from the outside as it was intimate on the inside. As such, the dinner ritual with the three of us was very important.

Chapter 3

My mother was a ferocious cook. And she stuffed everything! Spleen was one of her favorite and most labor-intensive dishes. But then again, there was also stuffed breast of veal, a classic, and we won't even mention what she did with fowl. There were many other stuffing targets such as beef heart, all sorts of fish, pastas and skins of God knows what. On the vegetarian front, she exercised her skills on every sort of root or leaf created by nature, including cabbage, squash, zucchini, tomato, eggplant, celeriac and artichokes. Conspicuous by their absence was corn, which was only fed to the hogs, and broccoli, an American invention. This passion for stuffing was not only time-consuming, it monopolized the kitchen for the duration of the preparation, to the exclusion of any other activity. Another consequence of the stuffing sport was that there were always prodigious leftovers. It was my father's sacred duty to eat them the next day, since there was no worse sin than throwing food away. The debate over the matter usually ended with my mother conceding that she would make the ultimate sacrifice and eat a couple of bites herself, whereupon she would make the leftovers more palatable by mixing about a pound of butter into the dish, generally elevating it to gourmet status.

This kind of cuisine presented quite the shopping challenge, launching my mother on heroic daily quests that would have made Don Quixote proud. I recall an incident at a public market where my mother was trying to secure detailed instructions from an irritable vegetable stand owner on how to stuff a an oversized zucchini. As one question led to another, and as the questions became more detailed, the man became aggravated, until he finally lost it. He suggested that my mother should take the zucchini, carve it carefully to preserve its voluptuous shape, and then "stuff it up her @%#"!

A lot of my time at home, beyond schoolwork, was devoted to toys and games. In particular, I developed a passionate interest in military operations. I had accumulated a humongous army of lead soldiers, complemented by weapons, battle matériel and equipment. When friends came over, we built camps and fortifications and we had great wars. While all the soldiers were killed, bombed and assaulted, no one in our world of play was ever really wounded, and they all lived to fight again the next day. My room was the theater of operations. I had two beds with one on either side of the room. The area under the beds became the opposing camps and trenches. The area between the beds was thus "no man's land."

Fighting our battles, we tossed various objects across the room, knocking out the lead soldiers arrayed in strategic formation within the camp areas. The forces were eclectic and anachronistic to say the least. There was the usual complement of World War I soldiers in French, German and British uniforms. There were also colorful North African troops or Zouaves, as well as American Indian warriors and cowboys on horseback. Napoleon's *Grande Armée* was well represented by contingents of the imperial infantry, the Hussar cavalry and the artillery. Even the Roman Empire was present and accounted for. Cap pistols and other devices like pots, pans and sundry noisemakers were used to create the din of battle.

My martial instincts may well have found their roots in my father's grim fascination with world events, which were not limited to Hitler's relentless progress towards the domination of Europe. He was also fascinated by the Russo-Finnish war, for reasons that have never been totally clear to me. At that time, Belgium was neutral, but stood in the path of a German invasion of France. The relevance of the Russo-Finnish war to our situation in Belgium was that a German invasion seemed inevitable to all but Chamberlain, the prime minister of England. Stalin, like everyone in Europe, feared an invasion. In Russia, this fear was manifested as a threat to Leningrad. Finland had a non-aggression pact with Russia. Hitler and Stalin had entered into a mutual non-aggression pact as well. However, the governments of these nations did not believe that the pacts would be honored. A German invasion of Leningrad would give the Germans access deeper into Russia through the Gulf of Finland and the Karelian Isthmus. To counteract both this and related strategic and territorial threats, Russia offered Finland land and other concessions in exchange for control over the areas Stalin required to enable an effective defense against a potential German attack. Finland refused, and Russia canceled its 1932 non-aggression treaty with its small neighbor and proceeded with the invasion of Finland. Sympathy ran with Finland, which was stigmatized as the underdog. Russia was considered the boorish big bad bear in the struggle, pushing a small, relatively helpless neighbor around. My father was, of course, on Finland's side, despite the fact that, if Russia won, it would provide them with the means to stop Hitler's juggernaut. I recall a large map pinned on our living room wall, filled with little flags that served to track the movements of the respective forces in that war. Peace, achieved with the blessings of the allies, arrived within a relatively short time. In

Chapter 3

March 1940, after Hitler's conquest of Europe was launched, Russia got what it needed. The peace terms were remarkably moderate. In fact, both countries gained significant strategic advantages because of the fortifications and rail lines built in the course of this war, creating a most unsuitable theater for the *Blitzkrieg* tactics that would soon follow in other parts of Europe.

Another interest of mine, far more constructive than the art of waging make-believe wars, was the assembly of structures and machines with the help of a well-equipped Erector Set. My collection of metal bars, angles, steel plates of various shapes, wheels, pulleys, nuts and screws was awesome. I spent hours with this toy, constantly challenged by the assembly guides that came with the set. My projects kept getting more ambitious, expanding into bigger and more complex structures and machines. Ultimately, this activity expanded all the way out into the covered portion of our little yard. I was reasonably skilled with this toy and, in some respects, this was my first encounter with architecture and construction. (While I would ultimately become an architect and later a real estate developer, my early passion for the Erector Set would prove to be a short-lived flirtation and not an enduring love affair. As an adult, I seem to have lost the ability, and therefore the interest, to distinguish nuts from bolts. I get lost immediately if I have to decipher instructions for even the simplest of assemblies, whether or not batteries or electricity are involved!)

Our house was blessed with a little yard, which opened off the kitchen. It was one of my favorite places. We created a small garden there to grow flowers, herbs and vegetables (oddly enough, no Brussels sprouts). This experience of growing string beans, squash, sunflowers and other produce from seed and experimenting with earthworms, butterflies and other insect visitors taught me the ways of nature. A masonry wall surrounded the yard, some six or seven feet high, opening up a very private and personal territory for me.

My mother and I frequently walked to the Parc Josaphat, whose well-groomed green oasis offset the dense dark brick and stony character of the neighborhood's environment. The park was located about three blocks from home. In addition to providing fresh air and grass, it doubled as a nanny hangout and as a place where my mother could catch up on daily gossip. However, organized sports simply were not part of our lives. As such, we used this public open space to fly kites, sail toy boats in a swan-filled public pond, enjoy walks and get the indoor mothballs shaken out in passive ways. This is where I learned to use a scooter as a preferred way to get around. I was still too young for a bike, even with training wheels, and I considered myself clearly too old for a tricycle.

On the weekends, we often traveled to Laaeken, a huge expanse of open space that contained the Brussels airport. This was usually a full-day affair, carrying a picnic lunch or dinner. Model airplanes, kite flying and observation of the takeoff and landing of real planes were the typical activities. Laaeken, more than five miles away and, therefore, not within walking distance of home, could be reached by bus or a combination of tramway and bus transportation. Also somewhat removed from home, but very popular with us, was Rouge-Clôitre, an ancient abbey in the middle of the Forêt de Soignes, a majestic forest. Unlike Laaeken, Rouge-Clôitre was totally surrounded by first-growth trees that were as stately as they were beautiful. On a few occasions, we pushed on beyond the forest to pay homage to Waterloo and Napoleon, who was considered probably more hero than villain, given his huge influence on the history of Belgium. Because we did not own a car, we either rented a car or went with friends who owned one. On one such occasion, we stopped for a roadside rest and I took a walk with the driver, who insisted on telling me how children were born. As we passed a cabbage field, he informed me, quite confidentially, that babies are born in cabbage heads and that, when grownups found them, they kept the children as their own. He described this as one of the many miracles God had brought about. Naturally, I swallowed the story hook, line

Peter with his father at the seashore (Ostend, Belgium, circa 1934).

36

Chapter 3

and sinker. Afterwards, every time we passed a cabbage patch I had to stop and check for babies!

During the summer months, we traveled to the seashore at Ostend, a port town on the English Channel with a wide beach endowed with heavy surf and extremely soft sand. Shelling was a favorite activity, as was the construction of sand castles and related public works such as moats, ramparts, tunnels, and bridges. The beach provided an ideal environment for magnificent dunes in a completely natural and non-commercial setting. Cokes, hot dogs and fries were unheard of, but it was possible to rent colorful cloth mini-pavilions or tiny wooden cabanas on wheels. At the beach, I busied myself building extraordinarily complicated sand castles while my father went into the water for a long swim. His daring deeds in the English Channel drove my mother crazy! One day he started swimming casually. Nobody was really concerned about this, until the realization dawned — first on my mother, then me, then the lifeguard and finally, everybody on the beach — that my father had totally disappeared from view! He was a tiny dot near the horizon — he had to be rescued, and fast. He was then severely chastised by my mother and he promised to never go that far out again.

The tragedy was that, despite his most heroic efforts, he never succeeded in teaching me to swim, even though he almost drowned me one day at a local indoor pool when he and a swimming instructor strapped me in a harness which was suspended by pulleys and attached to a rod that enabled the fearsome duo to raise and lower me into the pool while telling me to make swimming motions. This exercise was meant to demonstrate the buoyancy of water, but it did very little to teach me how to breathe while I was underneath the surface. I have always felt that this must have been an early form of water boarding, and I don't think I have ever swallowed as much water! (I still feel grief and considerable guilt that, by the time I had mastered the art of swimming and became an accredited Red Cross water safety instructor, my father was long dead and I could never show him my accomplishments.)

Unfortunately, my father's determination to see me swim was not duplicated in his zeal to collect the money that he was owed. He did not like to deal with confrontations, so he was notorious for not demanding to get paid, whereupon my mother became the primary and irresistible force used to extract performance from recalcitrant clients. I remember one in particular — Herr Posnanski. I must have been six or seven years old when my mother grabbed me by the arm and dragged me, full of fury and anger, to the construction site where she found the deadbeat discussing something with my father. She broke into the conversation starting with "Mein Lieber Herr Posnanski...." (My dear Mr. Posnanski), and then she launched into the most horrible tongue-lashing I had ever witnessed. I think Mr. Posnanski must have paid, because no murders were reported in the neighborhood that day!

Winters were long and on the dark side, with not much snow, but nearly constant rain. For the most part, we stayed indoors. School was in full swing and Christmas was the big event. Like Christmases everywhere, this involved a great deal of preparation. It was a time when department stores decorated their windows lavishly and festively. It was also a time for gifts. Without ascribing any religious meaning to the ritual, we always had a heavily laden Christmas tree, lit with real candles. When I was seven years old, I caught my parents getting ready to play Santa on the night before Christmas, wrapping presents with a lot of whispering. This was an epiphany. The jig was up! There was no Santa Claus! However, I realized that it was not in my best interest to expose my discovery. I was devious enough to continue openly to believe in St. Nicholas, using this stealthily acquired knowledge to extort all kinds of things from my parents and their friends. After all, what did I have to lose?

As an illustration of the extent to which I was a spoiled brat, I recall the huge disappointment I felt one Christmas when, after having gone to some trouble to be a very good boy, and making some painful sacrifices, I felt entitled to write a heart-rending plea in super-explicit terms to Santa, demanding an electric train. When the morning of the hallowed day arrived, I searched all the gifts that had been carefully arranged on the floor of the living room. I could not believe my eyes. All I got was the wind-up, spring version of a train. I had a tantrum; I cursed everybody and everything; I was inconsolable. Little did I know that five months after that Christmas, the gift of an electric train set and the perambulations of Santa Claus would lose importance and be relegated to an insignificant corner of my mind; we were about to be overwhelmed by the upheaval in human affairs which would become the Second World War.

Chapter 4

Blitzkrieg

Seven years in Brussels had slipped by without any earthshaking events to upset our lives. My tight short pants had continued to chafe my inner thighs and cause the collateral benefits previously mentioned; I still wasn't diligent in practicing the piano; my mother was as protective and obsessive about cleanliness as ever; and my father was well ensconced in his architectural practice. But, all at once, it came crashing to an end early one Friday morning when Germany broke the neutrality treaties that kept Belgium out of war.

I was a happy kid, surrounded by care, love and a bunch of toys — except for the electric train, of course, which kept eluding me. I hated school, as did most healthy male preteens. May 10, 1940, started as just another Friday, the day I dreaded not because my entire world was about to collapse, but because I had to perform at school, in front of the class. I awoke that morning to what I thought was the usual beer barrel commotion in the café across the street — but there was no truck, nor were there any barrels. Everything was quiet around the

Peter (Brussels, circa 1937).

little café. Minutes after the initial loud rumble awakened me, the noise multiplied and drew us into the street. There, as we chatted with our neighbors who were equally shaken by the loud rumbling sound, word spread that the noise we heard was the sound of the *Luftwaffe* Stukas bombing the Laaeken airport. It did not take us long to realize that we were in mortal danger and that we were in the middle of something called the *Blitzkrieg*.

Before long, it was all around us! The Stukas were diving, creating panic with their low-altitude strafing. The racket of the low-flying planes was terrifying. Worst of all, the whistling sound of the bombs had a paralyzing effect on our minds, robbing us of all sense of reason and rational behavior. The *Blitzkrieg* had struck us, and did so with complete surprise! I felt very small, utterly confused and helplessly lost. The terrifying whistles from the bombs were so loud and close, they magnified the illusion that each bomb would land directly on the top of my head. The dive bombers flew very low overhead, and were unrestrained in their enthusiasm to strafe hapless civilians caught out in the open. Suddenly, the hardships of school evaporated, and whatever anxieties I may have had over the homework assignment I would have had to perform in class that morning had dissipated completely. My life and its focus became almost instantly, and quintessentially, one of personal survival. My first instinct was to run like a headless chicken. I ran back into the house and out into the yard, where I had always felt so safe. I stood, completely still, flattened against the old wall that surrounded our little yard, fed by the adrenaline-fueled desperation for survival. I even tried to claw my way *inside* that wall, wanting to live the rest of my life there, curled into a fetal position.

The air raid sirens continued to blast their loud, unremitting, modulated and lugubrious whine, warning us that more incoming Stukas had been spotted. We heard the panicked shouts as the air raid wardens screamed orders. We knew this meant that we had about two minutes to reach a protected area before the Stukas were directly over our neighborhood. To be out in the open when the dive bombers were overhead was horrendously dangerous. If nothing else, the sound was paralyzing, thus leaving us extremely vulnerable. I don't remember how long I stayed transfixed there. All I recall is that my parents, with help from the air raid wardens and their staff, gently pried me loose from the wall and half dragged, half pushed me into the air raid shelter assigned to our district.

Chapter 4

Inside the shelter, the lighting was very poor. While the raid was in progress, the lights flickered at every explosion, and we held our breath on the dwindling hope that we would survive. There was a cacophony of voices — old, young, foreign, couth and uncouth — from the people who populated the shelter, maintaining a background buzz of discourse interrupted by the incredibly loud crashes of the Armageddon unfolding outside. A strange sort of fatalistic calm fell on the assembled neighbors after the initial panic had subsided, once people realized that survival was possible. Now that they had found shelter, they resumed the activities that had been interrupted by the alert. Knitting, baby feeding and reading were common ways of passing the time while the masters of destruction swooped overhead and brought noisy chaos into our lives. There were no toilet facilities in the shelter, and this became a preoccupation that almost exceeded our need for safety. The same sirens eventually gave us the steady monotone blast we knew signaled the all clear. The raid was over and they were sending us back to our homes. Like a brutal juggernaut, the German war machine had reached into the heart and soul of what I considered my home and my country.

Literally translated, *Blitzkrieg* means "lightning war." As the name implies, it was an assault tactic based on speed, coordination and movement, designed to hit hard and move on instantly. The aim was to create panic among the civilian population, as a civilian population on the move can create absolute havoc for a defending army trying to get its forces to the war front. Doubt, confusion and rumor were sure to paralyze both the government and the defending military. It required a military force based around light tank units supported by planes and infantry (foot soldiers). A tank commander named Heinz Wilhelm Guderian, who wrote a military pamphlet called *Achtung Panzer*, which was studied by Hitler, developed the tactic. Ironically, Guderian got the idea for the *Blitzkrieg* from two officers — one from France and one from Britain — and he had broadened what they had put on paper.

Hitler had spent four years in the First World War trenches, fighting a static war with neither side moving far for months on end. Because of this, he was enthralled by Guderian's plan, which was a dynamic kind of warfare that relied on swift movement. When Guderian told Hitler that he could reach the French coast in weeks if an attack on France was ordered, fellow officers openly laughed at him. The German High Command told Hitler that Guderian's boast was impossible. He was greeted with derision and told that he might not even reach the River Meuse, considered France's first major line of defense, and thought to be impossible to cross in a battle situation. Hitler, however, gave his full backing to Guderian. Ultimately, the *Blitzkrieg* proved Guderian right. It also proved that Hitler had chosen his commanders carefully, as they proved they could successfully execute a new tactic for war even though they did not initially support it.

The order of the day for Hitler's forces became "speed, and still more speed, and always speed," and that demanded audacity, more audacity and always audacity. Once a strategic target had been selected, Stuka dive bombers were sent in to soften up the enemy, destroy all rail lines, communication centers and major rail links. This was done as the German tanks were approaching. The planes withdrew only at the last minute so that the enemy did not have time to recover their senses before the tanks, supported by infantry, attacked. Half-track vehicles moved most troops, so there was no real need for roads, though these were later repaired so that the Germans could use them. Once an objective had been taken, the Germans did not stop to celebrate the victory; they moved on to the next objective. Retreating civilians would hinder any work done by the army being attacked, and civilians fleeing the fighting were attacked to create further mayhem.

As a tactic, *Blitzkrieg* was used to devastating effect in Poland and elsewhere in Europe. In the spring of 1940, the German army, aided by the infamous *Blitzkrieg*, succeeded in pushing the British and French forces, which had been positioned to protect Belgium and the Netherlands, to the beaches of Dunkirk on the English Channel, where many found their way back to England. In June 1941, the Germans mounted Operation Barbarossa, in which the Russian army was devastated in the attack on Russia. Part of the reason that *Blitzkrieg* was so successful was because Britain and France still had a First World War mentality. What tanks they had were of poor quality compared to the German armor. British and French tactics were outdated, and Britain still believed that, as an island, it was safe, protected by a historically famous and powerful navy. The high commands of both countries, dominated by the old traditional cavalry regiments, had powerful political pull. The cavalry regiments ruled supreme and were

Chapter 4

adamant that the tanks would not have any influence in their armies. Hitler despised this type of officer. He developed a strong bias against the old army cadre, and instead embraced his tank commanders, including one of Guderian's young disciples, Erwin Rommel. There is no question that Hitler much preferred the use of his armored forces to that of his infantry and artillery in the *Wehrmacht*, using Stukas as effective mobile artillery. In fact, tanks — or Panzers as they were called — were almost symbiotically linked to the *Blitzkrieg* because of their unmatched mobile and dynamic character.

Clearly, if Hitler's wishes were to be fulfilled, Nazi Germany would have to have a sufficiently massive war-making capacity, including tanks on the ground and planes in the air, to conquer Europe. At the same time, given his arrogant supremacist ambitions, he lusted to provide Germany with the necessary *Lebensraum,* or living space, that was necessary for the Third Reich to stretch its tentacles. To fulfill both these wishes required a strategy and a tactic of unstoppable speed and unthinkable brutality, deployed on a heretofore unheard-of scale.

In 1941, a diary kept by an unknown French soldier was found. In it were some comments, all written in just five days — May 5, 1940 to May 10, 1940 — that help explain this tactic, and how terrifying and successful it was. Below is a literal translation:

> When the dive-bombers come down, they [the French] stood it for two hours and then ran waving their hands over bombardment ... it was a superb example of military surprise.... The pace is too fast ... it's the cooperation between the dive bombers and the tanks that is winning the war for Germany.... News that the Germans are in Amiens ... this is like some ridiculous nightmare.

That Friday, the 10th of May 1940, found Belgium in a precarious position, with Germany threatening her borders. The situation in Belgium and the Low Lands had grown exceedingly fragile and perilous. All the German appeasement and disarmament efforts by France, England and the other nations at risk of attack by Germany had failed, as had the Versailles Treaty disarmament mandates. The final straws, the events that finally forced these nations to face reality, were Hitler's *Anschluss,* or the annexing of Austria into the Third Reich, punctuated by the invasion of the Sudetenland and Germany's lightning conquest of Poland. There was no doubt left about his ambition to conquer the world.

The threatened nations responded by creating an Alliance, reinforcing their respective existing neutrality pacts and committing to a mutual defense strategy in the case of attack. That strategy involved developing hardened defense lines like the one designed by Maginot in the path of a potential invasion from Germany. The First World War had taught Europe to avoid trench warfare at all costs. Unfortunately, they failed to recognize the signs that pointed to Germany preparing to use a new tactic for warfare — the *Blitzkrieg*.

Belgium did not want to be permanently occupied by the Allied forces until an invasion actually occurred, as it feared compromising its neutrality. This meant that Belgium needed lines of military retreat, on Belgian land, which could be defended by the Belgian army. This would enable the country to act as a vital buffer for the Allies in repelling the kind of massive attacks they feared would come from the east. What befell Belgium on the 10th of May is probably best described by John Keegan in his 1989 book *The Second World War*:

> Belgium was in an impossible position. Short of allowing France and Britain to garrison its territory from the onset — which would have compromised the neutrality it still believed to be its best hope of averting invasion — it had no option but to keep its military distance from the allies while fortifying its Eastern frontier as best it could against the Wehrmacht.

Although Belgian intelligence anticipated an attack, Belgium still claimed its elusive neutrality. Everyone was conscious of Belgium's vulnerability and strategic importance. Along with the other Benelux countries, it sat like a cork, directly in the path between Germany and France. These circumstances led the country, despite its standing as a historically neutral nation, to plan for an attack by Germany at its most vulnerable point. Accordingly, Belgium had to fortify its eastern frontier against the *Wehrmacht* to the best of its ablilty. This meant concentrating the Belgian army and defenses along the Albert Canal near the Dutch border. A little farther back, they could link up along the Dyle Line with the Maginot Line, thereby creating a base from which a counterattack could be launched to stem the invading tide. This strategy, however, would draw the Allies deep into Belgian territory, thus exposing their rears at the south and at the west.

In the late 1930s, recognizing the fragile quality of Belgium's neutrality and the disregard Hitler felt for treaties, which he considered to be mere "scraps of paper," King Leopold spoke to the people about Belgium's peril. Ever since the Versailles Treaty ending the First World War, Belgium's neutrality had depended on independent agreements with its neighbors. None of the options included the kind of firm anti-aggression commitment with enforceable dire consequences for the violators, which was so desired by the once-neutral country. The king informed his people that they must strengthen their forces and increase defense spending. To defend the most vulnerable border where the natural barriers of the Meuse River and the Albert Canal connected, Belgium constructed a modern fortress, Fort Eben Emael. An immense plateau of a fortress, studded with gun emplacements trained on the vital bridges and crossings over the Albert Canal and Meuse River, Eben Emael posed a formidable defense. Combined with its steel-protected guns, impervious to attack from the air, the fort possessed a sheer wall of rock on the canal side, making an amphibious attack impossible. Thus considered impregnable by any known method of attack, the fort — the key to any invasion from Germany — became the challenge for a determined and cunning enemy. And this enemy, Adolf Hitler and his general staff, was not only cunning but also inventive and ahead of their time.

Just as he chose aggressive and forward-thinking commanders like Guderian and Rommel for his tactic of *Blitzkrieg*, Hitler chose another officer with similar qualifications and an aggressive "can do" attitude — Karl Student — for a special mission. Student would be in charge of a new force, and a new attack concept — gliders! Hitler asked him a straightforward question, "Can you take Fort Eben Emael?" When Student answered in the affirmative, Hitler set him to the task of planning the assault and gave him anything he needed for training and weapons.

Student chose his force carefully and began training in secret more than a year before the attack. The gliders would land on the plateau of the fort with each carrying a team assigned to a specific gun emplacement. They would carry with them the new weapon promised by Hitler, a shaped charge to be fastened onto the rounded steel tops of the emplacements. When detonated, the shaped charge exploded into a void facing the target, driving molten steel through the emplacement steel, disabling anything and anyone inside. Prepared totally in secret, the raid went off as planned and, as dawn came to Fort Eben Emael on the morning of May 10, 1940, Student's gliders brought death and destruction to the great fortress in the first-ever glider assault in military history. Although all the emplacements were not crippled and some of the units inside the fort fought for over 24 hours, the main objective was achieved: the Panzers crossed the Meuse and the Albert Canal. The northern thrust into Belgium was achieved and the attack to encircle the Allies began farther south.

John Keegan continues the story:

> The availability of massive and efficiently mobile German Panzer Divisions and their complete air superiority made it feasible for the Germans to execute a remarkable swing of the bulk of their forces from the East and the Ardennes to the Allies' Southern and Western fronts. These plans and disposition of forces were the prelude to the Dunkirk Encirclement, and the subsequent debacle for the Allies that would lead to their ultimate evacuation from Belgium and eventually culminate in the fall of France.

The Belgian government had prepared a defense system against a land attack and also undertook a wide range of defensive measures to protect the civilian population against aerial attacks. Everyone in our neighborhood had participated in the trench-digging effort in the nearby Parc Josaphat, and we had learned how to tape our windows to minimize the damage and danger from broken glass chards and how to insulate our home from any light that might be seen from the sky. The Civil Defense authorities had designated a number of cellars as bomb shelters in case Belgium's neutrality was violated, but beyond that, there had not been any extensive training for civilians. Until the moment of the first air raid, we had been only marginally familiar with the emergency protocols and the location and access points of all the shelters. We knew that safety would clearly not be inside our house, yet the dangers would be magnified exponentially if we were caught in the open while trying to reach a shelter.

The Civil Defense establishment arrived in full force later that day, and we were properly briefed on all the procedures. We felt like hostages, totally dependent on our air raid shelters, terrified to leave our neighborhood for more than a fraction of an hour for fear of finding ourselves too far away to reach our shelter. Nor could we ever forget the sound of the sirens alerting us to the deadly threat from the sky. The modulated wailing produced an echo in the empty streets that suggested the coming of a biblical apocalypse.

Chapter 4

And, sure enough, later that morning, satisfied that the airport was useless and that any possible resistance that the Allied forces might interpose to prevent the invasion of Belgium had been disabled, the Stukas returned to the residential areas of Brussels in waves, at regular intervals. As expected, this panicked people out of the city and onto the highways, further impeding the Allies' attempts to stem the Germans. While civilians were being driven out of Brussels towards the south by the heavily mechanized German army coming from the north, the Allies were unsuccessfully trying to clear the very same roads, so that they could stem the invasion by moving north towards the Albert Canal.

For me, the main stage of the theater was not in the sky where the Stukas were circling, diving, strafing and unloading their lethal cargo of bombs; it was on the ground, in the streets and in the cellars. It was in those places where the paralysis of endless air raid warning sirens took its cumulative toll. I was completely focused on my immediate survival, and all my concerns were concentrated on the next air raid. I had no appreciation for the larger events that surrounded that traumatic day. And so it continued. Any time, night or day, the sirens blared out their alternating signals, making life a living hell for us. The feeling that the raids would go on forever filled us with a combination of fear and hopelessness. It was hard not to focus on the thought that, sooner or later during the course of one of these raids, it would be our turn. It wasn't until many years later that I came to realize that the amount of time one spends in pain is far more significant than the extent of the pain. While the *Blitzkrieg* was the perfect tactic for Hitler and his armed forces, it was hell on earth for the civilian population in the path of Germany's conquest of Europe and beyond. It is impossible for me to think of the *Blitzkrieg* without evoking the imagery of Picasso's mural masterpiece, *Guernica*.

The German raid on Guernica, a small village in Spain, was organized by Colonel Wolfram Von Richthofen, who took his pleasures in slaughtering innocent, harmless civilians while testing out new tools of warfare in the process. It is no surprise that after Guernica, the good colonel graduated to a critical position in the execution of the *Blitzkrieg*, where he became part of the main show, spreading unmitigated terror over a continent instead of flying an old Junker plane with a mission to flatten a small village. In many respects, the raid on Guernica served as the testing ground and prelude to the *Blitzkrieg*.

I had always found it difficult to put my personal experiences with the *Blitzkrieg* into words until, some 30 years after the war, I went to see the exhibit of Pablo Picasso's *Guernica* at New York's Museum of Modern Art. Picasso's famous painting commemorates the April 1937 aerial bombardment on the defenseless Basque village. The attack, using incendiary and other explosives, killed hundreds of civilian villagers (by some estimates, the casualties may have reached 1,600), and proved to be a horrific preview of what would soon be happening all over Europe. I was astounded to discover how vividly the gigantic floor-to-ceiling, building-wide mural painting mounted in the main lobby of New York's Museum of Modern Art had captured my recollections of the *Blitzkrieg*. Adding to the drama of the painting was the compelling dramatic audio-visual production, which transformed the static graphic into an experience that transported the visitor into the horrific environment of a city being destroyed by bombs. The combination of a painting only Pablo Picasso could create, the sounds of crashing buildings, flashing lights, projected psychedelic close-ups of scenes moving in and out of the canvas and a compelling voice-over narration of the event felt like an orchestration of instruments in a cataclysmic symphony. All of these diverse elements had been successfully combined, and they had replicated the sense of terror that I had experienced during the *Blitzkrieg*. Indeed, not even the passage of time will ever erase my memories of the day the Stukas came to our city.

Chapter 5

For those bored by peace, let them wish for a war and experience utter misery!

The morning after the initial raid on Brussels, my father, without much explanation, was asked to report to the local police station. We assumed that he was being drafted into the Civil Defense effort, and so he complied without hesitation. As it turned out, this was not a call to service, requesting that he once again perform a patriotic duty for his country and new homeland. To our profound shock, the Allies had arrested him. They placed him in military custody, classified him as an enemy alien and immediately sent him to an undisclosed internment camp, leaving my mother and me without any information about his fate or the location or nature of the camp. For my father, the arrest represented an act of supreme irony. The French and British Allies were in Belgium to help stem the German tide of invaders. As part of their security efforts, they vigorously sought to rid the country of enemy aliens. It was not surprising that my father was identified as one, as the authorities had a well-documented dossier from our legal immigration to Belgium, which included his heroic service record for Germany during the First World War. The fact that we were in Belgium because the real enemy, Nazi Germany, was hunting my father because he was a Jew was, of course, lost on the Allies.

For me, life, and indeed my whole world, would never be the same. The day the Stukas came would stay with me for the rest of my life. A strange new life, highly influenced by kismet, began to unfold like a fast-paced, action-driven dream. Years later, only after I came to terms with the fact that I must accept my new life as reality, did it become possible for me to accept the world as it had in fact become, allowing reality to creep back into my life in manageable bundles. It did so, gradually, moment by moment, until I understood that each day, and kismet, would bring me to yet another day in the life I was destined to live. Unfortunately for my father, neither kismet nor any other incarnation of fate had ever been in his corner. He was dealt so many cruel blows in his lifetime that it is hard for me to imagine worse treatment. As I ponder my life and how fortunate I have been, I often wonder if at least some of the unbelievable good luck I have experienced isn't an attempt by fate to set things right — atoning, so to speak, by being as kind and benign to me as she had been cruel to my father.

The skies were relatively quiet the rest of the day. My father was gone and my mother was hysterical. It would be several days later, during our disorganized escape from Brussels, before my mother would begin to piece together enough information to determine my father's whereabouts. We followed the instincts of most of the population. Accordingly, our first priority was protection of life and limb. More air raids were expected, presenting a constant danger that we had to address, both on an ongoing and emergency basis; the second priority was to recover whatever money my parents had in the local banks. We taped the windows to prevent flying shards of glass as one of our responses to the first priority, and then hung blackout curtains everywhere to maintain nighttime invisibility from the air. We tinted exposed shiny surfaces to minimize aerial observation. More importantly, we familiarized ourselves with all the hurriedly prepared bomb shelters in our area as well as the network of trenches in the neighboring Parc Josaphat that linked the shelters. We packed emergency equipment and supplies and, finally, we studied the information distributed by the Civil Defense workers, the police and the fire department.

Our second priority, the recovery of our money, was an epic struggle. The city was in a state of panic. There was a run on the banks, as everyone clamored to withdraw their assets. I recall my mother, holding my hand in a death grip, struggling with anyone she could collar, desperately trying to find someone who could help her get our money. We finally reached downtown Brussels and found the bank building. The mobs were brutal, too thick and too desperate. We couldn't get through the bank lobby. Our money was lost. We would have to make do with only the cash and valuables we carried on us or had hidden within the house. I have no idea how much money we lost; I just remember that any recovery was out of the question.

Chapter 5

Three days after the initial raid, the Stukas returned with increased intensity. Word was out that the Panzers were coming. The order of the day was to get ready to evacuate. We had no car, certainly no access to a truck, so we could take only what we were able to carry. My mother packed two backpacks and two suitcases. It was all we could manage. She was forced to make agonizing decisions regarding which treasures would be left behind, including those that had financial value as well as sentimental worth. My toys, of course, did not stand a chance.

We left our home on the morning of the fourth day, hoping to outrun not only the air raids, but also the Panzers that had massed to overrun the city. We knew that we would never see our house again and that it would be confiscated, occupied and maybe razed by the Nazis. As a gesture to properly reflect her excruciating frustration with what was happening to our family, my mother hung my father's Iron Cross prominently on the mantelpiece for the Germans to find. Then, we left the city, falling in with the thousands of others fleeing Brussels.

When we had been forced to abandon our home in Germany to escape from the rise of the Nazi regime, we had taken the train from Berlin to Brussels and we had enough advance warning to turn many of our belongings into cash and jewelry to assure our financial survival. This time, however, we were simply homeless, destitute refugees, part of an endless ragtag line of other refugees fleeing south, away from the German tanks that were advancing from the north. There was no United Nations organization, and there certainly was not a high commissioner for refugees. We were pariahs, left to the mercy of the land, possessing only what we were wearing and carrying. We kept our *Cartes d'Identités*, or government-issued ID card, and our ration cards. We formed passing acquaintances with fellow refugees while trudging with our bundles on the crowded Belgian roads. Along the way, we learned that many enemy aliens like my father had been sent to France. The rumor that many internment camps had been opened in the South of France gave us a further clue as to my father's whereabouts. With this new hope, we were propelled forward, ready to face whatever might lie ahead in our migration from a besieged Belgium towards the border of a seriously threatened France.

During the monotonous, exhausting trek along the macadam of the Belgian roads, my mother grieved for the time when our extended family had been all together, living in relative peace. She told me stories of her sisters and my father's siblings, and wondered what would become of them and if we would ever be reunited. Now, so many years later as I write this memoir, the best I can do is try to piece together those stories based on the scant information I have been able to gather over the years.

My mother's parents, Margareta and Leo Neustadt, came into this world around 1869. The family had lived in Spain, but fled to Breslau, Germany, in the early 1800s, a province of Lower Silesia in what is now Southwest Poland, in order to escape the Spanish Inquisition. The Neustadt family moved to Berlin before the First World War. My maternal grandfather was a superb cabinetmaker and craftsman, who created wood inlays for his furniture of such high quality that they were considered works of art. They fled Germany in 1930 for Israel when it was still called Palestine.

My maternal grandparents, Margareta and Leo Neustadt (circa 1869).

My mother was next to the youngest in a family of five girls. The youngest was Rosel (Rosa), who was born in 1907; she had one daughter, Aviva. They were able to flee to Israel when Aviva was about 11 years old. Fortunately for them, the German government was more anxious to get the Jews out of the country at that time than to kill them. Unfortunately, however, Israel proved not to be far enough for Rosa, who was killed during an Italian air raid on Tel Aviv in 1940. Gertrude (Trude) was born in 1895 and never married. She also left Germany, settling in Haifa with my grandparents.

My mother's oldest sister, Magda, was born in 1891. She

Chapter 5

From left to right: Kethe, my maternal grandmother Margareta, Trude, my mother Lily, my maternal grandfather Leo, Magda, and Rosel, front (circa 1916).

left Berlin relatively late in the exodus from Germany, and settled in Amsterdam around 1934. The last time we heard from her was when she telephoned my mother after the *Blitzkrieg*. I only overheard one side of this conversation, and it was mostly lost on me, as it was in German.

Kethe was born in 1892 and had one son, Heinrich (Heine) Lublin. They left Germany to join us in Brussels in the early 1930s, and escaped to France with us as well, but she was later caught and interned in Gurs, a French concentration camp in the Pyrenees, which served as a way station to Auschwitz and other death camps. She spent two years there before being sent to certain death at Auschwitz. During her last days in Gurs, she sent a heart-rending postcard to Heine, whose escape to Palestine she had engineered before her capture:

> Gurs, le 28, Mai, 1942
> Mein goldener Junge, Damit Du weisst wo Deine Mutti ist, sende ich Dir nun hier diese Karte.
> Nun musste ich das zweitemal fliehen, lebe mit Tausend den in einem Camp, wo fuer innere Sauberkeit gesorgt wird.
> Leider habe ich nun alles, was ich in Berlin gerettet habe in Bruessel lassen muessen. Es war mir, ob ich nun all dem noch einmal was wieder sehen wurde. Heinele wenn Du irrgendwas fuer mich tun kannst zu Dir zu kommen so tu es bald.
> Hoffentlich erricht Dich diese Karte. Meine Post aus Bruessel wirst Du wohl erhalten haben.
> Tante Lily, Peterle und ich sind zussamen ins Bruessel fort, nun sind wir getrennt worden, weil Muetter mit Kinder in ein weiteres Camp gekommen sind. Wir passen auch Mutti auf.

The following is a literal translation:

> Gurs, on 28th May 1942
> My beautiful son, in order to let you know where your mother is, I send you now this card.
> Now I had to escape a second time, live with thousands of others in a camp, where one worry about internal cleanness. Unfortunately I had to let all the things that I had from Berlin in Brussels. For me I wished if I could see them once again. Heinele, if you can do something for me to come to you, do as soon as possible. Hopefully this card will reach you. You would keep my post from Brussels with pleasure.
> Aunt Lily, Peterle and I had to leave Brussels, and we were separated because many mothers and children came into further camp.
> We care about Mother also.

The Korytowski family originated in Poland where, at one time, there had been a town called Korytow where the Korytowski family was prominent. My father's family, having moved to Berlin in the early 1900s, strongly identified with the German pre–First World War culture and Berlin society. Although my recollections are vague, I recall my grandparents surrounded by an aura of tenderness, affection and generosity. I remember being the recipient of oodles of gifts and a lot of love from them.

My father was the eldest of four children. He had three sisters—Liselotte (Lotte), Lucy, Lillie (my father's twin)—and one brother, Fritz.

Chapter 5

The Berlin crowd, from left to right: Gertrud, Al and Lotte (Cohen) Werner, Fritz, Lily Neustadt Korytowski and friend (circa 1920).

Fritz was an *enfant terrible*, the frivolous playboy counterpart of my earnest father. He was always in trouble, mostly with women, but in other areas as well. I have been told of jealous husbands coming after poor Fritz with shotguns.

My father's twin sister, Lillie, and her husband left Germany for Romania, which had been his native land before the war. However, they soon found that they had jumped from the proverbial frying pan into the fire when the Axis annexed Romania in 1940. They ultimately left Romania and immigrated to Palestine. My father's sister Lucy has remained a mystery to me, just as she was always a mystery to the others in our family. The one consistency was that everyone referred to her as "the eccentric one."

But it was my father's youngest sister, Lotte, the boss of the family, who turned out to be the real pioneer. She and her husband, Al Cohen, had been part of the Berlin in-crowd, but had the good judgment to be among the first to escape Nazi Germany, and the only ones with the prophetic wisdom to flee as far away as possible. The decision to leave the fatherland early made it possible for them to reach a true sanctuary — the Promised Land, the land of freedom and opportunity, the land of milk and honey — the

United States of America! Nearly a decade after our escape from Belgium, Lotte would become my savior and guardian.

But these reminiscences of families lost would have to wait; the hour-by-hour harshness of our situation yanked my mother and me back into the stark reality of our torturous trek towards France, safety and, hopefully, my father.

My mother changed into survival mode; she was preoccupied with the need to gather information about my father and protect us from harm and any further loss of our worldly goods. For me, it was constant hunger and thirst that occupied the front row of my concerns. We barely made it to Waterloo that first day, covering not much more than a dozen kilometers. As we passed small rural hamlets, we found a stable that the farmers had made available for the night. Village residents and good Samaritans along the road offered us water, bread and, in some cases, even fruit.

The second day on the road was more difficult. The month of May was still chilly and washing in the open with ice-cold water from a manual pump was not much fun. Stukas kept swooping in over the refugees, intermittently bombing and strafing, constantly maintaining the level of terror necessary to push us along towards the French border.

On our third night on the road, we bedded down in a church in the little town of Meslin Leveque. While the stone floor was cold and hard, we felt secure. The village priest walked up and down the central aisle amidst the pews during much of the night, assuring us that we were safe in the House of the Lord and under His special protection. We left early the next morning. That night, after another terrifying day on the road, we heard the unmistakable sound of massive bombings coming from the direction where we had been just that morning. We found out the following day through the refugee grapevine that indeed, not only had there been an air raid in Meslin Leveque, but the church where God had promised us safety had been destroyed. Some 50 people, including the priest who had comforted us the night before, had died in this senseless war episode. Although my dwindling belief in divine intervention didn't need a push, this event added substantial momentum to its downward slide.

After six days on the road, with every part of our bodies aching, our feet abused, our shoes worn far beyond their usefulness and the irresistible

Chapter 5

temptation to shed more and more of the baggage we were dragging along, we reached the city of Douai, some 60 kilometers from Brussels. Douai had just been bombed and was in flames. It was a gruesome sight. There were dead bodies and bleeding wounded in the streets. The city was in shambles. However, this was where we finally found relief. A fleet of trucks was waiting for us. The drivers, who were British and French military personnel, were milling around, together with Red Cross workers who were in a state of urgent disorganization. Without bothering to ask us, the soldiers unceremoniously loaded us on the trucks, and the Red Cross took charge of our welfare. We were on our way to Paris via Cambrai and Amiens. Most importantly, we were, for a short while at least, outside the combat zone. Unfortunately, it proved to be only the eye of the hurricane.

We did not know that our convoy was racing across the advance detachments of the German juggernaut that was driving the Allied forces relentlessly toward the English Channel. But the breakneck truck ride to Paris through the bombed-out territories and war-devastated landscapes of Northern France shed more light on the whereabouts of my father. Piecing snippets of information together during rest stops, my mother refined the earlier information she had received. She reasoned that he had been taken to a low-security seaside internment camp in Canet-Plage, used to hold a wide-ranging population, including enemy aliens, refugees and persons without proper identification. The small village of Canet-Plage was near the slightly larger one-steeple town of St. Cyprien and the good-sized metropolis of Perpignan. The latter occupies a strategic location on the Mediterranean south of Toulouse, with the Languedoc on its west. A short drive east of Perpignan, one encounters Marseille, the Riviera and a gateway to the Alps. And so, the destination for our uncomfortable journey became clear. It was to be Paris, followed by an eight-hour train ride to Toulouse in the South of France, then a brief "pit stop" in Perpignan and Canet.

When the Allied trucks finally reached Paris, they dropped us off at the *Gare D'Austerlitz*, the rail terminal that served destinations in Southwest France. For me, this was very exiting! It even beat a toy electric train. This was a real train! My first! Going to a real destination! An adventure! What fun! Alas, reality struck hard and fast. At first, we had problems finding anything; the right train, the right track, the schedule, the train access control, food, water. The experience turned my juvenile excitement into a black hole of uncertainty. The station was a nightmare, filled with a disorganized and frantic mob of military personnel wearing uniforms of all kinds; sailors with red pompons on their berets, North-African troops wearing their fezzes and colorful uniforms, Civil Defense workers also in uniform and armed local police wearing the shields and trappings of their units. The Red Cross was visible throughout and, of course, they too had uniforms. Permeating the whole scene were the throngs of refugees. Like us, many were wearing dilapidated rags. Others, strangely enough, were wearing business attire, but most of them looked haggard, their clothing frayed and sometimes caked with dirt. Most seemed hopelessly lost. Virtually all were lugging old valises, beaten-up trunks and hastily wrapped bundles; many were pushing or pulling assorted carriages and lugging devices.

Eventually, things got sorted out, we found the right train and we were on our way to Perpignan. At last I had my first train ride! Somehow, the model trains were a lot more attractive than the real thing. Our train was stuffed beyond description. There were no seats to be had, standing room near a window or exit was at a premium and toilets were inaccessible. Those with contortionist skills relieved themselves through the train's doors and windows. The other passengers had to be even more creative in disposing of their waste during the grueling ten-hour ride. The press of humanity in the confined, closed and airless space did nothing for the air we had to breathe. As the train wound its way to the southern regions of France, it started to get hot, far beyond the capacity of the fans. Sweltering heat added to the other delights of the trip.

Without a doubt, remembering the scene at the railroad station makes the meaning of Robert McNamara's term "the fog of war" clear to me. It felt like a nexus for the confusion and disorientation brought about by war. What we experienced that day was infinitely more complex than might be described in a typical novel or film on the subject, where a simplistic tableau of a train terminal might be portrayed. Unlike scenes from a novel, there was no clear distinction between good guys and bad guys, where the former are ultimately rewarded and the latter permanently damned; where the central space of the public area is filled with heroic action, ingenious spy plots, exotic weaponry and where intense romantic adventures reach highly emotional climaxes ... no, it was nothing like that! Rather, it was a time for massive anxieties, hopeless confusion, conflicting emotions, visceral fear, panic, loss of expectations, hatred, deprivation, losses of all kinds

Chapter 5

and painful discomfort subordinated only to life-threatening, immediate danger.

While war tends to induce a general loathing of the human condition, it can also bring out the best in humanity, extracting the most heroic acts and deeds from many who unsuspectingly keep this potential hidden deep in their essential being, until it is explosively released. Had it been immortalized on film, the chaos at the *Gare D'Austerlitz* and the train trip would have provided a cameo of the war not commonly seen, and a picture of the civilian front as it existed in 1940 on the eve of the German occupation of France.

Chapter 6

...But where is my father?

When we finally reached Perpignan, my mother bought me new shoes, as the trek through Belgium had ruined the old ones. This was, as usual, torture for me with my protruding big toe knuckle. However, as I could feel the intense heat from the southern sun pass from the burning sidewalks directly to the soles of my feet, I gave in to my mother's wisdom and endured the pains of breaking in new leather. Who would have thought that shoe leather would soon become all but extinct and more precious than gold; that war shortages would generate a new industry of manufacturing ersatz shoes with wood soles and cardboard tops that were about as primitive as any footwear could be, short of wooden clogs.

Without spending any more time than necessary in Perpignan, we took a bus to St. Cyprien and Canet-Plage, where we found the camp. The Canet internment camp was a men-only installation managed by the French government. Officials wouldn't allow my mother to enter the camp but they let me in, so she delegated the job of finding my father to me. Though not a high-security installation, it had all the trappings of a place of detention, including barbed wire fences, primitive wooden barracks, guard towers and a full cadre of jailers and uniformed security personnel. It held over 5,000 detainees in about a hundred wooden barracks that looked very much like those still found in U.S. Army camps; long one-story wood frame buildings with clapboard wall facing. Inside each barrack, some 50 bedding spaces were arrayed in uniform, military style. The bedding, known in France as *paillasses*, was a form of straw bedding that the condemned French royalists were given in the *Conciergerie* prison while awaiting execution during the French Revolution.

Chapter 6

I was allowed to wander freely, but finding my father among the rows of identical buildings and endless bedding spaces turned out to be a real challenge. I did not find my father during my first visit to the camp. I had no reference point, and I didn't know anybody. After several visits, however, I knew the layout of the camp and had met a few of the internees. By my third visit, I had befriended some of the guards. Most were older men, veterans of earlier wars or non-military policemen, who felt humiliated by their present job assignment. It was a job they neither liked nor understood. Their main interest was their own security rather than their mission to guard the likes of my father. What a way to end a heroic military life! Moreover, they disliked the German government even more than their assignment, and they had no confidence in the current French regime, which was on its way to becoming the infamous Vichy government. What really mattered to them was the future of France and their place in that future. The best they could expect, if the *Fritzes*, as the French called the Germans, completed their invasion of France, was to be drafted into a work camp somewhere in Germany. For them, losing this war was a lot more than defeat on the battlefield; it was a total reorganization of life as they had known it before the conflict.

By socializing with the men I met during my wanderings around the camp, I was able to give them enough of a description of my father to trigger recollections and sightings that narrowed my search, first to the section of the camp where he was located, then to the barrack he occupied. I was directed to his *paillasse* and, with my heart in my mouth, I sat next to it and waited for his arrival. Over an hour passed and, with the fast oncoming dusk, the darkness of night was threatening. As I was not allowed in the camp at night, I reluctantly left my vigil and met my mother outside the gate. At least I knew where my father was; I just hadn't seen him yet.

The next morning, I finally found my father. He was crouched outside the barrack while a fellow prisoner performed a dental procedure on him. I assumed that the man who was treating him was a qualified dentist, yet what gave me concern were the instruments he was using—they were completely primitive. Given the circumstances, this should not have been a surprise, but really, a mallet, pliers and a pair of chisels—that looked a bit too medieval for me!

Although my father saw me immediately, he could neither talk nor smile while he was being worked on. When he was able to communicate, he did manage to put me at ease — what was being done was nothing more than some deferred maintenance on his dentures. I felt wonderful about having found my father, and that he was in good health. Thinking back, I now realize that finding him did not have the expected emotional impact of a long-awaited reunion. After all, we were only separated for two or three weeks and there had been no suggestion that his life was in danger. No, finding my father was more of a comforting relief from the anxieties that prevailed during those turbulent times. At least we would now be able to function as a family once again, albeit marginally, as long as he was in the camp.

I was allowed in the camp to visit my father as often as I wanted. My mother had to wait outside the camp, but arrangements were made for her to see him. She kept herself busy by providing him with supplies and other necessities. There was never a problem bringing goods into camp, and we were even allowed to go on one or two special outings with my father. Most memorably, the village of Canet enjoyed the distinction of being the cantaloupe capital of France. Every year, the village, undeterred by wars, celebrated its exalted status with an extraordinary *Festival des Melons*. We attended one of these festivals and found it as delightful as it was offbeat. It was the kind of event that typically endears the French to food mavens of the world. Although my mother and I fully immersed ourselves in the festivities, the internees had to be satisfied with nothing more than a taste of melon.

Meanwhile, France was in chaos. In the aftermath of Dunkirk, the Allies left the continent, regrouping in England, leaving France isolated, with only ad-hoc forces that were unable to offer organized resistance against the German invasion. As a result, France collapsed on the 18th of June 1940. An armistice and terms of surrender were signed on June 22. According to the armistice, France was divided into two zones. One was to be left to the French in full sovereignty, at least nominally, and the other was to be occupied by the Germans. The unoccupied *Zone Libre*, or Free Zone, comprised the southeastern two-fifths of the country, with Vichy as its capital. Paris remained the capital of the remaining three-fifths of the country. Philippe Petain, the 80-plus-year-old World War I French army marshal known as the "Hero of Verdun," was placed in control of Vichy, as part of the capitulation process. At the same time, the less than heroic Pierre Laval, who actively advocated collaboration with the

Chapter 6

Germans, shared control with Petain as minister of state. Together, they represented a French puppet government at Vichy and thus defined Franco-German relations for the rest of the war. The way was open for the occupation of France.

The German invasion proceeded relentlessly and the occupation of France occurred with Teutonic precision. For my father, the armistice meant that control of the Canet internment camp would be changing from a French civilian jurisdiction to a German military authority. Under Nazi control, there was little doubt about the fate of the prisoners. Once the new order took over the camp, my father would be viewed as a Jew, not as an enemy alien who represented a military threat. He would certainly not be recognized or accepted as a World War I Iron Cross recipient! For him, the term "changing of the guards" acquired a whole new meaning. It was critical to get him out of there as soon as possible, before the change in control took full effect.

My mother vigorously engineered my father's escape. She succeeded in bribing an array of guards with packs of cigarettes and other goodies. At a propitious time, one dark night, they allowed my father to slip out and rejoin us. The day after his escape, the change in command occurred and the Germans took over the camp; the entire cadre of French guards and camp security personnel resigned their positions and scattered around the region to avoid the German labor camps — and we held our breath. I will never know for sure if my father's absence had been noted at roll call. All that mattered was that no one tried to track us down, nor did they organize any searches for us. We were once again free to start a new life in a new town with renewed hope that the war would end before we were found.

CHAPTER 7

Toulouse: A Less Than Perfect Solution

Once my father was sprung from the Canet internment camp, our destination was Toulouse. This picturesque capital of France's southwest was the most logical haven available, albeit only a temporary one, since the Germans were not as yet occupying Toulouse and the region was part of the Free Zone of France. We had very little money and no good means of earning any. A solid form of employment could lead to exposure, and that would have dire consequences. Yet, given our unfamiliarity with the area, there was really little choice, and Toulouse seemed to be the destination with the greatest potential for securing some sort of livelihood.

We moved into a tiny, one-room, fifth-floor apartment, a *pied-à-terre*, near the *Cathedrale St. Sernin*. My mother cooked on a small, single-burner Sterno stove. We established official residency by applying for ration cards, without which we could not buy food. Since those cards needed to be consistent with our Belgian *Cartes d'Identités*, which were in the name of Korytowski, they would be a liability in a Nazi-infected area. To prevent detection, my parents asked me to call upon the skills for which I had once been punished — my ability to forge documents, which I had almost perfected while trying to keep my parents from finding out how badly behaved I had been in school. They hoped that if I could alter my teachers' notes to them, I could alter the ration cards well enough to avoid detection. And so, I changed our names on the cards to Engglenger, a name we chose because it did not sound Jewish and also had the same number of letters as Korytowski, thus helping to mask the alterations.

I went to school in that same neighborhood, although my time in Toulouse would be short-lived. I started school in the fall of 1940. It was almost a religious school, being heavily influenced by its neighborhood in the shadow of the famous cathedral. Being a newcomer to the neighborhood, a stranger in France and not able to follow the religious rites which prevailed in this quintessentially Catholic country, it was not surprising that I was perceived as being "different." This, of course, got me into all kinds of trouble. Ultimately, the alienation rose to violence. The fighting rink was the sidewalk and the sport was either wrestling or bare-knuckle boxing. In either case, the target always seemed to be my nose, and there was always blood. I think that, despite the fact that there were subsequent instances of street or schoolyard fights, it was this particular period that cured me of any impulse towards physical violence. It was just too painful! But there was a bright spot in my life from this period. It was my participation in an art contest sponsored by a cinema on Toulouse's main street, Rue Alsace-Lorraine. I submitted a watercolor, and won fourth prize — a movie pass good at any time for one year. I would never get to use my pass, however, as Toulouse was fast approaching the point where it could no longer be considered a safe haven.

The German occupation of the region had ushered in an era dominated by fear, with foreigners looked upon with suspicion and antipathy. For those suspected of being Jewish, it was far worse. They were the untouchables and had to stay hidden at all cost. Any contact with them presented a threat to one's security. We met more and more people in the normal course of daily life who were either Vichy sympathizers or outright Nazi collaborators. They, and others who were anxious to endear themselves to the new regime, were a constant threat to us, since they could potentially denounce us at any time. After the armistice, when the outwardly benign-appearing Vichy government had been put in place, the Nazis and the French collaborators acquired an awesome capacity for ferreting out Jews. Their success in this sport was far greater in the large urban centers than in the countryside. We had become not only refugees from the German bombing raids in Brussels but also fugitives now in deep hiding from the German occupation forces in France, the French collaborators and the French chauvinists, who were genetically constituted to consider any stranger an intruder. There were exceptions, however. These were the heroes who refused to collaborate and who placed themselves at risk and in mortal danger should they be exposed for helping Jews. Indeed, despite a lot of conflicting stories told after the war, my own personal experience was that the Catholic Church and many in the clergy always behaved admirably and with great courage, and must be counted among the heroes.

Life inside conquered France and, more particularly in large cities like Toulouse, is hard to imagine. There prevailed a constant feeling of suffocating paranoia that hovered over all of us. Fear overwhelmed the population and followed all of our movements like a menacing shadow ready to engulf us at any time. Everything was a threat! Anyone wearing a uniform, either German or French, could ask for our papers on nothing more than a whim. Civilians all started to look like Gestapo agents or collaborators. Bars and coffee houses were potential traps and streetcars made us feel particularly vulnerable, as they were places with limited escape routes. There was risk in talking to anyone, especially strangers. France's capitulation to Germany had turned the country into a virtual prison. The borders with Switzerland, Spain, Germany, Italy and Belgium formed a net from which even the most daring escape was nearly impossible. We squirmed and struggled for several months inside this net, distressed to see it tighten all the time. Controlled beyond anything imaginable, travel within France was hampered by countless roadblocks, food shortages, train and bus searches, demands for identity papers and permits. Foreign travel required visas that were issued sparingly and gave rise to a great deal of suspicion. Most terrifying was the fact that the Vichy, or German collaborators, were visible everywhere. Clearly, the noose was getting tighter.

At the same time, my parents were led to believe that the war could last a long time. Goebbels's propaganda machine worked overtime. France was effectively in a news blackout and a movement straitjacket. German censors sanitized all news. There was little good news filtering down and it was always overwhelmed by the crowing propaganda interjected into all manner of radio and newspapers. Even the tiniest glimmer of Allied success, of which there was a paucity, was extinguished by the Nazis in what we now call "spin." Radio programs, dominated by Vichy and Nazi martial music, broadcast news designed to impress us with how terrible things were for France. According to the pronouncements from the Nazi propaganda machinery, the Allies somehow had no capacity for victory of any kind, and the Reich was on the verge of becoming masters of the world.

As our situation deteriorated, escape seemed more and more impossible. Yet, after several conversations with people my parents had learned to trust as kindred souls, there seemed to be two possible avenues of

Chapter 7

escape — one through Switzerland, the other through Spain to America. Switzerland was one of the few European countries that were still neutral. In fact, it was reputed to be a bastion of neutrality. It managed to remain generally unscathed by the war, as its safety rested in the need to keep the Swiss's precious international banking establishment out of harm's way. With interests and tendrils throughout the Western world, the Swiss were protected against adversity in a way that no other country could match in those times. Ironically, it was this virtue, namely the perception of safety from the events unfolding in the rest of Europe, which made it impossible for us to move there. Everybody wanted to live in Switzerland, and Switzerland went to extraordinary efforts to keep immigrants out, if for no other reason than to maintain its pristine neutrality and protect the banks. They were exquisitely draconian in preventing anyone from setting foot on their soil. Clearly, escape to Switzerland was out of the question.

We then considered the second, more complex escape option. It meant trying for America. But to accomplish this would involve many moving pieces and a lot of money. A large network of relationships operated secretly on an international level. It included guides, local contacts in most cities, and suppliers of identity papers, safe hiding places supplied with food and survival equipment, means of transportation and a communication system. My parents arranged to meet with a guide connected with the Toulouse network. The man seemed a little old but very animated. He was well dressed but he sported tattoos on his arms and a beaded necklace around his neck. Fortunately for us, he turned out to be one of the good guys. He painstakingly explained the details of the escape plan. He told us that we would first have to make our way across the Pyrenees and cross the border into Spain. Generalisimo Fransico Franco, Spain's dictator, did not espouse Hitler's obsession against the Jews, and many refugees who tried to cross into Spain from France had succeeded. The next step would involve making our way to Casablanca in North Africa by boat. There, the guide told us, the network had access to transatlantic ships that would take us for the crossing to America. The price for this adventure was, not surprisingly, commensurate with its risks and far more than what was left of our limited supply of money. My parents concluded that, while this second option seemed technically feasible, the odyssey of reaching America in this convoluted manner was extremely chancy. For the plan to succeed we would need more than luck; at the moment, it was unaffordable. Until we could find the means to replenish our badly depleted money, we would have no choice but to continue to live in France under precarious circumstances. We would need to find a hiding place in the countryside, much safer than a large city, as the Germans had concentrated their activities in the cities, where house-to-house searches were easier and more productive. The village needed to be small enough to be ignored by the world, but large enough to offer some form of employment. After considerable research, my parents decided on Mane, a tiny, one-street village about 30 kilometers from Toulouse and St. Girons, in the foothills of the Pyrenees. It was time for us to prepare for a long stay there, in deep hiding. We created a cover story not too far from the actual truth, whereby our home in the North had been destroyed by the *Blitzkrieg*, and that our stay would be temporary. We certainly did not want anyone to know that we were Jewish or that we hoped to safely stay hidden in the village until the end of the war.

And so, in late summer of 1941, the Engglenger family left Toulouse and moved to Mane. I finally felt that my encounter with Hitler's *Blitzkrieg* was over. Little did I realize that the real terror of life under Nazi occupation was just beginning.

CHAPTER 8

Mane: The Daring Dairy Odyssey

And so, early on a cool fall morning in 1941, we packed our meager belongings and quietly disappeared, hopefully without leaving a trace. We caught the bus from Toulouse to Mane. I had just turned ten and, like most children, I was looking forward to the adventure with wonder and anticipation, even though it meant yet another new school. While that thought did not fill me with pedagogic excitement, it was an opportunity to make new friends. More accurately, Pierre Engglenger would make new friends, as we had decided to keep the name a bit longer in order to avoid unnecessarily testing my forgery skills. Mane would be a fresh start, a promising new place into which we could go into even deeper hiding.

The bus dropped us off in front of the post office building on Mane's main street. My parents rented a ground-floor apartment in a modest two-story, three-family house located towards the end of that street, somewhat removed from the center of activity. While our new home was a small, one-bedroom apartment with a living room and an eat-in kitchen, it felt like a palace. We had considerably more space than in our last abode, where our kitchen consisted of a sink and a Sterno stove, and where we all shared the same bed.

My parents knew that their first priority was to find a way to replenish our badly depleted funds, not only to provide for food, rent and basic necessities but, if we were to have any chance at all to escape from France, we would also need a considerable amount of savings. For my father, practicing his profession as an architect in the little village was out of the question, as was any possibility for my mother to create and manage a day care facility as she had done in Germany almost 15 years earlier. I am not sure how the idea emerged, but my parents saw an opportunity to produce and

Peter, revisiting the home where he last lived with his parents (Mane, France, 1996).

sell dairy products made from the abundant supply of milk from the many small farms around Mane. No one in the village had gone into this business, probably because the lack of one or two large dairy farms meant that milk needed to be collected from many small, widely dispersed farms, making profitability more of a challenge. Although the relationship between architecture and cheese was exotically remote, my parents jumped into it with great vigor. They learned the technology of the dairy industry from whatever

Chapter 8

sources they could lay their hands on and, after a few false starts and much experimentation, production finally got underway in our little apartment. We would each have our respective jobs in the new enterprise; my father would be in charge of production, my mother, quite naturally, became the business manager (with the secondary self-assigned responsibility of enforcing sanitary standards), and my role would be procurement of the milk from the suppliers and delivery of the end products to our customers.

Clearly, it would not be possible to walk between the farms, which were spread over a 15-kilometer radius, and the local bus system was not viable for this purpose either, as the schedules were too rigid and the stops often too far removed from the farms. A bicycle, which was as much a necessity in those days as owning a car is today, emerged as the principal means for accomplishing this. Because this represented a sizable outlay for my parents, the purchase had to be a practical one. It would not be a children's toy, a racing bike or a fancy touring one; it would be a grown man's bike, primarily suited for my father, since my mother would never ride such a dangerous contraption. I had never ridden a bike in my life, but I knew I must bond with it — and quickly. This turned out to be an important, but somewhat painful, step on my road to adulthood. I felt particularly proud of this new challenge because, in addition to endowing me with a new level of mobility, it would enable my entry into the hallowed world of private enterprise. I would become an indispensable cog in our dairy adventure. But it was not a bed of roses.

In order to perform my mission, I had to first learn to ride the bike. As a full-size men's bike, it was too large for me but, according to my mother, I would soon grow into it. In the meantime, I had to cope with that miserable horizontal bar that does not exist on women's bikes. It was too high and it consistently hit me in the crotch when I slipped off the pedals. Until I became proficient, I was condemned to a painful black and blue crotch, made worse every time I had to change positions on the bike. Eventually, I did master this wondrous equipment, and it soon evolved from a necessity into an amusement device and, in the years to come, a critical survival tool. While my father had confidence in my role in our new enterprise, my mother was, as usual, nervous about turning me loose in the countryside. As for me, the bike gave me a newfound level of freedom, independence and mobility. When riding, I became welded to the saddle; I felt naked, small and awkward when I dismounted.

Every day, I would pedal the 30 or more kilometers required to commute between the farms that sold us the milk. The bottles — empty wine bottles — hung inside sacks which my father had made to fit over the handlebars and the rear wheel like saddlebags. When empty, they clanged together noisily and, when full, they made a clunking sound as I went over bumps. I learned to repair the tires, which were constantly beaten up by ill-maintained roads. Flats often plagued me and, on frequent occasions, I had to ride at night. This was a very disconcerting experience, as the only source of light on the pitch-black roads came from a tiny bike light my father had mounted on my handlebars. Power for the lantern came entirely from the sweat and tears of my pedal action, which gave life to the small generator powered by the turning of the bike's front wheel. But, within a short time, all the farmers knew me and were grateful to have found a new outlet for their milk.

Once the milk was collected and brought back to our apartment, the bottles were emptied into a larger bowl-like container, where the cream rose to the surface and was separated from the rest of the milk. Next, my father skimmed the cream off the milk and poured it into another bottle, which he used instead of a churn, shaking it until specks of butter started to form. I will always remember the comic scene of my father dancing around the apartment in his underwear, moving to the rhythms of whatever classical sounds could be extracted from an old phonograph we had found. Eventually, the churned cream clumped into butter and the remaining liquid became buttermilk. Butter was in great demand, and thus very easy to sell. Buttermilk was less popular, but here too, there was sufficient demand and nothing went to waste. After the cream was skimmed off and turned into butter and buttermilk, the residue was allowed to coagulate and curdle over a period of about 24 hours. The product was separated yet one more time into solid curds and liquid whey. The latter with its solids was then turned into cottage cheese, and the bigger curds were kneaded and shaped into cheeses. It was at that point that the cheese was flavored, and where each became endowed with its own special character. The final step was to allow the cheese to ripen under the pressure of variable weights until each cheese had fully developed. My father's homespun operation succeeded in producing a kind of hybrid between a very runny Liederkranz and classic Brie that was really quite respectable. The various cheeses, the butter and the cottage cheese were incredibly popular. The milk was, of course, neither pasteurized nor homogenized. This lack of modern technology produced the kinds of delicious flavors that our current over-sanitized and ultra-pasteurized world has long since forgotten.

While our new enterprise was growing, I was getting to know my new school, which, as usual, I didn't like. But then again, I never liked any of my schools, nor was I particularly fond of the village and our humdrum life there. Clearly for a ten-year-old boy who had just survived the *Blitzkrieg* and eluded the Nazi manhunt, this was anticlimactic and there seemed very little about Mane to get excited about. Luckily, I soon became close friends with a local boy my age — Robert Soula. We explored everything together, sifting through the most remote corners of the countryside. I knew that my parents were under great financial stress, while at the same time fearing for our lives but, as a child, I was able to subordinate both stress and fear to the thrill of experiencing a new and very different environment. Robert taught me all about his favorite pastimes and showed me his secret hideouts, and it was fascinating. I would never have known the thrill of sledding if I had continued to live in a city, nor would I have had the opportunity to construct a ridiculously crude version of Frank Lloyd Wright's architectural masterpiece "Falling Waters," which he built outside Pittsburgh in 1934. Our "Falling Waters" was a shack we used as a *No Girls Allowed* clubhouse, which we built in great secrecy on top of a riverlet in the middle of an open wheat field. The water was allowed to run underneath the shanty-like structure and the effects of this arrangement were spectacular! This was where we learned to smoke and discussed the many things parents don't always share with their kids. In fact, on one occasion, when we snuck off to our lair, we caught a German soldier with one of the local maidens. Startled by our intrusion, he jumped up and pulled out his Luger — and we ran for our lives!

In the process of exploring all the activities this new environment offered, Robert and I managed to stay out of trouble — more or less — except for my encounter with the sport of sledding, which would turn into a disaster. Racing down a hill on a few slabs of wood that had been nailed together was an unimaginable activity for a city boy. But here in the countryside, it was popular among both school kids and adults. Within a short walking distance of the village, there was an old water tower sitting on top of a fairly impressive hill. The latter inspired all kinds of daring feats performed by friends and schoolmates on their sleds. During the few occasions when it snowed or rained, the hill provided the opportunity for kids to haul out their little homemade wooden sleds, called *Luges*; nothing like the slick version used in Olympic competitions, but the barebones kind that anyone could make with a hammer, a saw and some nails. Robert and I had fabricated a sled with used boards and other secondhand material. Like the rest of the kids, we would drag this improvised contraption up the hill and then slide down the slopes at furious speeds ... with no control whatsoever! The rides were thrilling, even if their endings were often humiliating, and we survived unscathed. Always out of control whether on snow, mud or wet grass, we ended our rides sprawled at various levels on the glide path. Only on rare occasions did a ride end with anyone left standing at the bottom. Now it must be said, riding these improvised sleds was indeed dangerous, given their primitive construction and the hazardous nature of the terrain, not to mention the chancy weather conditions. But we were prepared to ignore all the dangers and safety warnings in the name of peer pressure. After all, hadn't my parents told me that it was essential for me to blend in?

It took a fatal construction flaw in our sled to end my career. I have always found it convenient to hold poor Robert — my best pal, playmate and all-around companion — responsible for what happened. But truthfully, in our fervor to complete the job, neither of us noticed a large rusty nailhead protruding from the side of the frame near one of the runners. And so it happened, on the occasion of an exceptionally good spill, the rusty nailhead ripped out an appreciable piece of my calf. This was not a mere cut that could be stitched. It was a large, open gouge that had to heal very gradually, with the ever-present danger of tetanus and other infections, during a time when antibiotics were not generally known or available. Naturally, my mother swung into action and, once again, displayed her medical and nursing wizardry. There is nothing like profuse iodine and various other disinfecting alcohols on an open wound to discourage heroic behavior! For some reason my mother did not use hydrogen peroxide. Maybe it was rationed out of existence? We shall never know, but after three weeks or so in bed, I was able to go back to school, limping, with my leg heavily bandaged. Some three months later, the wound had closed, but so had any further chapters in my sledding career. The experience reinforced once again that "mother" meant security, protection and the ultimate sense of being in the right place at the right time!

Chapter 8

While on the subject of accidents, there was yet another episode during this period that required my mother's ministrations. This one, however, left a more serious scar, not on my body but on my psyche. There was a shallow, fast-running stream nearby, brimming with trout. Fly-fishing became a passion, and I became an expert. I knew how to make rods, I knew the hooks, the lures, the baits, the different kinds of lines, the corks and floaters and the techniques for different kinds of fishing. To catch trout, I stood in the cold stream and tossed the line out, again and again, until there was life at its end. Then, I used my net to capture the fish, removed the hook and drop it in a pail that I usually left on the riverbank. Deep down, I always felt that this was a cruel process, and I empathized with the fish and the live bait. However, I managed to rationalize all this by convincing myself that I really had no idea how fish actually felt. Then one day, all that changed.

Standing barefoot in the stream, balancing on the slippery stones, I lost my footing and the big toe on my right foot had to take my full weight. Unfortunately, I landed on a piece of glass that, forced by the weight of my body, cut my toe almost by half. Blood was gushing, and the water was turning red. I barely managed to keep from fainting, but finally clambered onto the shore and hobbled home as best I could. There, of course, I was in good hands in the ever-present care of my mother. But, the thought that repeated in my mind during this incident was that my pain was nothing compared to the pain I had caused the fish on the hook and, more significantly, that what I had experienced was not just an accident, but God telling me to stop hurting His creations. This thinking, reinforced by my swaddled toe, induced such a sense of guilt in me that I never wanted to go fishing again. In fact, this empathy business has always been a burden for me. I did manage to avoid becoming a vegetarian, although I came close to becoming one, perhaps even a vegan, because of the empathy I felt for all living things. Fortunately, or maybe unfortunately, the realities of war and deprivation submerged these humanitarian instincts and, once food was plentiful again, I realized that I was doomed to remain devoid of any qualms about eating fish — or beef, or lamb chops, or even *foie gras*, for that matter!

There was very little question that, over time, our dairy business could have developed into a highly profitable concern, since my mother was an outstanding success in displaying and marketing the growing product line that emerged from our tiny apartment. Alas, success is always accompanied by notoriety, and for us that meant deadly danger. We had moved to Mane to hide, not to seek fame; the last thing we sought was notoriety. But, in the final analysis, Mane turned out to be a good hiding place for a short time, as it was too small for the Germans to care about. On the other hand, the war seemed endless, and the Nazi determination to cleanse the world of people like us was unrelenting. We had become well known in Mane, not as Jews, but as strangers. And that was enough to rekindle all the fears that had originally led to our attempt to find sanctuary in the countryside. We simply could not dismiss the fact that the Nazi presence was all around us.

As we built up our dairy enterprise, we had dared dream that Mane would be our permanent shelter from the war. Alas, this was not in the cards. The Germans, who had shown little interest in France's internal political arrangements as long as public order was maintained, were becoming a great deal harsher in their governance. Threatened by the prospects of invasions from the Mediterranean as well as the Atlantic, security was of paramount concern, and the Nazis intruded more and more in local governmental affairs, seeking a far tighter level of control. There were several factors that led to this tightening of the screws.

First, in 1942 after Hitler abandoned the *Blitzkrieg* phase of the war, Germany started to convert all the territory it had secured into a full-scale war economy. This meant that all occupied territories had to supply workers for German factories. It also meant that heretofore-peaceful regions such as the Toulouse countryside in so-called Free France were now swept into the collaboration agreement with the Petain-Laval Vichy government, and France became the de facto collector of forced labor for the German war machine. For us, this was a significant threat, since the risk of being identified as either Jews or immigrants grew to virtual certainty in Vichy's new eagerness to please the conquerors. Neighbors, school acquaintances, friends — anyone we might encounter socially or in connection with our business — could give us away inadvertently, or worse, deliberately.

Second, our anxieties had reached a crescendo with the elevation of Hitler's threats to exterminate all the Jews. The avowed rhetoric and the scope of his threats resonated throughout France. At the same time, any news of German setbacks never made it through the net of German censorship. With Teutonic zeal, the implementation of Hitler's extermination policy had been embraced by both the German establishment and the French collaborators. The latter were given incentives, such as additional privileges and generous financial rewards, for information about Jews hiding in France. We had become highly vulnerable, not to mention profitable, targets for capture, and our notoriety as cheese-makers extraordinaire dramatically increased the likelihood of discovery.

The third factor that led to the tightening of the screws was the growing vigor and organizational power of the French Resistance, which heightened the Germans' nervousness and vigilance over security. As a result, there was increased paranoia among the German leaders, who left less and less responsibility to the French police, and significantly increased their presence amidst the civilian population. They were everywhere. Repression, torture, hostage taking and door-to-door searches became commonplace. They increased pressure on the resistance, now reorganized as the FFI (*Forces Française de L'Interieure*). The FFI was the successor to the maquis, and they had combined their resources to conduct raids and sabotage activities. It wasn't long before the resistance was able to link up with London, where Charles de Gaulle and other French heroes held court. To the German and the Vichy governments, members of the resistance were considered and treated as terrorists.

As if the German military and the collaborators were not enough, there was also the *Milice*, a para-military militia formed at Hitler's personal request by Pierre Laval, Pétain's generally despised first minister, to fight the resistance and wipe out terrorism. The *miliciens* emerged mostly from the ranks of the French Foreign Legion and were generally considered German allies. They were mostly boorish mercenaries, organized to fight *Maquis* nests and become a countervailing force against the FFI. The *Milice* acquired official status in November 1942 and, shortly thereafter, Hitler overruled the Vichy government's independence. At the same time, the Allies invaded Morocco and Algeria, requiring the Germans to demand more men for the factories. Draft-aged locals tried to avoid this fate at all costs, including assuming a clandestine life and joining the resistance. The *Milice* would go anywhere to run them to ground and, if in the process, they happened upon some Jews in hiding—*tant pis*...! (no matter), it would be all to the good.

These worsening conditions made us revisit our options for escape to safer havens. Alas, we found that little had changed. Switzerland was more out of the question than ever before, and our situation in France was growing more tenuous every day. Our presence in Mane was no longer a secret. Our success in making cheeses and dairy products may have been the envy of any would-be entrepreneur, but the activity was also a red flag that could bring attention to us and lead to the discovery that we were Jews. It was only a matter of time before the inexorable efficiency of the relentless German search apparatus would catch up with us. Within the broader context, conditions had worsened for the Nazis, both in North Africa and, on the Eastern Front, in Russia, where the battle of Stalingrad was not only raging, but also proving that the super race was indeed vulnerable. This added even more urgency to our decision to leave, as we knew that a wounded enemy in fear of losing its power could be far more lethal than a secure one, bloated with the confidence of military success. As the Vichy puppet government was gradually marginalized throughout the former Free Zone, German military units moved to take up positions and bases all the way to the Mediterranean, their olive-green uniforms appearing where none had been seen before. Both *Wehrmacht* and *Waffen SS*, the armed military branch of the SS, could turn up anywhere. Life had become much more perilous for all of us as 1942 turned into 1943.

I was well aware of what was happening around us from news broadcasts, dinner table conversations and discussions with friends and immediate neighbors, and knew that we could not go on much longer in hiding.

My parents determined that, as before, the only escape from the ever-tightening Nazi noose was across the Pyrenees into Spain, then on to Casablanca and America. Fortunately, our dairy business had given us enough resources to hire a guide, and we lived relatively close to the Spanish border. We knew from rumors that, once in Spain, the Franco government, unlike the Swiss, did not rebuff refugees and allowed them passage to and through their country. My father lauded Generalissimo Franco, who had publicly expressed a benign attitude towards immigration into Spain from France. The only remaining challenges were to find the safest means to get us over the Pyrenees and, once safe in Spain, to make sure that the remaining elements of the elaborate escape plan were firmly in place. My parents recognized that the escape plan would be fraught with danger and uncertainty, and even considered the possibility of splitting the family up, leaving one of my parents behind to secure help for those on the journey

Chapter 8

should anything go wrong. But in the end, the decision was made that we would leave as a family, or not at all.

My parents found a guide who was unlike the first guide we had met in Toulouse when our escape plans were thwarted by the lack of resources. He was a middle-aged man with a weatherbeaten face who looked and acted more like a local farmer than a gypsy. He spent about an hour in our home, absorbed in a very animated discussion with my parents. I sensed that it was the mountains that really held his interest, but much of the hour was spent in tense negotiations about how the proceeds of the payment would be meted out. The rest of the time was spent on detailed instructions about how the escape plan would unfold in order to assure our safety ... and his own. When he left, he was folding a wad of money that my father had given him, a sum sufficient to get all of us to Casablanca!

While I was excited at the prospect of another new adventure, I couldn't help but sense my parents' fear that the plan was unrealistic, but I trusted them so completely, I did not share their anxiety. And at the age of 11, I had no idea how long and arduous the trek over the mountains would be, nor how hard it would be for my parents, who were now in their mid-forties, and not in the best of health.

Unbeknownst to me, they had prepared our neighbors in Mane for the possibility that we might be separated, and they had found an older couple in Toulouse who had agreed to give me shelter should that become necessary. Before we left, my father gave me a slip of paper on which he had penciled the name and address of the couple in Toulouse, and told me to take it to our neighbors in Mane if we were separated or the escape aborted. There was nothing else on that slip of paper: anything more than that might prove dangerous for the people who had agreed to help us. I pocketed the note without a word. Precautions were one thing, but failure was unthinkable, so we discussed it no further.

We studied the maps until we had them memorized. Finally, we received notice that the time for escape was right — we were set to go. On the night before Easter there was no moon and, in the spirit of Easter, the Germans had reduced the number of mountain patrols along the route from four to three. We rehearsed our cover story before we left Mane; we were going away for a few days — a leisurely hiking trip in the mountains for a short holiday. Packing for the trip required very little, as just a few things would be necessary for hiking, and anything else we carried would arouse suspicion. We began our escape in the early afternoon by taking a bus from Mane to the neighboring town of Salis du Salat, a thermal spring only a few kilometers from Mane, but too far to walk. In Salis, we connected with another bus that took us to St. Girons, a small city with a population of about 8,000, located some 100 kilometers south of Toulouse, at the very base of the Pyrenees.

The bus from Salis du Salat to St. Girons was not crowded, which was not unusual. Except for market days and festivals, when everybody either jumped on the buses or hung onto their sides from their bicycles so that they could be pulled up the hilly inclines instead of having to pedal, the buses had few passengers. There was a lady of a certain age, dressed entirely in black and engrossed in her knitting, and two older men dressed in farmer's blues, their ubiquitous Basque berets on their heads. One was chewing tobacco; the other was relieving his anxieties by smoking something he had created from cornhusks, used in lieu of cigarettes and tobacco that were rationed or simply unavailable in France at the time. There was no conversation; everybody boarded as a stranger and left the same way. There was always the possibility that the Germans would stop the bus to check identity papers, or that there would be collaborators posing as fellow passengers, but not today. We reached St. Girons without being discovered and proceeded to the agreed-upon intersection where we were to meet our guide.

He was there waiting for us, prepared with more specific information on the mountains, the road we would be hiking, the pattern of German patrols and the schedule of the French border guards. It was clear that he was well-schooled in the subtleties of the hide-and-seek games that were constantly afoot between the local smugglers and the border guards. The smugglers and the guards actually knew each other well and usually drank together the morning after their nocturnal escapades, celebrating their respective exploits from the night before. Most of the exploits did not involve refugees, as the smuggling of goods generally available only on the black market (including liquors, tobacco, silks and leather wares) were considered more desirable and far less risky cargo than human beings seeking sanctuary from the Germans. When we left the guide, after agreeing on where we would meet at dusk, we had an early dinner in a small café.

Finally, it was time. Carrying our minimal baggage, we ambled out on what was designed to appear as a leisurely stroll through town. We

Chapter 8

spotted the guide and, staying some distance back, we followed him along the paved road until he turned onto a dirt road in the direction of the mountains. I had to make a conscious effort to remember that this was not simply "a walk in the park," that our lives were in danger as never before, and I had to be diligent in watching for any signs of potential trouble. If we were careful — and very lucky — we were on the path that would take us out of France, right under the noses of the Germans and the collaborators!

Chapter 9

A Night to Remember

As dusk began to settle, two other couples joined us in our leisurely walk. Eventually, the dirt road crossed a junction. On one side, there was a paved road, with carefully designed and well-maintained switchbacks. It was for motor vehicles rather than pack animals or people on foot, and was heavily patrolled by the Germans and border guards. The other side was a narrow, unpaved path which was also patrolled, but minimally so. The guide turned onto the unpaved path and it quickly became much steeper. As the church steeples of St. Girons melted into the dark of the night, the group began to slow as we climbed the mountain. The guide was oblivious to the extra effort, as this was his home territory. I was also oblivious to the exertion, being full of energy from the recent dinner and expectations of a great adventure, one that would surely keep me from school for quite awhile.

For me, this was a lark, and for reasons I will never understand, the gravity of the situation never really struck me. My parents had shielded me from the fear of being caught. But for them, the dangers and uncertainties of the journey were all too clear. What it meant to be caught was too terrifying for rational thought. While they knew that they could abort the escape and turn back at any point, the guide had pointed out that they would almost certainly run into a patrol in the process. In the final analysis, there was one compelling reason for pushing on, regardless of the effort required — there was simply no alternative!

Our path, used only by mules and smugglers, was not a well-worn path. It was full of brush, thorns and rocks, and covered with second growth trees. The steepness of the path varied a great deal. My parents had problems keeping up with the pace set by the guide, particularly on

Chapter 9

the steeper parts, and the temptation to stray onto the paved area was ever-present.

Meanwhile, I cavorted along the mountain path with the guide, out in front of the group. As the path became more difficult, my parents trailed farther behind with every step. As we continued to rise, the path twisted to break the angle of ascent, and it was not long before the rest of the group had dropped out of sight, and the guide and I were walking alone. When we realized this, we stopped, hoping everyone would soon catch up. When they didn't, we doubled back. We found the other two couples, but my parents were nowhere to be found. It was as if a mysterious hand had swept through the mountainside below us, swallowing them up. The reality was as stark as it was frightening. My parents were lost, most likely intercepted by a German patrol like injured prey hunted in the African bush.

I wouldn't have the luxury of time to dwell on the situation. The guide demanded an immediate decision from me — continue on with him and the other couples or stay behind — because if they had found my parents, it would be only minutes before a French border patrol or worse, a German *Wehrmacht* patrol, would intercept our path. For the first time a life-or-death decision was entirely up to me! I was shocked into the realization that there would be neither a mother nor a father with whom to deliberate the matter.

I had two options, but no information about what had happened to my parents to help me make a choice. I could stay with the guide and the rest of the party and continue the adventure. If I opted for this alternative, I felt that I would be plunging into a black hole of uncertainty — an epic mountain trek across the French/Spanish border followed by an unchartered voyage through Spain, a country with which I was completely unfamiliar and one where I neither spoke nor comprehended the language. If I survived that, the future got even blurrier — I would be alone in a large port city in Africa, hoping to catch a boat for the crossing to America, with no money or anyone to meet me once I got there. Alternatively, they would leave me behind to make my way to the nearest traveled road and wait for a bus to take me back to St. Girons. From there, I could return to Mane, impose on our friends there, and face the hazards of Nazi occupation. What if my parents were later found to be safe and I had chosen to go on without them — they would not know where I had gone and would never be able to find me! The guide pressed me for a decision. Only one option made any sense to me, and that was to abandon the escape into Spain and to take my chances in France. The guide proved to be a decent man, and he gave me the money my parents had paid him, but kept the fake ID cards and travel documents, as they would only have landed me in even more hot water if I were captured. And so, I set out alone with my little bundle of possessions, searching for a bus stop on an isolated road in the middle of the Pyrenees, not far from the Spanish border.

I retraced my steps, descending the rough path alone toward the road leading back into St. Girons. Somewhere along that lonely stretch of road I found a small, unobtrusive bus sign, an indication of eventual transport. As I waited, it began raining. It was the depth of night and the cold was penetrating. The only sound came from an electrical transformer perched on a nearby pole. The mournful beep sounded with the regularity of the drip in a Chinese water torture. I wasn't sure if a bus would ever come. If it did, I didn't know where I would go. I was in hostile territory and I felt unimaginably, hopelessly alone.

The wait seemed endless. So did the rain. It is that rain, beating relentlessly on me, that is etched in my memories of the moment. After what seemed like an eternity, at the crack of dawn, I could hear the sound of a tired bus as it managed the hairpin turns of the mountains. As the noise of the engine was upon me, I desperately hailed the oncoming bus. The driver obeyed the little stop sign on the side of the road where I had been waiting and, after a brief moment of anxiety for me, brought the bus to a halt. I climbed aboard, dripping wet from the rain and dew, stiff from the cold. I paid the fare to St. Girons with money the guide had given me and scrunched into a seat somewhere near the middle of the bus by one of the large windows so characteristic of European busses in those days. We slowly began our trip down the mountain, rain pelting the wide glass window, blurring the view and my senses.

Somewhere along the way the rain stopped, but I didn't notice. The soul-wrenching night finally ended and the bus reached St. Girons around mid-morning and stopped in the town square. Through the bus's wide window I could see the whole of the town square. The day was in full swing and the square was crawling with olive-green uniforms and steel helmets — *Wehrmacht* — German troops in combat gear and carrying rifles in port position, as well as armed French police and a disparate crowd of civilians. It was there that I saw my parents. They were standing, under

Chapter 9

Wehrmacht guard, along with others who had been caught that night in the mountains. My first instinct was to leap out of the bus and run to them. In that moment I had to make the most agonizing decision of my life — do I run off the bus and join them, or do I stay hidden?

I knew that any sign of recognition from either my parents or me would bring the authorities down on top of me. The situation was extremely dangerous, as anything could set off the *Wehrmacht*'s search instincts, which lay close to the surface at all times. I was paralyzed. After an all too brief glimpse of my parents through the window of the bus, I saw a fleeting look in my direction from my mother, and I saw her quickly squeeze my father's hand. It would be the last I would ever see of them. My only consolation was that they knew I was safe — at least for the moment. The bus lurched forward, continuing on its journey. Still damp, but safely tucked into my pocket, I found the note that my father had given me. I crouched deeper into my seat, staying hidden below the windows for as long as possible. Several stops later, when it seemed safe, I switched busses and headed back to Mane.

A lifetime later, as I began research for this memoir, the rest of the story emerged. Thanks to the "Holocaust and War Victim Tracing and Information Services" of the American Red Cross, I found that the French Red Cross had uncovered an SS telex dated June 23, 1943, which read: "...handed over to Obersturmbannfürer Eichmann o.V.i.A...." and a telegram stating:

"Re: Jews evacuation Transport from France,
On 23 June 1943 at 10:00 A.M., transport train number D901 left the station Le Bourget-Drancy for Auschwitz with a total of 1002 Jews. The Jews on this transport correspond to the evacuation rules for France. The transport leader is Master of Security Police, Richard Urban with 20 men, who were given a single transport list with the names of the people on the transport. The escort group of Urban was replaced at the border of Germany and France at the border station in Neuburg by the group from 1/20 Security Police Metz. Rations were as usual per Jew for 14 days."

The telex was signed *I.A., Röthke, SS-Obersturmfürer.*

Both my parents were on the list of names for Convoy 55, which left Drancy on June 23, 1943. With Teutonic precision, their names were spelled correctly, and their respective birthdays, professions and last legal address in Brussels were correctly recorded.

The telex serves to illustrate the stark efficiency with which the

R.F. SS
Security-Service
News Transmission

23 June 1943

Number 3?785

Telegram

IV B -- SA 225 a
Rö./Ne.   Paris, 23 June 1943

1. To the   Urgent!
   SS Headquarters   Submit immediately!
   IV B 4 a
   handed over to SS Obersturmbannführer Eichmann o.V.i.A.

   B e r l i n

2. To the
   Inspector of the Concentration Camp in

   O r i e n b e r g

2.) To the
   Concentration Camp in

   A u s c h w i t z/O.S.

Re: Jews Evacuation Transport from France

On 23 June 1943 at 10:00am, transport train number D901 left the station Le Bourget-Drancy for Auschwitz with a total of 1002 Jews.

The Jews on this transport correspond to the evacuation rules for France.

The transport leader is Master of the Security Police, Richard Urban with 20 men, who were give a single transport list with the names of the people on the transport. The excort group of Urban was replaced at the border of Germany and France at the border station in Neuburg by the group from 1/20 Security Police Metz.

Rations were as usual per Jew for 14 days.

                               I.A.:

                               Röthke
                               SS-Obersturmführer.

English translation of train manifest showing Peter's parents' deportation transport to Auschwitz (circa 1943).

- 33 -

512-	KNOBEL Herz	1.12.93-VARSOVIE Polonaise	9, Rue St Sauveur Brocanteur
513-	KOHN Jean	21.3.14-PARIS Franç.Option	66, Avenue de la Motte Picquet- Clerc d'Avoué
514-	KOHORN Otto	1.11.05-VIENNE Indéterminée	23, Rue des Oules MONTAUBAN- S.P.
515-	KOHORN Ruth née David	24.11.09-BERLIN Indéterminée	23, Rue des Oules MONTAUBAN(- S.P.
516-	KONSZTADT Lajb	14.10.26-KALISZ Polonaise	6, Rue Mercoeur S.P.
517-	KOPYT Abram	16.7.03-PRASCOROV Réf.Russe	12, Rue Papillon Chauffeur taxis
518-	KORB Rosa née Edelman	15.1.93-SOLOKI Lithuanienne	51, Rue de Lappe Couturière
519-	KORMAN Suzanne	2.12.28-PARIS 12° Franç.Nat .	34, Rue Ordener S.P.
520-	KORNBERG Bernard	12.6.32-PARIS Franç.Nat .	2, Rue Déodat de Séverac-PERPIGNAN- Ecolier
521-	KORNBERG Isaac	7.7.05-WLODOWA Polonaise	2, Rue Déodat de Séverac- PERPIGNAN Coupeur en chemises
522-	KORNBERG Marie née Minska	12.6.05-VARSOVIE Polonaise	2, Rue Déodat de Séverac-PERPIGNAN S.P.
523-	KORNBERG Maurice	12.5.26-PARIS Franç.Nat .	2, Rue Déodat de Séverac-PERPIGNAN- Etudiant
524-	KORYTOVSKI Lily née Neustadt	12.7.97-BRESLAU Indéterminée	323, Rue du Coteau BRUXELLES- Assistante sociale
525-	KORYTOWSKI Erich	9.2.96-BERLIN Indéterminée	323, Rue des Coteaux BRUXELLES - Architecte
526-	KOSTJUKOWITSCH Emilie née Firkser	5.11.87-RIGA Réf.Russe	10, Rue des Accacias Couturière
527-	KOTLARIS Abraham	17.12.74-ASTRAKAN Réf.Russe	29, Rue Navarin S.P.

Train manifest showing Peter's parents' deportation transport to Auschwitz (circa 1943).

Germans were pursuing their "Final Solution." The full story of this episode in human history continues to be uncovered, bit-by-bit, as more survivors become authors. And so the chronicles abound. Among the mountains of documents that have been recovered, there is the following letter, written in pencil and thrown from one of the cars in Convoy 55, perhaps the very one in which my parents had traveled:

> In the box car, on the way to Metz.
> Dear friends, last night we slept 100 in a room in Drancy, where we were placed after the search. Some of the people were transported by stretcher. All pell-mell, sleeping on the floor ... we are 50 to a cattle car, sitting on the floor or on our baggage. It is impossible to move. Three people escaped by jumping from a train moving at 40 to 50 mph. We don't know if they are safe. They tell us we are going towards Metz, where there will be a selection.... I am strong in spite of the terrible heat, without any facilities or water.

Chapter 10

Enter the Countess

When the bus arrived in Mane, I went directly to the house of our neighbors, Simone and Jules La Bounce. I rang the bell. Simone answered and hugged me — she knew what must have happened if I was standing there alone at her door. We went into the kitchen, where she gave me milk and bread while I haltingly filled them in on the harrowing events of the night before. They were devastated by what they heard yet, given the perilous times, they were not surprised. I gave Simone the note containing the name and address of the family in Toulouse, which my parents had given me in the event they were captured, and Simone gave me the money my parents had left with her for me to travel and on which to get by. That address became my next destination, my sole focus and the key to my safety.

I had no idea what arrangements had been made. All I had was the name of a family, Monsieur et Madame Dubois, and an address in Toulouse. I knew not who they were nor why they were doing this. Were they poor, affluent, working, retired, old, young, French or foreign? The questions went unasked between the La Bounce family and me, knowing that the less they knew the safer they would be. The answers wouldn't have been relevant to me anyway, as there were no other options. And so, later that same day, Madame La Bounce put me on a bus to Toulouse, where I would meet Madame Dubois.

The family was a childless couple who, despite the risks involved, had agreed to take me in. They were extremely kind and loving, almost doting — and I recall them as quite elderly. They had lived in Toulouse all their lives, in a small townhouse on the Canal du Midi near the main railroad station, la Gare Matabiau. At the time, I thought that they were in their eighties but, considering the subjective distortion that time assumes for a child, it is more likely that they were much younger.

I stayed with the Dubois family for about two months. It was a very small taste of interim normality during a time when fear of capture dominated my thoughts. Although located in the falsely labeled "Free" or Unoccupied Zone, Toulouse was crawling with Germans, collaborators, *miliciens* and Vichy agents. It was impossible to avoid contact with them on the crowded streets, in the streetcars and other public places.

I was reasonably safe, however, as long as I stayed out of public restrooms and away from urinals that held the danger of someone seeing that I was circumcised. Hiding this fact made walking the streets a particularly unpleasant experience, as I had to spend hours in precarious discomfort until I found a place secure and private enough for me to go. I also had to refrain from speaking or giving any sign of understanding German. I had been warned that merely showing an understanding of a simple "Good morning" or "Hello" spoken in German had entrapped many Jews. All of this was terrifying — I was back in a large city, living with virtual strangers who, though they opened their home to me at great risk to themselves, knew as little about me as I knew about them. This was certainly not a bonding experience; it was a circumstantial relationship, which had all of the hallmarks of an interim arrangement. As such, there was nothing remarkable about this interlude in my life, except that it acquainted me with obsessive behavior.

The lady of the house must have had a case of obsessive-compulsive disorder so severe that medical intervention would probably have been justified had we been living in more normal times. However, we were not in normal times and her irrational aberrations were benign compared to the lethal atmosphere that prevailed outside this sanctuary, so I wasn't about to do anything that would jeopardize my welcome there. Accordingly, I cheerfully submitted to my host's harmless obsessions without the least bit of hesitation. *I washed my feet constantly*— before meals, after meals, when coming in from outside, before going to bed — and for any reason, at any time. Madame Dubois must have had some sort of foot fetish, and it was okay with me. In my memories, she and her husband will forever remain among the heroes who risked their lives to protect me, a total stranger.

One day, after my feet were thoroughly sterilized, Madame Dubois asked me to walk with her across the canal to *la Gare Matabiau*. On the sidewalk in front of the railroad station, Madame Dubois told me that I would soon meet two ladies who would henceforth see after me. Because they lived away from Toulouse, she explained, they were in a better position to protect me from the dangers of the city. She assured me that she and her husband loved me, but that everybody would be safer if I went with the ladies I was about to meet. So we hugged, said our goodbyes and she introduced me to the ladies waiting for me on the sidewalk.

I can only describe them as two *Grande Dames*. One was Madame Rotte de Neuville, who told me that she was there to represent the American Joint, more formally known as the American Jewish Joint Distribution Committee (JDC). I learned later that the organization was related to the American Quakers. While this would prove to be my only meeting with Madame de Neuville, I would soon get to know the other lady better than I could ever have imagined.

Madame Dubois then introduced me to the second woman, Tante Lily (Aunt Lily), formally known as Madame La Contesse Alix de Bonnefoy. She was known as Madame by those who worked with or for her, and as Lily by close associates and friends. For the children she had snatched from the jaws of the Nazis, however, she was known as Tante Lily, and meeting her would completely change my life.

Tante Lily was an attractive, elegant lady in her forties, regally poised and clearly accustomed to being in charge. She had a high forehead and a demeanor that inspired respect, projecting an aura that compelled obeisance by all who dealt with her. But nothing in what she did could hide the depth of kindness and caring that exuded from her. What was not so obvious was the heroism and courage she exhibited in the course of her clandestine activities related to saving Jewish children from the clutches of the Nazis. I learned later that she was part of a large network, organized and supported by such organizations as the International Red Cross, the American Joint and other similar non-governmental organizations.

When Tante Lily told me that I would be living with the de Bonnefoy family, it became instantly clear that my life was about to take yet another wild spin. It was the beginning of a different existence — a clandestine one — wrapped in the patina of France's old wealth. My relationship with Tante Lily would last until the end of the war and beyond. It would enable me to transcend the ever-present fears and anxieties of the German occupation and to fill the vacuum I constantly felt since losing my parents. I would go underground, assume a new name, another religion and a different persona. In the process, my life would be turned into that of an heir in a very old and respected French noble family, a standing that the de Bonnefoys had enjoyed for as long as anyone could remember. In fact, it hailed back to the days of the Norman invasions of France, prior to the turn of the first millennium.

Tante Lily had kept her car at the sidewalk curb. When she invited me to climb into the back seat, I almost felt as if I was being kidnapped — but in a most benign way — destined for Shangri-La or Camelot. It wasn't exactly clear to me where we were going, except for the fact that I would probably never see the Dubois family again. But I felt safe with the *Grande Dames*, as they both exuded warmth and strength and they were clearly on the side of the "good guys." So I piled into the car without the least hesitation, together with Madame Rotte de Neuville and Tante Lily.

The car was a tiny Citroën Rosengard. Since my parents never owned a car, I was really impressed. It even had an automatic starter instead of the more common manual crank still prevalent in those days. Once snugly installed, Tante Lily took the wheel and off we went, out of the city, on our way to a small village called Auriac-sur-Vendinelle, some 35 kilometers south and east of Toulouse, near the somewhat larger towns of Caraman and Revel. Tante Lily skillfully drove the little Rosengard out of the city along the national roads, lined with the tall sycamores Napoleon had planted well over a hundred years before. During the ride, she briefed me on my new identity. I would go by the name of Pierre Boivin. I liked that, because it sounded quintessentially French, and far removed from anything Polish, Jewish or German. I was to be the nephew of the Count and Countess de Bonnefoy, whose family had been killed in an air raid on Douai in Northern France. She told me that I would have to study the geography of that city, so that I could describe it in enough detail to convince a perfect stranger that I had lived there. She also told me a lot about her family and the people I would be meeting. She said they would adopt me eventually, but in the meantime I would live as a member of the family in the château. Of course, I would have to act as a devout Catholic even if I lacked the faith behind the religion. Not a problem! I felt quite sure God would forgive me this deception on Final Judgment Day. And, oh yes, I

Chapter 10

was to continue calling Madame Tante Lily, and her husband, Monsieur Le Comte Antoine de Bonnefoy, Oncle Nino. She assured me that there were no Germans in Auriac presently, but one never knew where collaborators or *miliciens* were lurking. It was, therefore, critically important to maintain my true identity as a deep secret. Only Tante Lily, Oncle Nino and the village priest, Monsieur le Curé, would know that I was Jewish. Before I knew it, we were arriving in Auriac-sur-Vendinelle, the place that, henceforth, would be my home.

When I saw the château for the first time, it was obvious to me that kismet was in the process of intervening once again, in a most dramatic way. At that moment, my early-life encounter with the Brandenburg Gate, my childhood in Brussels, the *Blitzkrieg* and, temporarily at least, even the pain of the loss of my parents, dropped back into the hidden recesses of my consciousness. The new realities forced themselves to center stage with all the urgencies my new situation demanded. Meeting Tante Lily and that first look at the château would have been a defining moment in my life in and of itself, but under my current circumstances — having just dodged events that surely could have ended it — this was truly miraculous.

Having been exposed to so many dangers at such a young age, everything about Tante Lily took on the trappings of a real sanctuary. I became a chameleon, slipping into this new, strange life with remarkable ease. I melded myself into this new persona and started to live it, both physically and psychologically, to the fullest. It was truly a transforming moment. I was now in the de Bonnefoy orbit, and it was instantaneously a mutual acceptance of our respective roles, together with all the ground rules this implied. I knew, instinctively and beyond any doubt, that the convulsions of recent events would be subordinated to a new, deep sense of security. It was a case of instant bonding — I felt that this was where I belonged.

The de Bonnefoys had many intimate friends in the region, all of whom were willing to help. They were all part of the old aristocracy and they were steeped in ancient traditions. All were intensely patriotic and despised the Vichy regime. They also had a visceral disgust of the Germans ... in or out of uniform, stemming not only from this war, but all the others as well. They owned large, imposing mansions and châteaux throughout the region and were all involved, in one way or another, in the French Resistance. For them, hiding Jewish children was an honor and a mission they considered heroic as well as patriotic.

The children that were in hiding with these families were mostly, if not all, Jewish. Most had lost their parents and families in war occurrences like bombing raids, and all were in dire and constant peril of being caught in Nazi roundups or entrapments. The bond that developed over the war years between these hidden children and their rescuers was truly remarkable and lasted for life. Everybody was keenly aware that they were all together in a life or death situation. As such, it was important to project the appearance of calm and normality in everything; it was critical that we blend in. As one of these children, I spent a lot of time on my bicycle, pedaling from château to château, visiting others like me and acting as an important communication link in this network of those determined to resist the occupiers.

The term "hero" for those involved in hiding Jews understates their deeds. All were in mortal danger of being denounced and caught, thereby facing the same fate as those they were protecting. Tante Lily and her friends were, of course, keenly aware of this and, in my mind, I have always felt that they represented the very best of French nobility.

CHAPTER 11

Auriac-sur-Vendinelle and Its Château

Auriac, which has changed little in the nearly 70 years since that first day I saw it, was a quaint little French village in the Languedoc region of Southern France. It was the kind that today appeals to those interested in experiencing a typical, small French community. As the car approached, the village was really not easily discernible. It was well hidden on the lee side of a large hill, with the only telltale sign of its existence being the square, moss-laden, medieval bell tower that served as the steeple for an equally ancient church. The tower came into view some distance away, signaling our arrival in the village.

Bigger than a hamlet but smaller than a town, Auriac was a tiny village that dated back to the dawn of France, when it was not much more than a grouping of about two dozen feudal farms that served and were protected by the lords of the château. The village plan was not complicated. We reached the heart of the village by veering off the *Route Nationale* (the main highway), and almost immediately encountered the old bell tower and church. Tante Lily explained that the church had served the village's ecumenical functions for as long as there had been a village. In France during those days, these functions were limited to those rigidly ordained by the Catholic Church. The church held court at the highest point of the village. The car felt out of place, as we drove down the narrow, crooked street that led to the village's covered public market that served as the community's principal activity center. As we drove down the street, she explained that this narrow street between the church and the market also served as the ceremonial path for public events. It was not hard for me to imagine a wedding, a funeral, or a parade marching down that path, starting with rituals at the church and ending with celebrations at the covered market. Tante Lily told me that such events were always well attended and quite orderly. Those who did not march would line the sides of the street and express their thoughts and feelings in whispers and, sometimes, quite loudly. Giving this tableau even more life, color and sound were the brass and percussion instruments, beating to the rhythm of the marchers.

We passed what would become a popular pit stop for me along the path — the village's bakery. It was famous for its meringues, a deliciously sweetened and beaten egg white frothing, molded and slowly baked to a pale tan crispness with a luscious soft center. Whether for a wedding or a funeral, no one could resist a stop there. Other popular locations were the cafés. There were three of them, each equipped with a billiard table and an unlimited supply of *Pastis* (Pernod) and beer. One of the important missions of these cafés was to serve as the *yenta seat* for the local women — a vantage point where gossipers were able to follow what was going on around the billiard table without missing any of the activities, like disturbances, fights, parades or other events that might unfold in the street. On such occasions, patrons of the cafés would usually bunch up at the doorways to observe and comment, often mockingly, about their parading friends and neighbors.

The square where the covered market was located was the undisputed village center. This was where the post office was found, and where *Monsieur Le Maire* (the mayor) and his buddies could be seen playing cards or *Petanque*, a very popular game played with steel-clad balls the size of small cantaloupes, which players took turns tossing as close as possible to a peg planted in the ground. There was also a barbershop and a solitary grocery that supplied the village with an endless supply of olive oil and wine out of barrels as well as food products and household goods. The covered market had a hip roof, but the sides between the columns that supported the structure were open. A permanent bandstand was used as a dais for musical events as well as ceremonial and political functions, and occupied a good part of the area under the roof. Adjoining the market place, there was a tall wall of fieldstones and a small iron gate to a private pea-graveled park. This park was the backyard of the de Bonnefoys' château. It was there that the countess and her friends enjoyed their afternoon tea and where, on hot summer days, in the shade of two gigantic sycamore trees, a lot of reading and knitting took place. With its location close to the center of the village, between the market place and the Vendinelle River, the château enjoyed a highly prominent but not domineering location in the village. We had finally arrived!

The Vendinelle River flowed — if that is the proper term — in front of the château. It would have been nice to attribute more heroic qualities to the little stream and endow it with the qualities of a defensive medieval moat, but alas, it wasn't so. The Vendinelle was quite small, and dried up almost entirely many times during the summer months. In reality, it was neither a river, a moat nor a stream; it was more evocative of a drainage ditch, although it did have a stone bridge that had to be crossed when approaching the main gate to the château. The Vendinelle separated the estate from the village's elementary school, located across the half dried river. It occurred to me that getting there would be entirely too easy for someone like me, who abhorred anything to do with school; all I had to do was walk across the little bridge!

The little Rosengard entered the château through the main entrance, crunching on the pea-shaped gravel, past the main iron gates, which were usually kept open. Tante Lily stopped the car in the courtyard of the main entrance. Most of the château building was ancient, constructed over 800 years before, during feudal times. The courtyard was U-shaped, with one leg of the U originally containing riding stables and a hayloft. But horses had been abandoned some time before in favor of automobiles. The stables had been anachronistically converted into their contemporary equivalent, a four-car garage and a machine shop. This was where Madame's Citroën Rosengard slept, in the company of Monsieur's suped-up Citroën *Traction Avant* (front wheel drive) and the family's all-purpose old Citroën, the workhorse for the fleet. The Citroën was a vintage boxy four-door sedan, which had to be started manually with a crank. Monsieur wouldn't deign to go near it and Madame usually enlisted Jorge, the chauffeur, to start it and drive her on her rounds when she visited the muddy farms of the estate.

The other leg of the U was the oldest part of the château. It was a two-story stone wing with a prominent round tower at its end, an imposing, marble-carved doorway which reflected its position of dominance in the hierarchy of spaces, and where the lords made their formal entrance.

The base of the U was a mixture of old and new, containing a large

The chateau (Auriac-sur-Vendinelle, France circa 1944).

formal ballroom filled with genuine antiques and chandeliers from the regal eras of the kings and the Napoleonic Age, styles appropriately called *Empire*. There was also an intimidating dining room, equipped with everything needed to properly entertain the many dignitaries who visited the château, including a large ceramic wood-burning space heater. This part of the building also contained the facilities required to service and maintain the château, including an enormous kitchen, a laundry room and several storage rooms that served as walk-in pantries. Finally, the second floor of this part of the building was where the help was quartered.

When I gazed at the front courtyard for the first time, my imagination took flight. It was easy to visualize the arrivals in olden times; horses majestically rearing and noisily scattering the pea-gravel, surrounded by romping and howling hounds, with the château staff in full regalia, lined up to greet the return of the lord. Alas, in my case, there was nothing so dramatic. The golden days of chivalry, as well as the pomp and decorum that characterized those times, were long gone. Unlike the typical movie scene,

Chapter 11

where the house personnel stiffly stands at attention waiting to be introduced, we merely stepped out of the little car without any ceremony and Tante Lily introduced me to the staff as a group, saying that I would meet them in the course of their respective daily service routines as we toured the château and farms.

We entered the château from the frontcourt and stepped over the marble-carved threshold into the formal vestibule. The floor was impeccably waxed herringbone parquet and the walls were silk covered in a rich wine-berry hue. Original oils and portraits of family ancestors hung on every wall, and tradition echoed from each and every time-beaten stone in this, the oldest part of the building.

The formal vestibule led to a large relatively modern and more informally welcoming oak paneled library, used much as one would a family room. Its seating was comfortably cushy and it was equipped with an electric space heater as well as a big standing radio. Naturally, there were many books, though I have no recollection of the titles. It was an ideal place for knitting, reading and quiet conversation. At one end of the formal vestibule, outside the library, there was a passageway, equipped with a small vanity and commode that led to the *Petit Salon*—a cozy little sitting room with a fireplace, where friends and family could gather informally, sip cognac, sit and stare at the fire until it died, as sleep would overtake them. It was, in many respects, the family's way station to slumber land.

Five of the ten bedrooms were reached from the vestibule by an imposing, monumental marble staircase whose treads were hollowed out by centuries of use. Three were arranged as suites, with their own bathrooms. One, the Blue Room, was in the Round Tower, and bathing and ablutions had to be shared with the occupants of the fifth room, next to the tower. The suites were usually reserved for visiting relatives or distinguished guests. I was told that the Eschelbourne family, who were very close friends that I would meet at dinner, occupied the Blue Room and the adjacent one.

Still on the second floor, but accessed from another wing of the château, were three more rooms; Tante Lily had the biggest bedroom, with a view of the marketplace and the large mature sycamore giants that adorned the front yard of the estate. Monsieur de Bonnefoy had a much smaller room. He spent relatively little time at the château, being in constant motion in and out of the village on important business. It had been many years since the count and the countess had shared the same room — or the same bed. Their bathrooms were separate as well. I slept in a tiny room, almost an alcove, between the bedrooms of Madame and Monsieur. While I had the least amount of space, I certainly appreciated the strategic advantages of its location, as I could always sense what was going on ... on both sides of the psychological fence.

The ground floor, as I had mentioned earlier, housed the kitchen, the cellars, the laundry and a lot of storage rooms. It was during this part of the tour that I met the first, and the most important, staff member — Albertine Garrig, the cook. Actually, she was much more than that. She really performed as chief of staff. One might say she was the soul of what made the château function. She was the "Clerk of the Works," the "Mother Earth" and the overseer in charge of food logistics, management and preparation. Her domain was indisputably inside the kitchen of the château. Albertine had two children; a daughter named Alice, who was a little older than me and who was part of the upstairs staff, and a son, Elie, who was my age. Elie and I quickly bonded, and he and I soon became inseparable.

Adjoining the kitchen were the storage rooms. One led to the family's treasure trove of *foie gras* (fattened goose liver) and other homemade delicacies, including sausages, hams and confit. Also adjoining the kitchen was the laundry room. Of course, neither Maytag nor any other washing or drying machines were available at that time. And certainly nothing was sent out. This meant that everything was done at home. Similarly, like the laundry, the homemade food products were processed right at the château. We had a respectable food preparation center where, among other delicacies, fattened goose livers were cooked and canned, and meats were preserved in salt. When it came to pasta, everyone — Albertine, her daughter, even her son and I — pitched in to roll, spread and shape the dough into the various kinds of pasta strips she served at the château.

On the second floor, above the kitchen where Albertine and some of the other help lived, there was a mysterious, locked room which no one was allowed to enter, out of respect for the ancestor for whom it was named. It was called "The Colonel's Room," and nobody had any idea why the room was locked or what the mystery was all about. Little did I know then that, in a few short months, my mischievous nature would cause me to spend several long, painful and embarrassing weeks in that room.

Chapter 11

The château was absolutely brimming with wondrous places. Above the second floor, spanning the full area of the château's footprint, was the attic. The attic faithfully followed the roof structure, with all of its beams and support elements creating a very dusty obstacle course that endowed the space with an aura of mystery. It was not well lit, which added to the sense of mystery. In the years to come, visiting this part of the old structure would be an adventure for me. It was like my own private museum, containing the relics of prior ages — obsolete tools, broken cooking gadgets and discarded clothes, hats, fabrics and furniture. Nobody ever went up there, but my friends and I frequently did, hoping to find a ghost or a fabulous treasure. The attic was not the only place we explored; there were many secret passages hidden behind the walls that interconnected some of the rooms. While we were able to explore them, their function had to remain a mystery, as I never wanted anyone to know that I was aware of their existence, fearing it might be considered trespassing in private family areas.

Beyond the château and its immediate surrounds, the Vendinelle defined the boundaries of a large park and a huge vegetable garden, both of which were part of the château's immediate property. This was where I met Ludovic, a rough, tough handyman with a drinking problem, and his wife, Denise, whom he beat regularly. Denise was the other upstairs maid. I also met Augustin, the tenant farmer and his family, who lived on the grounds and who took care of the château's vegetable garden, as well as the geese and other fowl. The geese were force-fed to produce an abundance of precious *foie gras*. The livers were stored in gallon-sized cans, stacked from floor to ceiling, in a ten-by-twenty-foot Fort Knox-like room, which adjoined the château's laundry and linen room. The practice of force feeding geese to enlarge their liver is currently going out of style, as it has raised the hackles of animal rights groups. More and more people now consider this cruel and inhumane. Nevertheless, *foie gras* remains much sought-after by epicureans throughout the world. I have always been ambivalent about the practice. I can certainly empathize with the goose, but I must admit that there are not many food products that come close to *foie gras*!

The de Bonnefoy family also owned over twenty tenant farms scattered over a radius of about 15 kilometers. They supplied the château with wheat, corn, wine, milk and livestock. The management and administration of these farms represented a major commitment of time and preoccupation for Tante Lily, who was referred to as *La Patronne* (boss-lady or owner). She was very diligent in visiting and inspecting her domain, not only to check on production and general conditions, but also to address the social, health and family problems and issues of the tenant farmers. Income and expenses had to be counted and analyzed, supplies had to be purchased, livestock traded and cooperative harvesting and marketing operations had to be organized and coordinated. As we prepared to tour the farms, I met George or, more accurately, *Jorge*, the chauffeur and mechanic extraordinaire who could fix anything ... as long as it wasn't new. He was also the manager of the hog compound and the woodshed that he adopted as his home on the estate. The old four-door boxy Citroën was George's baby. He was the only one who could make it go. George was an exile from Spain and the Spanish Civil War. He spoke a little French but was fluent in *patois*, an indescribable mixture of French and Spanish, which was prevalent in the Languedoc region. He was also most certainly fluent in cursing, which he did like a drunken sailor, both in patois and in unadulterated Spanish. He was particularly creative when he exerted himself in the extreme while hand cranking the old Model T-like Citroën into life. Unlike the cute little Rosengard, the old Citroën was the car that took Madame on her inspection tours of the tenant farms.

Tante Lily's territory was both inside as well as outside the château. She was the penultimate ambassador at large for the family, not only in the management of all the help at the château but also that of the tenant farms and the many who, on occasion, had to deal with the family or some aspect of its estate. In this capacity, she felt that the old Citroën symbolized a kind of historical culture compared to the more playful qualities of the newer and sportier Rosengard and Uncle Nino's impetuous *Traction Avant*. This immersion into farm life had led to Tante Lily's participation in the festivities that marked the important annually recurring events in a farm's production cycle.

One of these was the Threshing Day Feast. On that day, the farm whose wheat was being threshed usually hosted a huge feast, served outdoors on a long wooden table, celebrating the day when the rickety behemoth that was the communal threshing machine pulled into the farmyard near the hayloft. Once properly anchored and connected to a tractor by pulleys, the mechanism set into motion, separating grain from chaff for

Chapter II

six to eight hours. By the following day, all the guests would have departed, their hangovers from the feast would have abated and the grain would be neatly bagged for disposition at the local grain cooperative. The shafts, by then turned to straw, would have been bailed and stored for future use. In the meantime, after biding adieu to the farmer, the lumbering threshing machine was back in motion, being pulled by oxen to its next destination.

Another recurring event, which I would come to love, was the grape harvest. The region around Auriac was not known for its wine. I, for one, can attest to the fact that, at that time, I thought we produced the most undrinkable quaff in creation. It really wasn't until after the turn of the second millennium that the *Vins Docs* started to come into their own and were appreciated. In spite of this shaky beginning, the cultivation of grapevines and winemaking was big business on the farms owned by the de Bonnefoys. But for me, what mattered was that the process of transforming a fruit into something intoxicating gave rise to a level of merry making that only Bacchus himself could be expected to match.

The vineyards covered about 15 acres, and the harvest of the grapes was the ultimate communal event, involving more than two dozen men and women, as well as children of all ages. Their tasks were divided. One group would do the reaping, snipping the grapes from the vines and unloading the baskets of harvested grapes into a large four-foot-high round wooden vat, about ten feet in diameter. It was then the job of screeching and overexcited maidens to step into the vat with bare feet and stomp the grapes, to extract from them the juice that would ultimately become wine. Finally, a third group would collect the rendered juice into barrels that were dropped at a cooperative depot for processing and later distribution to the contributing farms.

In the process of stomping the grapes in the vat, however, a lot of very potent alcoholic fumes are generated. As this was inhaled by stompers, reapers and others in their immediate vicinity, what started out as a communal work project always degenerated into a drunken ribald celebration that erased all inhibitions that might otherwise prevail.

After the outlying farms finished the harvesting and processing of grapes, the activities adjoining the château were focused on distilling what was left once their juice and been extracted. This was called *marc*. Every year, after the grape juice was on its way to become wine, the local farmers dumped the marc, over a period of a month or so, one cart at a time, into a two-block-long, three-story mountain of grape skins, stems and other residues. This created the most awesome breeding ground for bees and a wide variety of other insects that were attracted by the emanations from the aromatic pile of grape marc. In Auriac, the marc collection site was the bank of the Vendinelle, directly opposite the château's entry gates. It wasn't long after the mountain of marc reached its intended size that the fermentation process would begin, all on its own, exuding the most enticing combinations of fragrances.

Eventually, an ancient mobile distillation still would rattle up to the mountain of marc. It had the appearance of a stationary locomotive, but it did not take long to appreciate its true function: to turn grape residue into ... you name it—firewater, hooch, grappa or, as the French call it, *Eau de Vie* (water of life). While the distillation took place, it was the custom, for all who passed, to accidentally or on purpose stop at the spigot and sample the end product, inevitably causing coughing, throat clearing and perhaps a choking spasm! The stuff was really strong! I never asked about the business arrangements governing this cooperative enterprise, nor am I sure it really mattered, as the most important thing seemed to be the sense of camaraderie and sinfulness the ritual engendered.

The farms were of critical importance to the château, especially in wartime. In addition to what was grown, they also produced income that was shared with the tenant farmers and used to buy supplies and other goods that could not be raised on the farm. Dependence on the outside was mostly limited to coffee, olive oil, gasoline, tobacco, sugar, spices, cosmetics, and cleaning and pharmaceutical products. Wine was a mixed bag, since the farms produced some really bad stuff, hardly fit for consumption by more refined palates. No matter how bad things got during the war, food was never a problem at the château, as we were virtually self-sufficient.

While this entire setting recalls the social systems of the Middle Ages, it was completely consistent with the natural order of things there and at that time. The family was widely respected by everyone in the region, not only as a matter of age-old feudalistic tradition or legal imperative but, more importantly, as a manifestation of its exemplary values, life style and universal respect. The name de Bonnefoy evoked such sentiments as honor, courage, service and chivalry. The word arrogance or anything suggesting an unwarranted exercise of power had no place in the family. There was only one other family that hailed from old nobility in Auriac — the d'Arails. They did not live in a château, but in their ancestral mansion located at the other end of the market square. It had deteriorated beyond hope, the family struggling with destitution, lacking the ability to cope with modern times. I have no idea what became of this family, but it exemplifies the fate of so many families that had met oblivion in the aftermath of the French Revolution.

By late afternoon, exhausted from the excitement of the trip from Toulouse and my tour of the town and the château, I was shown to my room for a rest, with the promise that I would meet the rest of the family at dinner that evening. Tante Lily came to get me around 7:00 P.M., the traditional time for dinner at the château. Waiting to meet me was Oncle Nino. He was not only Tante Lily's husband, but also her distant cousin. Also present were Nino's mother and father, both quite elderly, and Nino's spinster aunt, referred to as Tantishe, who was also quite old and a bit addled. Marthou, the de Bonnefoys' daughter and only child, lived away at school most of the time, but was also there to meet me. I was introduced to the assembled family as *Le Petit Pierrot* (little Peter), and Tante Lily explained the details of my cover story and the importance of keeping my real origins a deeply hidden secret. These brave, wonderful, sometimes quirky aristocrats would soon become my second family. This was what kismet had ordained for my new life.

Chapter 12

Château Life

I could never describe what life was like at the château without beginning with Oncle Nino. Although he was seldom there, he was the most unforgettable character I was to meet. He had a face made interesting by a missing eye, which he had lost in a bow and arrow accident when he was a boy. He refused to wear a glass eye, an eye patch or any other kind of prosthesis and, as a result, the gouged eye was always opaque, lifeless and somehow fearsome in appearance. Everybody liked to believe that he lost the eye in a moment of glory during World War I, and only a few of us knew that it was not some heroic deed that brought about the disfigurement. Nino was always impatient, to the point of being fidgety. He had a way of acting like a man of great importance, which of course he was in many respects. This self-importance in his mannerisms transcended everything he did; from the way he ate to the way he organized his shoes and clothing. He was steeped in politics, and the serious nature of his wheeling and dealing left little time for the kind of warmth that exuded from Tante Lily.

He had served with distinction in the First World War. Always a soldier at heart, after the humiliating fall of France in the summer of 1940, he and select groups of French officers refused to disarm; the humiliation of the capitulation of France to the *Boches* (barbarians or uncouth animals without conscience, and how the French referred to the Germans) was simply too much for them to bear. They buried whatever weapons they had or could find and became outlaws. This was the birth of the French Resistance, and Oncle Nino was right in there during the seminal stages of the effort. He spent the World War II years heroically involved in a number of resistance operations in both the occupied and unoccupied

Chapter 12

sectors of France. As such, he was badly wanted by the Germans, and the Nazi command would have considered his capture a trophy.

Nino always traveled by car, driving the black Citroën *Traction Avant*. This was a remarkable car with respect to cornering capabilities and power, making it the ideal vehicle for the French Resistance. His resistance activities often took him away from the château, to Lyon and, less frequently, to Paris in the German-Occupied Zone. When at the château, he could be found communicating by clandestine shortwave radio with the de Gaulle contingents in England.

But there was another side to Oncle Nino. He was a merciless joker and tease. His resistance activities meant that Nino would only be present at dinner about half the time, but he always made sure that his presence was felt. For example, he made it his mission to regularly infuriate Tantishe by kneading balls of fresh bread at the dinner table and flicking them with great force at her nose. When one landed, it would cause her *pince-nez* glasses to fall, inevitably landing in her soup!

To say that Nino treated me like a son would not reflect the reality of the relationship. Somehow I always felt like a waif in his presence, and his tokens of affection did not ring true. I actually dreaded their display. Nevertheless, he was an important man, always engrossed in important business and he was very proud of me when I risked my life by participating in the activities of the French Resistance. That was the common bond we were able to share; the relationship, while always on rock-solid ground, was simply not based on a great deal of affection, but on the risks we were willing to take for our country and freedom.

Mornings at the château usually began early, with Nino's father the first to rise. He was well into his eighties, and usually spent his mornings hunting on foot with an ancient, double-barreled shotgun slung on his shoulder. In the afternoons, he recovered from his hunting exertions, and rested among the sycamores in the park at the rear of the château, cleaning what he had killed so that Albertine could prepare it for dinner. The old count's hunt was not the kind stereotyped by Hollywood. There were no rearing horses, blaring horns, romping dogs, no army of bush beaters were roaming the countryside and there was no noisy crowd of guests and participants. No, there were no extravagant or colorful displays during the pursuit of some poor little fox. Monsieur's daily hunt was not nearly as exciting ... but it was just as unfair for the prey. It involved a pack of about 20 basset hounds, howling their way over to a rabbit hole that they had sniffed out, and converging upon it. Once such a warren was uncovered, the hounds milled around until the old man caught up. The moment a rabbit emerged, Monsieur blasted it to oblivion with his shotgun.

Invariably, Albertine had to deal with the trophies, which would end up on the oak dining table, transformed into incredible, wine-soaked meals. On rare occasions, the battle went aerial, and some hapless pheasant or other flying fowl got in the way of the lead pellets, providing an even tougher victual for Albertine to tenderize and cook into submission. When this happened, Albertine tenderized the birds before cooking them by hanging them on a hook for days, until the wings fell off on their own. Lead pellets were a normal accompaniment to the meal, and so was the consequential damage to the teeth. Sadly, to my knowledge, neither the great Escoffier nor Emily Post have been able to develop a technique for spitting out these pellets with fitting decorum and refinement!

Daily life revolved around Albertine and her kitchen. Clearly, this was center stage in the daily routine of the château. Her cooking mastery took place on the surface of a very large wood-fired cast-iron stove which she lit every morning before dawn and kept going until late into the night. The stove had an oven that could reach the extremely high temperatures necessary for her fabulous cognac soufflés. Her meals were prodigious and endlessly varied and creative. She was particularly talented with the tough, gamey fowl of which there was abundance. She had remarkable methods of tenderizing the meat and preserving the excess. Refrigerators, iceboxes and freezers were almost unheard of. Preservation of food was achieved in the ancient and traditional ways by salting, drying, cooking and canning. Smoking, for some reason, did not fit the regional culture. The making of *confit* to preserve fowl was elevated to a fine art. This method essentially preserved meat in its own fat after it had been rendered. And then, of course, there was the glorious *foie gras*, which was canned with lots of pepper, then boiled and stored for a long time. Often confused with pâté, which is a kitchen-prepared concoction that usually contains various things including goose or duck liver, true *foie gras* is the actual liver of the goose or the duck. It is as smooth as velvet and melts in your mouth, delivering a unique flavor that would qualify as ambrosia from the gods. Albertine must have produced a cellar full of these cans over the years, as they

Chapter 12

somehow survived the German occupation and, like a paradox, remained our main source of food right after the war, during the time of extreme food rationing.

Any cooling, notably for wine, was achieved by hanging food and liquid containers in fairly deep wells or cellars that hadn't seen daylight for centuries, and thus were able to maintain a relatively low ambient temperature. There was very little fish or seafood, and virtually no tropical products such as bananas, pineapples or citrus fruits.

My favorite dishes prepared by Albertine were *Pintade* (guinea fowl) and *Civet* (wild rabbit) in wine. She wasn't deterred by the challenge of creating new kinds of dishes, nor perfecting the traditional ones with unique innovations. She was a master at preparing all the dishes typically enjoyed by the French elite. She could cook anything on and/or in her old-fashioned wood stove and oven, moving pots and pans about on top of its surface to various positions, knowing exactly where she would find the temperatures she wanted for any particular dish. Everything always came out tasting and looking like something out of a Michelin star-rated eatery.

The meals, their preparation and presentations were always regal. There was always an ample supply of *charcuteries* (the terms cold cuts or deli products just does not seem to fit). Some of the dishes for which Albertine was famous included stuffed, baked tomatoes, rabbit stew, cassoulet, pork loin and roasted guinea fowl. Albertine was also famous for her cognac soufflés and floating islands. All of this was made from products homegrown or hunted on the property, and always cooked or baked in the ancient cast-iron stove.

I would not say that she went about her culinary feats in a quiet and demure manner. A massive and powerful woman of about 45, she was loud and gruff. The expenditure of the enormous energy required in coordinating these complex meals made her impatient, and she bossed everybody around. But that was the soul of her performance, and we certainly forgave and accepted her sometimes-excitable temperament. In fact, this was part of the charm of this very active kitchen, which she had turned into the most interesting and lively place at the Château. Despite her bossiness and turbulent kitchen life, Albertine had a heart of gold. She was extremely sensitive to my situation and, although I was told that she was not in on the secret of my true identity, I always suspected that she knew the real story all along. Nonetheless, I knew that I could trust her with my life.

Last in the order of appearance every morning were Nino's mother, Jeanne, and his aunt, Tantishe, who were late risers. Once they came down from their second-floor bedrooms in the old wing of the château, they were served breakfast, usually in the library, while listening to the news on the old radio, which was always full of static. The technology of frequency modulation (FM) had simply not yet reached the Languedoc at that time, nor would it for another few years. After breakfast, the old ladies proceeded with what they did during most of their days — needlepoint and reading.

Rounding out the cast of characters living at the château were the members of the Eschelbourne family, who lived with the de Bonnefoys like members of the family. Their bedroom suite was the Blue Room, and they sat with us regularly around the dinner table. Mr. Eschelbourne was a large, massively built man, who was nearly bald. He was quite verbose, garrulous and strangely reminiscent of the actor Sydney Greenstreet. Mr. Eschelbourne's wife was shy and diminutive, with an unremarkable personality. They seemed to be in their fifties, and had two daughters who were intimate friends with Marthou, the de Bonnefoys' daughter. Like Marthou, they seldom graced the ancestral dining table, as they were usually away at school. I was never told how the families had met, and I was given very little background about them, except that he was a diamond merchant from Holland, which explained a Dutch or Germanic accent.

Life at the château was always very busy. The de Bonnefoy family entertained a lot, plus their time was filled with the demands required for the viable management of the estate and the clandestine pattern of activities from which they dared never to stray very far. The dinner meal was very important at the château. It gave structure to the behavior pattern of the occupants and it was the key to the rhythm and normality of the place. Unlike Oncle Nino, Tante Lily was almost always in residence, and she presided over meals ritualistically and with great dignity and aplomb. The "old folks," Nino's parents and Tantishe, attended dinner every evening — religiously — they never missed a meal. I fell into that category as well.

Everyone would gather in the formal dining room, where they had their designated seat around the great polished oak table. Albertine and either her daughter, Alice, or Denise, the upstairs maid, served meals. The ritual always proceeded as follows, without exception: Tante Lily was served

Chapter 12

Peter (center) with Marthou (to the right of Peter), Countess de Fournasse (to the right of Marthou) and Dédé (end, right) (circa 1942).

first, to make sure everything was in order, then Nino's parents and Tantishe, then Oncle Nino, if he was there, then Marthou, if she was home from school, then the Eschelbournes and, finally, me.

After saying grace, significant announcements were made by Madame, such as, "Pierrot was a bad boy today and he won't be having any dessert." More importantly, Tante Lily managed the sprawling estate, and she would use this time to communicate information and coordinate all the matters that needed sharing and discussion. Everyone knew that, without the estate and the farms, the lifestyle to which everyone had become accustomed would be in danger of collapse in those turbulent times. Then, the conversation would drift into the events of the day, and invariably transition to politics, with the war as the primary topic, as it was always uppermost in everybody's mind.

News and discussion moved with great animation around the table as Albertine presented the three or four courses for both a first and second helping, serving each from the left, while her helper would take the empty plates from the right. My parents had trained me in table manners, but the château and the elaborate table setting were a challenge that required more than a routine recap. What was needed was a whole new education in order to even the playing field for my table manners, and Emily Post was nowhere to be seen. But I knew instinctively that it was incumbent upon me to study hard and quickly learn my table manners. I didn't want to be relegated to the kitchen to eat with the help. The art of eating elegantly must be a skill acquired genetically by old French families. It is difficult to master for those who join late into the game, and nearly impossible to ply with the kind of fluidity that engenders respect. The ultimate test was the ability to eat anything, but particularly squab, guinea or other small boned fowl, with only a knife and fork, without use of the fingers, which was considered gross and was simply not tolerated. (I am reasonably sure that the term "finger-lickin' good" was not known at that time.)

Beyond Albertine's famous desserts, there was always some sort of bleu cheese, usually Roquefort or Gorgonzola. Danish and Stilton could not be found locally, as their provenance hailed from a different region with a colder climate and different culture. The cheese most closely identified with the area where the château was located was Cantal, a mild, uniquely flavored hard cheese for which one needed to acquire a taste.

After dinner, the sated crowd usually retired to the Petit Salon for coffee, cognac or anisette. There was almost always a fire going, which endowed the room with a sense of coziness that contrasted sharply with the cold stone of the château's ancient walls. On cold winter nights, everyone left the cozy Petit Salon to go to his or her respective bedroom. As central heating was about as common as central air conditioning in those days, namely virtually non-existent, my expectation on my first cold night at the château was for a very cold room, followed by an hour of shivering in bed until the sheets finally warmed up. However, instead of an icy shock, a helpful soul, probably Alice or Denise, made sure that toasty warm sheets greeted my body, providing a delightful invitation to sleep and proving, once again, that the best pleasures are often nothing more than a relief from pain! This magic was accomplished thanks to a contraption called a *moine* (which translates into monk). It was a sled-shaped hollow framework within which a container of embers was suspended, thus warming the sheets without burning them. The moine was placed under the covers about 45 minutes before bedtime. The effect of slipping into a preheated bed when you are expecting to be frozen stiff defies comparison with any other kind of luxury.

Chapter 12

My own day typically started with breakfast in the kitchen, watching Albertine stoke the stove back to life, determining whether the embers from the night before would roar back to life or if a whole new lighting would be necessary. This was the time to catch up on the gossip, as the rest of the help drifted into the kitchen to find out about the occurrences of the night before.

My breakfast usually consisted of a bowl of hot milk, into which I would dunk some very fresh and crusty bread. The milk was not pasteurized, homogenized or otherwise rendered safe, but it was delicious! The bread, which came fresh from the bakery every morning, was sliced from a large, 18-inch round loaf after Albertine, in a kind of ad hoc consecration ceremony, had scratched a sign of the cross on the bottom. After breakfast, I walked across the entry courtyard and over the old stone bridge that spanned the Vendinelle. Once on the other side, it was a very short walk to school.

As always, I was a very bad student. This time, the challenge was even greater, as I was also learning to be an accidental Catholic. I had always had an aversion to rites, and never understood the relationship between mysticism and religious faith. It wouldn't be until much later that I would study Auguste Comte, and come to espouse his philosophy of Positivism, rationally suggesting that there are things we don't know and were simply not meant to know. While a gross oversimplification and highly limited view of his philosophy, this approach has indeed provided me with a *modus vivendi*, at least until science and religion can make their peace and fill in the blanks. In the meantime, I spent a lot of time in Auriac's medieval church. It is significant to note, however, that no one in the de Bonnefoy family ever, not even once, attempted to convert me to Catholicism, although they did spend a considerable amount of time teaching me enough about the Catholic religious rites to enable me to convincingly pass as a Catholic. Unfortunately (or fortunately), even the pope could not undo my circumcision. I managed to become an altar boy, and each week I would swing the burning incense during Mass, following the service as faithfully as I could. But I eschewed confession, and faked the prayers and communion.

True to form, I could not stop my naturally mischievous nature from coming to the fore, and it wasn't long before the ceremonial wine mysteriously began to disappear, prayer books were glued to the pews and, horror of all horrors, on heavy snow days, huge balls of snow were dumped on worshipers from the church tower as they exited the church.

I was 12, and my best friends were Elie Garrig, Albertine's son, and Maurice Coret, the village grocer's son. The three of us were the same age, in the same class in school and we did everything together; we were inseparable. We explored everything — every nook and cranny — not only of the château, but those of any member of the opposite sex we could coerce. We avidly participated in every fad that hit the village, and everything turned into a contest or a game.

Spinning tops were very popular because they were easy to get. But they could also be dangerous. Making things fly — like kites, model planes and slings and arrows — filled the summer months with endless contests and thrills. At one point, the entire youth of the village went on a stilt-walking rampage. The covered central market appeared to be full of human storks, milling around in random patterns like a scene from a zoo; it was hilarious.

An ongoing obsession of ours was playing marbles. The schoolyard was usually the favored venue for these contests, and many ended in muddy fights. We played various forms of the game all year round, with periodic formal competitions that sometimes triggered the emotional involvement of parents and adults — sort of like Little League today!

Swimming was also a preoccupation. The Vendinelle, however, fell far short of providing a swimming environment. There were only two places where swimming was possible. One was a large, man-made reservoir the size of a lake. It had become a fashionable resort area called St. Ferreol, near St. Girons, about 20 kilometers away. The test of fire for burgeoning swimmers was to swim the mile across that lake without a boat to assist. Succeed, and you were dubbed a real swimmer. The other spot, much closer to home, was an old but really deep millpond, less than a hundred feet across, located within a short bike ride of Auriac. The problem was, it was privately owned and used by its owner as part of a watermill and flour-production operation. The owner used dogs and shotguns to keep kids like us away. Then, we discovered a third, completely different, possibility.

The château's vegetable garden and farm was served by a shallow, 12-foot square concrete cistern filled with rain and well water, and was about three and a half to four feet deep. It was used to water the vegetable crops,

Chapter 12

but there was always enough water to experience the feeling of water buoyancy, and thus give the impression of swimming while actually hopping on one unseen foot on the shallow bottom of the cistern. Anyhow, that's how I learned to swim.

After months of practice in the cistern, I was ready for the real test — to swim for real across the millpond. In my imagination, it became deeper and more ominous every day. In fact, it was a source of major anxiety until the day of THE BIG TEST! I had brought all this on myself, with an act of foolish bravado, by defiantly throwing down the gauntlet and announcing, unabashedly, that I could easily swim across the bottomless millpond any time I wanted. It was, of course, pretty much of a bluff, but I got caught up in my own fantasy and now, I would have to pay the price. And so, on the agreed-upon day, I set out with my friends for THE BIG TEST. I got in the water and, miracles of miracles, I was actually able to make it across with nary a problem. The whole event started to feel almost anticlimactic, until our jubilation upon my completion of the return swim back across the millpond awakened the miller. He came out screaming, with unrestrained anger and his shotgun ready for action. In a panic, we ran for the wall protecting the pond and, as I tried to climb over it, I managed to impale myself on the spikes the miller had so conveniently placed to discourage juvenile delinquents like us. When my friends succeeded in disengaging me from the spikes and we were safe from further danger, I felt blood flowing profusely from my crotch, into my pants and down my leg. We rushed back to the château to find Albertine ready to unleash a long and noisy tongue-lashing. Instead, I was so covered in blood that a doctor had to be called to control the flow from my crotch. By the time he got there, my genitals had distended to frightening dimensions, swelling to twice their normal size.

I was allowed, just this once, to sleep in "The Colonel's Room" over the kitchen, instead of my usual tiny alcove between Madame's and Monsieur's rooms. The large, cushy bed in that room enabled me to lie with legs appropriately spread to accommodate the source of my dilemma. I spent about three weeks healing in that bed, convinced that I would never be able to sire an heir for the de Bonnefoys or myself. This, of course, turned out to be wrong, as my son, Erich, and my daughter, Lisa, can now attest. But none of that really mattered because now, I could swim!

I still don't know the reason for my obsession with swimming. Perhaps it was the anxieties caused by my father constantly swimming too far out at the beach at Ostend, or perhaps it was his stubborn and futile attempts to teach me to swim by strapping me in that ridiculous medieval contraption and dunking me into a pool like a fish on a line. (Much later, well after the war, I continued to swim, making the varsity team for my high school and my college and then, for good measure, I swam for the U.S. Army. Finally, I became an American Red Cross swimming and water safety instructor. It's a miracle that I never had ambitions of becoming a Navy Seal!) This passion for swimming would, unfortunately, spawn an uncomfortable, recurring dream — I can see my father, very much alive and proudly watching as I demonstrate my swimming skills for him. And then the dream ends. In the dream, there is never any response from my father, leaving me with an empty sense of deep regret, mixed with indefinable guilt that I would never be able to bring him satisfaction on this score.

And so, the months passed. My life had assumed a sense of normality, as each day neatly unfolded in a more or less predictable fashion. My parents were gone, and this was an inexorable void. But it was filled by daily routines that were never really routine-like. School was always a challenge, but the important thing was that I was alive, I was loved and cared for and, most important of all, my cover story was holding.

CHAPTER 13

The Resistance

The year of 1943 was turning into 1944 without my noticing the passage of time. I had arrived at the château in time for the new school year, and now we had already finished the Christmas celebrations!

In Belgium, Christmas is known as St. Nicholas Day; in France, it is Noel. In this profoundly Catholic country, Christmas is considered the holiest of all holidays and a great deal of effort is always devoted to this celebration. Easter is almost as important but, given the nature of what is feted, this event was somewhat more somber.

Christmas at the château was a schizophrenic affair. On one hand, the endless Masses in the ancient church, laden with choir chants and a wide range of ceremonial rites, gave overwhelming respect to the glorious birth of the Christ child. On the other hand, it was an equally glorious opportunity to turn Albertine loose in her kitchen and allow her to create one of the inestimable feasts for which she was so famous. The menu consisted of many parts, but the most unforgettable dish was always braised goose, stuffed with a chestnut dressing ... turkeys were not even on the radar screen, and sweet potatoes, well ... nobody would ever think of eating that!

This lavish supper was served after the midnight church service where, for what seemed like hours, we had squirmed, hungry and cold, on the hard wood of the church's pews. And all we got in exchange for our liturgical efforts was a *crouton* dipped in holy water, which was piously passed among the faithful by the altar boys ... of which I was one.

As 1944 unfolded, the war and the simmering anger with the German occupation of France continued to overhang our lives, despite the illusion of normality that prevailed in Auriac. The concept of a free France, à la

Vichy, had been debunked. No more illusions. The fact was, all of France was now an occupied zone. Despite the complete German occupation, the Vichy government would continue to exercise jurisdiction until the collapse of the regime after the 1944 Normandy invasion, when the United States ceased to acknowledge Vichy as the official government of France. Nonetheless, there still existed a sense of normality, and many were tacitly accepting France's new status as a completely occupied territory.

People were sick of the war (which had been going on since 1939), sick of living in constant fear, sick of the privations and discouraged by the fact that, except for the underground leadership in the resistance, we were cloaked in a blanket of isolation that made it impossible for anyone to appreciate the full scope of events taking place in the world. We had no ready access to information on the war; we could not see beyond the events of our lives and our tiny region.

What we did hear, over and over again, were the daily pronouncements from *Der Füehrer* and his propaganda establishment detailing the secret weapons he would unleash to bring victory to the Third Reich. He ranted about the *Flying Bombs* (the V-1 and the more advanced V-2), which he planned to drop on London and other British cities. He would make good on this threat in June of 1944, ushering in an era of terror from the sky, as powerful explosives fell without warning on civilian areas, causing widespread death and destruction. (Ironically, the science and engineering that produced the rockets that powered these flying bombs was the same that was used nearly half a century later to get America to the Moon, and thanks to the same German scientist — Werner Von Braun!) Hitler's boasts did not stop with the V-1 and V-2 flying bombs. He had far more sinister plans, including the development of an atomic bomb that, mercifully, never came to be. He did succeed in perfecting much of his capacity for destruction; he developed the *Tiger Tank*, a monstrous killing machine that nothing in the Allied armor arsenal could match, and a jet fighter plane unrivaled among the Allied air forces.

On the bright side, however, resistance efforts throughout Europe had proved to be not only possible but also more and more common. And, in France, it had become a passion to find ways of fighting Germans. With the war beginning to turn, Oncle Nino was absent from the château more frequently than normal during the winter of 1944. While it was whispered that the reason for his absence was important resistance business, most of

Chapter 13

what transpired remained a mystery to me. These precautions were for everyone's protection and security, since to be captured meant a fate worse than death for anyone associated with the resistance. The Germans had no hesitation in using the most barbaric means possible to extract every last piece of information in one's possession. We were told of the tortures and ordeals that the SS inflicted upon those unlucky enough to end up in their clutches. After the war, those in our circle of friends who had been captured (but managed to survive) confirmed much of this. The Germans, the *Milice* and the collaborators had indeed refined their torture skills to the level of a fine art. Asking too many questions of resistance fighters was not only unpatriotic, it was dangerous.

In spite of the great secrecy, one thing was clear to me: Oncle Nino had a significant role with the French Resistance, specifically the unit known as the *Maquis de la Montagne Noire* (Maquis of the Black Mountain), which had set up its headquarters in a thickly forested, hilly area in the Tarn Valley in the Languedoc region of Southwestern France. He was part of a network of partisans and saboteurs known as *Maquisards*. These members of the *Maquis* had refused to accept the Vichy government of France and refused to acknowledge the leadership of Maréchal Philippe Petain, Admiral Darlan and their cohorts, who had surrendered the country to the Third Reich in 1940, ushering in the era that was to hold France in chains until August of 1944. They refused to lose their freedom like so many men of draftable age, who had been rounded up and forced to serve in the infamous German work camps that went by the pompous, bureaucratic name of *Service du Travail Obligatoire* (Obligatory Work Service).

Literally translated, the term *Maquis* refers to thickets, underbrush or bushes in the countryside or in the mountains. But in the context of the French Resistance, the term referred to a guerrilla unit in hiding from the oppressor. Before their formation into more formal units, members of the *Maquis* were known as *Partisans*. They were involved at the very dawn of the resistance. More than anything else, it was the fear of the German work camps that had forced these able-bodied men to escape conscription and flee from their homes into the mountains and forested hiding places throughout France. Initially, they had acted as individuals, but had widespread help and support from the local rural population in the regions, where they found shelter and were able to hide, despite the existence of collaborators who were always around to curry the favor of the occupiers.

Most were armed with old, obsolete weapons like hunting shotguns, and nothing more. The veterans from the defeated French Army who had hidden their weapons, however, were better off. They had modern repeater rifles, grenades and steel helmets. It wasn't until later, in mid-1943, that Sten and burp guns made their appearance as the emblematic weapon of the *Maquis*.

Beginning as early as 1942, the individual Partisans began to coalesce into bands committed to fight the occupiers and their collaborators. They became known as the *Maquis*, and they eventually grew into a network sufficiently well organized to become an increasingly serious thorn in the side of German military operations. Once they were able to establish contact with London, where General Charles de Gaulle was leading the French army in exile, the resistance took on the semblance of a military force of some consequence. In 1944, the Allies began parachute drops that supplied the *Maquis* with vehicular mobility, radio communication, medical supplies, dynamite, detonators, and other explosive capacities, as well as an ample reservoir of ammunition. They were now an effective fighting force and a real threat to the Axis.

Ultimately, capitalizing on the reverses that were battering the German Army, the *Maquisards* grew into fearsome, enraged and vengeful killers; the hunted had become the hunters. It would not be until after the Normandy landings in June 1944 that the *Maquis* would become formal, disciplined members of the Allied Army, and they were officially designated as a member of the *Forces Française de l'Interieur* (FFI).

The symbol for the FFI was the Cross of Lorraine. It was seen everywhere; on the armbands of partisans, on their berets, painted on cars, trucks and busses — anything encountered by the resistance fighters became adorned with the cross. The cross came from the Lorraine, the companion region to the Alsace in Northeastern France. These regions have always been referred to as one, the Alsace-Lorraine, and have for centuries represented a land in bloody contention between France and Germany. Historically, control of the Alsace-Lorraine has seesawed between the two countries, depending on who was winning the most recent war. But the Alsatians, despite their Germanic traits, customs in food, proper names and wines, always considered themselves quintessentially French. They were fierce, if not belligerent, in this conviction. Ask any Frenchman, for example, where brasseries came from! The Lorraine, on the other hand,

Chapter 13

has always been French, without any trace of ambivalence or German traits. Located in the path of virtually every German invasion of France, it has always been at the forefront of heroic battles and defense works like those surrounding the Maginot Line. The Lorraine was a major player in epic battles between France and Germany, such as those fought in the war of 1870 and the First World War for the cities of Metz, Toul and Verdun, and for the defense of such hermetically fortified cities as Sedan. The cross quickly became an iconic and dreaded signal for the Germans and the collaborators to run for their lives.

The *Maquis de la Montagne Noire* unit was located perhaps 25 or 30 kilometers from the château. Periodically, Oncle Nino would use me as a bike messenger to convey information and instructions to the leaders of the *Maquis*. On such occasions he would entrust me with coded snippets of information. These had to remain undecipherable to assure the security of the *Maquis* as well as my own, should I be captured. But, despite the danger, I never hesitated. I never had any doubt that completing these missions and delivering the information was very important, so I was always well-prepared. I usually concealed the messages inside the hollow pipes of my bike, which I accessed through its saddle assembly. I never felt in danger of being discovered by the Germans; I was just a typical 12-year-old ragamuffin on a bike, riding a country road with a fresh baguette in my saddlebag! Carrying bread was always an effective ploy to allay suspicion and evade the attention of the Germans. Bread was, after all, the universal staff of life, the wholesome substance of sustenance. And the aroma of recently baked French bread would undoubtedly combine innocence with mouthwatering temptations, thus getting me past any check points interposed by the occupiers.

Fortunately, I was stopped only once. One night, I was stopped by two sweaty *Boches* reeking of stale sauerkraut, who asked me for a taste of the baguette I was carrying. I assured them that, while it was quite fresh and delicious, it had no weapon hidden inside, but I refused to share it with them, exclaiming, "Grandma will be so mad when I get to her house with only half a loaf that she will beat me senseless!" The ploy worked successfully, and they set me free, to continue on my way to "Grandma's." Truthfully, the fresh baked bread always smelled so good that, all too often, it would be all gone by the time I reached my destination. Of course, there was no "Grandma," but had there been, it would not have made any difference — to this day, I still cannot resist the smell of a freshly baked baguette!

Once I was sure I was clear from any German eyes, I would meet my contact near, but outside, the inner security perimeter of the camouflaged *Maquis* encampment. As my contact was always alone and was expecting me, recognition was not a problem. Yet, we still used passwords as an additional layer of security. After these minor formalities, I was escorted to the leader of the *Maquis* cell. Once the greetings were done, my bike was taken apart to yield the concealed information. Then, it would be reassembled, with a return message inside to be delivered to Oncle Nino at the château.

The exchange of information and messages had once again worked without incident; everything had gone well, I would live to see another day! If I had been caught, if something — anything — had gone wrong.... My constant fear was that, if the war did not end soon, living in the *Maquis* would likely be my fate.

The road between the *Maquis* and Auriac was quite hilly and the bike ride was always arduous. By the end of the return trip, it was painful to the point where the dangers of the missions were subordinated to the physical pain of the journey. But, in retrospect, one of the most difficult aspects of my role as a courier for the *Maquis* was the fact that these experiences were never warm or rewarding. Fear of attack ... from without and within ... did not make for cheerful dispositions, and the *Maquisards* were not, by and large, gregarious. They were not at all like the merry men who surrounded Robin Hood, nor were they Boy Scouts, helping old ladies and doing good deeds. They were not paragons of virtue; they were a tough and ruthless bunch, one where discipline was always a challenge. The hardships many had suffered before joining the resistance, those they were currently experiencing in hiding while living away from their families, the acts of brutality they had witnessed — all this combined to harden their outlook on life. Their dominant desire was to see the war end and to see the viscerally hated enemy excruciatingly punished and dispatched into Hell. In the final analysis, what the *Maquisards* were was heroic. Their sacrifices were instrumental in helping save the world from the horrors of the Third Reich.

My missions for the *Maquis* would often take me to other estates owned by relatives and friends of the de Bonnefoys. When this occurred, the plan was always for me to stay for an extended period of time. We

Chapter 13

would often play checkers, chess or endless games of Monopoly and cards to pass the time. It was not only a way of disguising my activities for the resistance, as discovery would have put me in deadly peril from the Germans, the Vichy occupation authorities and, of course, any friend or neighbor who might be a collaborator, but also a pleasant way to end a strenuous journey, particularly on winter's cold and rainy days.

In the course of these visits, I had the privilege of meeting a number of distinguished personalities and their families who, like me, were in hiding. Most were so modest that I had no idea of their fame and reputation until after the war. At one of my favorite stops, Château de Redon, a neighboring château where Tante Lily's sister Nicole lived, I met Marc Chagall. After the war, he was officially recognized as France's Artist Laureate, a title and honor of the highest degree the state could bestow. On a different occasion, I met Darius Milhaud who would, after the war, become my shipmate during my immigration to the United States. These princes of the art world were badly wanted by the Germans not only because they were Jewish, but also because their participation in the resistance was notorious.

While visiting one of the châteaux hiding Jews imbedded in France's southwestern countryside, I was introduced to Jean Cassou, who was to become the director of the Paris Museum of Modern Art after the war, and his daughter Isabelle, who I remember as a whiz at Monopoly, a quintessentially capitalistic game. Ironically, after the war, she turned into an ardent communist. My friendship with the Cassous outlived the war. The last time I saw them was in 1958 in Paris, in their *Quartier Latin* Left Bank walk-up flat, surrounded by the mementos of Jean Cassou's career — museum quality paintings, drawings, sculptures, maquettes and a wide variety of original art treasures from Picasso, Miro, Chagall, Brancusi, Calder, Matisse and so many other contemporary heroes of the Impressionism and Expressionism eras.

There was also the Abraham family, Marcel and his two sisters. Marcel was a distinguished educator who became minister of education after the war, as well as Poet Laureate of France. He and Tante Lily were lovers. This was no secret, nor was Uncle Nino's reputation as a Lothario. And in a country as profoundly Catholic as France, divorce was not an option. Long after the war, when Marcel died, he was given a very public state funeral, including a eulogy full of poems he had written honoring Tante

Lily. He was truly the love of her life, and I decided that, in his honor, I would make Marcel my son's middle name.

Finally, there was a Benedictine monk, Père Jacob Clément. His monastery was the Abbaye D'Encalcat in Dourgne in the Tarn area. Père Clément was an extremely talented pianist. He was also a prodigious writer, maintaining a steady flow of correspondence with such world-class contemporary religious philosophers as Jacques Maritain and others concerned with the direction of religious thought. Even though the monastery maintained a vow of silence, Père Clément was far too worldly, gregarious and extroverted for such restraint. In fact, for a Benedictine prelate from the straight-laced order steeped in self-discipline, he displayed a remarkably secular spirit! He loved to get out and mingle with society, flirting and getting "involved with" members of both sexes. Indeed, he was charming and enormously respected for his intellect. I helped encourage his unusual behavior by conspiring to spring him out of the monastic life from time to time, and acting as a carrier pigeon, delivering his correspondence.

It was not until long after the war that I learned that Père Clément was a converted Jew, and thus in mortal danger, not of losing his soul, which he may well have deserved, but his life, which he did not deserve, every time he left the sanctuary of the monastery. Perhaps God could forgive him his straying, but the Nazis would not!

Meanwhile, as the war raged on throughout the winter, the Eschelbourne family made the château at Auriac their second home. Mr. Eschelbourne entertained us with the details of his frequent trips to Holland and South Africa for what always sounded like very important and exotic business, while his wife stayed behind at the château. Over time, the relationship between the families became even more intimate. The Eschelbournes were among the very few people Tante Lily trusted completely — they were not only familiar with Nino's resistance activities, but also with Tante Lily's work hiding and rescuing Jewish children — including me.

The Eschelbournes would join us after dinner as we huddled conspiratorially in the Petit Salon, listening to the clandestine, cryptic broadcasts on the family's crackling short wave radio. We would listen, as London would broadcast "personal messages" meant to be picked up for use by the resistance. Our hope was always that the magic code words would be heard, announcing the date of the Allied invasion of Europe. That date, as well as the location of the Allied landings and other details about this anxiously

Chapter 13

awaited event was, of course, cloaked in the deepest of secrecy. Only a few people, those who had a "need to know," had that information. Even with Oncle Nino's high-level involvement in the *Maquis*, we were not part of that group. Only after the landings had begun did we find out what the code words were. They were built into the almost musical lines from a famous Paul Verlaine poem — "Les sanglots longs des violons, ... Blessent mon coeur d'une langueur monotone" — which translates "The long sobs from the violins wound my heart with a languorous, monotonous mood."

But during that winter of 1944, the invasion was still a dream, and by mid-winter, Auriac's tenuous sense of normality would be shattered.

Chapter 14

We've Got Company

The village school, a small primary school with four classrooms and a walled yard, was located across the Vendinelle River, opposite from the château. The school was so close that I could walk to it, and even watch what was going on there from the château. On this particular morning, I was eating my breakfast at the kitchen table, getting ready for school. Albertine was looking absentmindedly out of the kitchen window in the direction of the school, when she called my attention to movement across the Vendinelle. We saw a German military staff car drive up to the schoolhouse. While this caught the interest of Albertine and others in the kitchen, for me it was not mere interest — it set off a strident alarm! My alarm increased in intensity as we watched four uniformed German officers walk into the school. The alarm reached its crescendo when we saw the Germans walking out with the headmaster, who was pointing repeatedly in the direction of the château.

The Germans climbed back into the staff car, crossed the Vendinelle and headed straight for the front yard of the château. I was petrified. Had somebody denounced Tante Lily? Had the *Maquis* been infiltrated and Oncle Nino captured? The entire château and all its occupants were going to be arrested, and I would be sent to a death camp! Who was at the bottom of this ... Albertine ... the village priest ... the tenant farmer — I knew I shouldn't have flirted with his daughter, Marilou. Who could have possibly committed an act so vile, so perverse? I didn't know what to do or what to think, and it really didn't matter. There was no place to run without giving myself away. But I was paralyzed with fear, rooted in place. I couldn't move; I felt an unstoppable panic rise in my chest.

The German staff car approached the château gates and drove noisily

Chapter 14

onto the graveled frontcourt. I watched as the four German officers climbed out and approached the kitchen. My knees were shaking; all I could do was sit at the kitchen table and stare at the half-eaten breakfast in front of me, waiting for events to unfold.

The officers were covered with ribbons, chains and medals symbolizing their valor. They conveyed an aura of discipline and authority. They were dressed immaculately in crisp, neatly ironed olive-green uniforms and they wore brilliantly shined black boots and belts with brass buckles, as well as dress daggers. They wore no helmets, only the officer kepis, a small, soft hat with a stiff visor similar to that normally worn by civil officials. They bore no weapons other than the requisite holstered Luger. The uniforms evoked memories of St. Girons and my parents; but it was the headband on their hats that carried an even more sinister message. The headbands were adorned with the fearsome death-head symbol, identifying them as members of the *Schutzstaffel*, the feared and loathed SS, famous for their ferocious, Doberman-like blood oath to Hitler and the Nazi party.

But, to my astonishment, these officers seemed extremely polite, given their fearful reputation. They clicked their heels smartly and informed Albertine that their mission was to secure living accommodations for what turned out to be a regiment of *Waffen SS* soldiers, an elite branch of the *Schutzstaffel*. They would be quartered in Auriac for a limited period of time, just until the troops could rest and then move out to their next battle theater. In this manner, new recruits could be trained and war-weary troops could rest. Their regiment was being held in reserve, and it would be refreshed with additional troops and shipped to the Eastern front to stop the Russian advance toward the fatherland. The Russian front was a destination that inspired unimaginable terror for the German military ... even for the fearsome SS.

After the advance guard assessed the village, planned where and how the regiment would be encamped and held meetings with various residents and local officials involved in securing the housing arrangements, the rest of the SS unit arrived. Field-grade officers along with their aides, orderlies and all their military paraphernalia were housed with us in the château, and most of the enlisted troops were accommodated in the schoolhouse. But as this was not enough space for nearly 1,000 troops, every available nook and cranny was utilized. Any empty village shops, second-floor vacant space, public offices ... but not the church ... were all commandeered for housing. Even space in the outlying farms was requisitioned ... as long as it was within reasonable bicycle reach of the village. The château also served as regimental headquarters. Quite naturally, the officers took the best and most prestigious section of the château, its ancient stone wing around the tradition-laden vestibule with its ornate, monumental marble staircase. The Eschelbournes were unceremoniously moved to other, less comfortable rooms, and life in Auriac — and at the château — would never be the same.

The Germans were as class conscious as the French, and had no qualms about treating their ordinary soldiers, the non-aristocrats in the enlisted ranks, abominably. The discipline and the harassment of the troopers was overbearing, constant and painful to behold. Punishments were frequent and humiliating; drillings and training were incessant and, behind it all, we could almost feel the obsessive fear of their next deployment! It loomed more and more menacingly as the war lingered on. The German officers, in contrast to the much-abused ordinary troopers, indulged in every possible luxury and pampering on which they could lay their hands. Curiously, they did everything possible to impress us, their vanquished hosts, with the notion that they were not like *Boches*. In fact, the German colonel in command of the unit took great pains to inform Tante Lily that, before the war, he was a professor of history at Heidelberg University, and that he had great respect for French culture, traditions and, how to best say it, the noble breeding of the de Bonnefoy family. While this attitude did not reflect the image and reputation of the *Boches*, it did little to calm our fears.

They also went to great lengths to demonstrate their appreciation for Albertine's cognac soufflés, which they requested at all hours of the day and night. I will always remember her grumbling and cursing while she was turning out one cognac soufflé after another, all night long, as the orderlies serving the SS officers continuously came and went from the kitchen. There was one benefit for me in all this manic activity. I got to help Albertine in the kitchen, dipping a finger in the luscious egg and cognac mixture, which she whipped so vigorously that you would have thought the bowl was full of her worst enemies! Not surprisingly, the officers were also great aficionados of *foie gras* and all the other wondrous French specialties we kept stored in the larder of the château.

Chapter 14

For us, it was the dawn of a new reality. With the arrival of the regiment, there were no more fanfares or parades; the shops stayed open, but gingerly so; the church performed its rites and the priest continued to say Mass. But it felt as if a pall had fallen over the village. Like the rest of France, we were plunged into what became known as the *Dark Years*.

The dual occupancy of the château by its owners and by the invaders turned Albertine's obsessively well-ordered kitchen into chaos. The German officers always ate in the library, never with us. Sometimes, to the exasperation of everyone, they even demanded different dishes. Their food was prepared with much under-breath cursing from her. The orderlies were virtually slaves to their masters and they served them accordingly, with a degree of obsequiousness inconceivable to someone as independent and defiant as Albertine! Indeed, the latter would have flung their ill-gotten food in their faces and ended up shot to death if left to her natural instincts.

As the Germans had occupied the Auriac school building, classes were moved to temporary space above a row of stores on a street that flanked the château. The village streets were no longer quiet and peaceful; they were ringing out with the martial songs that German soldiers delivered in cadence with the thump, thump, thump of their jackboots on the pavement. From my classroom, I could see and hear everything that was happening in the street below. The normal daily activities of the village were accompanied by the tramping of German boots, marching in military cadence down the street and around the corner, where they entered the château through the short pedestrian bridge across the Vendinelle. This linked the vegetable garden with the large rear court of the château where the ancient sycamores cast their everlasting shade. Along with the rhythm of the boots, the troopers were always singing the kind of songs that inspire the military to seek a glory that transcends life and death. This kind of choral music might have been moving under different circumstances. In this case, however, the singing did not sound as melodious as had probably been intended by Beethoven or Mozart. It was unduly martial and guttural; these were unmistakably songs of the conquerors, not of the vanquished. And they certainly were not the music of art lovers. It was easy to understand why they did not resonate well with the villagers or me.

The rear, park-like enclosure in back of the château offered a three-acre surface of loose pea-gravel. When the soldiers reached it, they broke their single formation into ten or 12 smaller ones. Then, they proceeded to undertake their daily drills, accompanied by orders bellowed by subalterns at the top of their lungs. Non-commissioned officers and officers used the opportunity of having the bulk of the troops assembled in one place to harangue them and mete out humiliating punishments to be witnessed by the assembled company. It seemed as if all the troops occupying Auriac passed the commanding officer in review at least twice a week. After that, the troops were usually dismissed and they dispersed to resume whatever activities they were engaged in prior to the drill. One such occasion occurred on Hitler's birthday. The morning drill and the harangues and the speeches were particularly heated, and they were endless. The marching and singing sounded exceedingly vigorous. Tante Lily asked me to join her in her bedroom, which overlooked the drill area where the troops were assembled. She asked me if I could translate what was being said. Drawing on what little German I still remembered from when I had lived with my parents, I did the best I could. I must have been successful because, long before the Germans were finished with their speeches and harangues, she hugged me hard and melted into tears. Her ancestral home was being raped and the invader was bragging about it. It was humiliating. It was an excruciating, highly charged emotional moment for both of us. Once again, I felt helpless and unable to change anything.

The orderlies who served the officers in the château were a busy bunch. There were five of them. They spent most of their time shining boots, polishing belt buckles and cleaning weapons. They seemed to have no personal life. They did not, unlike the officers, speak French, but they managed to communicate very well with us in other ways. I was impressed with how young they all were. Most of them seemed to be between 15 and 18 years old and had not seen combat. They did not seem hardened like all the others I had encountered. I found out during some quiet, one-on-one moments with them that they were quick to express hatred for Hitler and disgust with the war. It was interesting to see the dreaded enemy this close — practically from inside the monster's maw.

I still remember how the soldiers smelled. They emitted an aroma that was like an acrid combination of shoe polish coupled with sauerkraut and machine oil, with the latter owed to the maintenance of their weapons. In the final analysis, it was impossible to escape the fact that they were human beings with normal desires, fears, emotions and attitudes. Under different circumstances, we might even have been buddies. But to think in those terms at that time would be considered heresy or, in some quarters, treason!

I recall one particularly young orderly with curly blond hair. We called him "Blondie," and he was extremely likable. We became so familiar with him that we sometimes forgot that the skull and bones adorned his uniform. One day, I almost asked him how he felt about Jews; however, conditioned reflexes immediately and thankfully interfered with this notion and I never did anything that stupid. After all, they were all, including Blondie, members of the *Waffen SS,* and thus part of Hitler's elite military. It would have been a very dangerous game to pull the tail of that tiger.

But fear of the Germans did not deter some fools in the village from indulging in the sport of sitting in the public cafés and openly mocking the Germans to their faces, using jokes and satire about Hitler, their national traits and their personal conduct in conquered territories like ultra-chauvinistic France. This kind of bravado was rare, however, and they could take some degree of comfort in the fact that most German soldiers neither spoke nor understood any French.

With the Germans spread throughout Auriac and with their headquarters in our home, we had to be particularly careful. We stopped listening to *Radio Londre Personal Messages,* but never stopped hoping that, one day soon, London would announce D-Day and our deliverance. Meanwhile, we had to take whatever comfort we could from each rumor that came to us about an Allied victory or a German defeat. This gave us all, and particularly the resistance members, new energy to face the future and continue the fight for freedom. It also made us more daring and we were willing to take more risks in communicating with the resistance network, though we really had no idea about the progress of the war.

We saw less and less of Oncle Nino, as his work with the resistance intensified. Fortunately, my cover story was holding. As German security tightened, my bicycle rides for the *Maquis* were curtailed to only the most critical ones, but I had fallen into a new role. I knew enough German to understand much of the speeches the German commander delivered from the improvised dais built at the parade grounds in back of the château. Hitler's birthday celebration and my performance as Tante Lily's "translator in chief" had proven that my linguistic skills enabled me to provide a rough translation, but this fact had to be kept a deep secret. While my translations were very useful for military intelligence, there would be questions about my origins should this talent be discovered, and the consequences for everyone at the château would be dire.

Henceforth, every time the German troops were assembled, I stood with Tante Lily at one of the upstairs windows and did my best to provide a simultaneous translation of the harangue as the commander stood at attention before his assembled troops, proclaiming his message in the harsh and authoritative manner so common in the German military. And every time, Tante Lily would cry her heart out, so great was the humiliation, particularly when the assembled troopers intoned "Deutschland Uber Alles," the Hun's national anthem. The sounds echoed from the proud walls of her ancestral home, which was in the hands of an enemy she despised with every fiber of her being. It was on these occasions that a violent hatred for the Nazis welled up within me, impelling a desperate and very foolish impulse to escape from the village, seek out the *Maquis*, jump into a traction-avant and, with a burp gun, wreak havoc by spraying the Germans in the village square with a blizzard of bullets.

It became nearly impossible to get news of the war. The Germans controlled all the sources, and their propaganda made for very depressing listening. If we believed what they said, the Allies somehow had no capacity for victory of any kind ... ever ... and the Reich was on the verge of becoming the master of the world. The reality, however, was quite different and some of it managed to leak out slowly.

Names like Stalingrad oozed out of the news blackouts imposed by Goebbel's propaganda machine. Thanks to Oncle Nino's resistance network, we learned of the German surrender of the entire sixth Army in January 1943, even though the German propaganda claimed the sixth Army had fought to the death a year later. In early 1944, there was hush-hush talk about the Allies and the deeds of the FFI; graffiti showing the Cross of Lorraine made its appearance with impunity more and more frequently. Charles de Gaulle was more openly emerging as the principal icon of France's liberation; and the prospective landing by the Allies in Northern France was no longer a question of if, but one of when and where! The Allied landings that occurred in Sicily in the middle of 1943 and the eventual withdrawal of German forces proved that the invincible machine could, in fact, be defeated. The Italian landings and other successes by the Allies, if cited at all, were mocked and dwarfed by large posters plastered throughout France showing a map of Italy with a giant snail trying to wend its way up the iconic boot-shaped peninsula that defines Italy's coastline. The caption made reference to the Allies' lack of vigor by borrowing from the popular Irish song "It's a Long Way to Tipperary." The message was clear: the Allies were mired down and not getting anywhere.

Most French citizens had no idea that what they thought of as the war in Europe had truly become a world war — they didn't know that Australia had been involved since 1939 ... and on our side! It was only because of the dribble of information from underground sources that we knew of America's official entry into the war in Europe in 1942, nor did they know that America was at war with Japan, although it had begun over two years before; they had not heard about Pearl Harbor; they did not have the slightest inkling that America had been working on an atomic bomb, even though the Manhattan Project had been initiated in 1942. While we knew that captured Jews were being taken to what were euphemistically referred to as *work camps* by the German and Vichy governments, we did not know that Hitler's Wannsee Conference in January 1942 had sealed the fate of Jews and other *undesirables* with the creation of his *Final Solution*, and that the *work camps* were actually death camps. We knew nothing about the battle of Stalingrad, one of the great turning points in World War II when, in January of 1943, over 90,000 German troops had surrendered to the Soviets.

Today, the battle of El Alamein is well known. (When Joyce and I were driving through Egypt some 60 or more years later, we stopped at a museum built in the middle of the Libyan desert that commemorated the battle.) But in early 1944, in German-occupied France, we were only dimly aware of the war in North Africa and we were even less aware of the epic desert armor duels between Rommel and Montgomery. We had no idea that the Axis forces in North Africa had surrendered in May 1943, nor did we know about the Allied campaigns in Italy that ended with a victory for the Allies in the fall of 1943. We knew nothing about the Warsaw Ghetto, so eloquently described in Leon Uris's 1980 tome titled *Mila 18*, which told the story of the 750 Jews who fought back against the Germans for almost a month in 1943, demonstrating to the world that, to some degree at least, resistance was possible.

In fact, 1943 had really been the year when the tide of the war had begun to turn from the Third Reich and the Axis to the Allies, who were by then committed to obtaining the unconditional surrender of not only Germany but also of Japan, the Empire of the Rising Sun. Massive carpet bombing of German cities, beginning with Hamburg in July 1943, would continue throughout 1944 until, early in 1945, most of the German industrial centers would be totally incapacitated. Of particular note was the firebombing of Dresden, which killed at least 135,000 civilians (then later became the subject of a cult science-fiction book by Kurt Vonnegut, called *Slaughterhouse-Five.*

The year 1944 was nearly half over, the Germans were still in Auriac and we were still unable to listen to the radio. One day, a disheveled man dressed in a farmer's blue denim frock with the ubiquitous beret on his head burst into the château in a state of high agitation and demanded to see Madame or Monsieur de Bonnefoy. He was escorted into the Petit Salon, which was usually avoided by the Germans. As he stepped into the intimate room, he could barely contain himself. The moment he saw Oncle Nino, who knew the man as a partisan who had somehow managed to keep a short-wave radio stashed away, he blurted out his news: he had heard the anxiously awaited verses from Verlaine's poem!

News that the coded pronouncement had indeed been issued unleashed a bolt of raw energy on the population of the country. It had been subjugated for so long that the prospect of freedom reached deep into the soul of France and awoke every tendril of the French yearning for resistance and retribution. With the massive D-Day invasion of Hitler's Fortress Europe from the north on June 6, 1944, the Italian Campaign from the south and the debacles the Germans were experiencing all over the Russian front, it became more and more clear that there was a big bright light at the end of the tunnel ... and it was shining on all of us.

The enthusiasm that had previously energized the triumphal German martial songs the troops intoned while marching through the village quickly evaporated, leaving behind merely the mournful sounds of boots tramping on the pavement. The changes in the German officers' daily lives were immediate and profound. Germany was beginning to taste defeat everywhere, and a new attitude was pervasive. The handwriting was on the wall—bold and unabashed, both figuratively and in vivid, colorful graffiti.

The more intelligent among the German military soldiers had by now accepted the idea that Hitler was a madman and that Germany could not

Chapter 14

win the war. Yet they were trapped in their loyalties to the Reich, their fear of the regime, and their fear of the retribution they expected from the conquered victims. Gone was the arrogance, and with it the passion for the exercise of power and terror. Nonetheless, this was not yet a defeated enemy. The occupation of the country would continue a bit longer. Moreover, the Germans had acquired a vigorous zeal for retaliation. The most evil and notorious example of this might well have been the horrific burning of 653 innocent civilians who, on June 10, 1944, were ordered to assemble in the Town Square of Oradour-sur-Glane. After being forced into the village church and two barns, the Germans locked the doors and openings and torched the three buildings. Nobody survived the atrocity, which was purportedly committed by the Germans as an act of retaliation!

A few weeks after D-Day, the occupation unit piled into their trucks and left Auriac, headed for the Russian front. They did so without fanfare or incidents. While it had been less than six months since they had first arrived, for me it felt like a lifetime. Word reached us not long afterwards that the entire regiment, including poor Blondie, had been killed fighting the Russians. I felt no jubilation about this news, as it could not have brought my parents back. I could also conceive that, under different circumstances, Blondie might have been a friend. Once again, this points out the ultimate truth about war — it's war as an idea that is the real villain, those who perish in it are the victims, and, in the final analysis, there are no winners.

A few weeks after the Germans left, the Eschelbourne family mysteriously left the château. Everybody was shocked. They were picked up by a stranger driving an old Peugeot, into which they packed much of their belongings and left, with only a perfunctory expression of affection. We were all mystified! But our surprise was nothing compared to our shock when, about two years after the war had ended, the Toulouse newspapers came out with a screaming banner headline proclaiming:

COLONEL ESCHELBOURNE, Long Wanted by the Allied Authorities, Finally Captured!

Reading further, we learned that he was no diamond merchant. He was an *Abwehr* spy in the German naval intelligence, and was deeply involved in the November 1942 scuttling of the French navy in Toulon, an historic event the German and Vichy governments undertook to prevent their ships from falling into Allied hands. Wide-ranging speculation notwithstanding, no one has really offered a credible explanation as to why the colonel did not turn us in. Here again, I see kismet in action! This remains one of the great mysteries of my life and belies my instinct that, on rare occasions, unlike Voltaire's poor Candide, all indeed does happen for the best, in the best of all possible worlds. I can't help but believe that a positive kismet does exist.

With the good colonel and the Germans gone, Auriac had to be put in order again. The village school that had served as an army barrack had to be thoroughly rehabilitated and this had to be done with some urgency, since it had to be ready for the fall of 1944 when the new school year was scheduled to begin. At the same time, the second-floor space we had been using for classrooms had to be cleaned and prepared for rental, in the hopes that someone would show interest. In general, the village seemed ready to sink back into its normal state of somnolence.

I hadn't liked the improvised classrooms in the little street that flanked the château any better than the official schoolhouse, but it didn't really matter. I was in my last year of primary school, and in July I would receive my *Certificat d'Etudes*. Tante Lily was busy making arrangements for me to start the lycée or collége (secondary school), either in Toulouse or, more conveniently, in Revel. I would soon be off to another new adventure!

CHAPTER 15

Revel

In the fall of 1944, after I received my *Certificat d'Etudes* attesting to the fact that I had successfully passed all the primary school tests, Tante Lily decided, quite wisely I thought, that I would be safer if I started secondary school as a boarder instead of a day student. As a day student, I would have needed a place to live, since the nearest secondary school was too far from Auriac for a daily commute. Additionally, we could never forget that there were always hazards involved on the roads in the region. Although the Germans had left Auriac, they could still be found on the roads and in the public transportation systems. And so, we concluded that I would be better off and out of harm's way if I lived at a school, which was separated from Auriac by only a short car ride of ten to 15 kilometers.

The secondary school in Revel met all our needs. The city was easily accessible to and from Auriac, and the rigidly enforced uniform French national curricula and teaching standards that prevailed in the country, even under the Vichy governance, removed any anxieties that might exist about differences in quality of education in the other schools within the broader Toulouse region. In fact, Tante Lily believed that Revel would offer better teachers, smaller classrooms and better facilities than most other schools, a belief shared by most of her friends and neighbors in the region who had sent their children there.

I had never been in Revel and I had heard of the school only in the vaguest terms. The idea, however, appealed to me. I really would not miss the château that much; Revel was so close and easily reachable. Moreover, it was an opportunity for me to experience a new environment where I would be in the company of others who, like me, would be separated, cast out of the family nest, albeit benignly, by parents or guardians, and who were looking forward to a new freedom with mixed emotions. In this respect at least, I found myself in the same boat as my fellow boarders. It was a warm feeling compared to the relative isolation within which I had lived for most of my life.

The French secondary schools typically comprise two kinds of institutions, called either lycées or collèges. The distinction lies in the fact that a lycée covered the entire seven year course of secondary study, typically catering to students between the ages of 11 and 18, while a collège typically covered the first four years of the secondary education and requiring a transfer to a lycèe at the end of that period. While this distinction may be moot, what is important is that it is in these lycées and collèges that the foundation of the French education system is laid.

Secondary schools could be public or private and they could choose to focus on technology, liberal arts or philosophy. Further, they specialized in a particular vocational field, and some chose to associate with larger institutions so students would then be positioned to pursue higher levels of education towards a specific professional career.

The boarding school in Revel was a private institution named *Ecole de Garçons* (Boys School), and it was a collège, not a lycée. The course of study was general education, and it was not associated with any other institutions. The student body was small, consisting of about 130 students, with two-thirds of these being boarders. There was nothing unusual about it; the National Education Ministry dictated its curriculum and I would have to transfer to a larger institution after the first three or four years there.

After completing Primary School in Auriac, I would have normally started my secondary school education in the *sixième* (sixth grade), the beginning level in the secondary school system. But because of the disruption caused by the German occupation of Auriac and the pressure from Vichy to show the world that they had gotten all students to complete the requirement for the *Certificat d'Etudes* on time (as if these were normal times!), the school master overshot the mark and had actually covered much of what was normally taught in the sixth grade during the last year of primary School. To my joy, this led to the decision to allow me to skip the *sixième* entirely and begin my secondary education in the *cinquième* (fifth grade).

One of the many differences between the French and American school systems was that scholastic levels in France were numbered in reverse, descending order as one climbed the academic ladder. Thus, when *la premiere* (the first grade) was reached, the end of that school year marked the end of one's secondary education. This achievement is crowned by a horrendous examination—the dreaded *Baccho* (Baccalaureate exam), colloquially more often referred to as *Le Bac*.

The *Baccho* was then followed by a second exam, *Le Deuxieme Baccho* (the Second Baccalaureate). This was where the student chose between curricula focused on either philosophy or mathematics, in preparation for an advanced level of education at a university, such as *la Sorbonne*. Passing *Le Bac* was not something that anyone took for granted. In fact, many failed. If they did, they were required to try again; if they continued to fail or gave up completely, they would be forced to alter their career paths from a professional one to that of a common tradesman. In terms of academic standing, the *Baccho* was equivalent to the SAT or college board exams administered at the end of the American high school course of study. But this was deceptive. In many respects, the *Baccho* was equivalent to the education level of a sophomore in an American university in terms of the analytical efforts required to cope with the curriculum.

Physically, the school in Revel had an almost military quality. There were several two- and three-story blocks of buildings grouped around an open quadrangle, interlinked by a tall 18-foot stone and concrete wall. The effect from the street, except for an elaborate front gate, was a monolithic façade of blank walls interrupted only by rows of grilled windows. Each of the building blocks had its own primary function on the campus; one for classrooms, one for the dormitory and two organized to accommodate everything else, such as the refectory, study hall, administrative offices, infirmary, locker room and storage space. Visually, the buildings resembled those of comparable institutions and were not architecturally remarkable.

The quadrangle surface was a combination of pea gravel and unpaved soil, ideal for soccer practice, marble matches and the inevitable fights boys are prone to get into. I enjoyed the games we played in the quadrangle. I was pretty good at marbles and, over time, I collected an impressive treasure trove of agates, thus provoking a dangerous level of jealousy among my friends. But sports—organized or otherwise—were clearly subordinated to serious academic studies. I was shocked to learn years later that, in American schools, participation in sports was actually required as a class. While I might have preferred this, it was not to be — French grammar, mathematics and geography would be where my priorities would be focused. As a matter of fact, the differences went beyond sports. Underlying the French pedagogic culture was the conviction that to spare the rod would spoil the child. Discipline and inflexibility were very much at the root of that culture. In contrast, I found American schools endowed with a more pragmatic bend of mind, where results from teaching matter more than academic and theoretic principles.

The same tendencies showed up in the way knowledge was drilled into us. French as a language was taught with a ferocious zeal and focused on grammar. This involved, among other joys, figuring out the ending of verbs and other words, depending on a plethora of conjugational and situational circumstances. Grammar was always looked upon with particular horror. The French language is a quagmire of rules. But there are more exceptions than there are rules, and every rule impacts yet other rules and each of those carries its own exceptions. To cope with this challenge, we had to learn grammar by taking dictation and then spend hours analyzing the text, justifying sentence structures and spelling everything by the rules. American students did not have to undergo such rigors. There are a few rules, of course, but compared to French grammar, they seem like child's play. France frequently staged formal grammar contests that were avidly followed like a national sport, so complex is the French system of grammar. Unlike the American spelling bee, these contests were infinitely more challenging in that the contestants had to be grammarians as well as spellers and had to complete a document dictated to them by the event's judge. In contrast, my exposure to high school English grammar in the American schools was basically limited to spelling bees. Even as an immigrant who was desperately trying to learn English, I was able to be brilliant without too much effort.

Things did not get any easier in the study of French literature. We had to memorize classic plays and other works that have defined French culture from the dawn of its history. We covered the great playwright Corneille, who wrote such plays as *Le Cid* and *Horace,* both written in rhymes that endowed these works with an almost musical quality and sometimes even inspired a syncopated delivery. We ventured into comedy with Moliere and such plays as *Le Misanthrope* and *Le Malade Malgrè Lui* (*The Malingerer*). I even had to memorize some Shakespeare without a really clear idea of the text's meaning, as that was years before I immigrated to America where I acquired a more intimate familiarity with the English language.

Our study of literature was further enriched with works from political intellectuals and critics, including Voltaire's *Candide*; Lamartine, who participated in the founding of France's Second Republic and whose romantic poetry combined political realities with idealism; and Madame de Stael, who was recognized through her letters, critiques and the discussion salons she hosted and which had such profound influence on the political climate during the Napoleonic era. And, of course, who can forget such giants of literature as Victor Hugo with his classic novels and epic poems like *Les Châtiments* (*The Punishments*), which provided inspiring critiques of the political figures of those times. Our studies of literature also ventured into the early Middle Ages, with the poetry of François Villon. It sent shivers down my spine when I read his famous epitaph, *La Ballade des Pendus* ("The Ballad of the Hanged"), which so vividly describes the brutal nature and spirit of that age.

We not only had to do a painful amount of memorization of the classics, we were also steeped in the historic context of many works. We read the flamboyant orations of Mirabeau, Danton and so many others inspired by the French Revolution. All one has to do is note the names of streets in Paris to understand how important these writers were to the French. Nor can anyone who grew up in France forget *La Chanson de Roland* (*The Song of Roland*), a legend dating from the dawn of France's history. It gloriously depicts the hero, Roland, desperately sounding his martial horn in a narrow Pyrenean pass at Ronceveaux. He blew so long and so hard that his lungs burst. But his efforts paid off, and he succeeded in alerting the French Emperor Charlemagne and his army that the Moorish invasion through the historic pass in the Basque region of the Pyrenees was under way. (Just a few years ago, some 60 years after I had read this snippet of French history and literature, Joyce and I found ourselves in Basque country. I could not resist the temptation of seeing the actual place where Roland performed his deed of valor. So we braved the French police, the Basque Separatists and the armed checkpoints and proceeded up into the valley that would lead us to Ronceveaux. It was nothing like what we had imagined; the place was deserted and it wasn't even French. It was Spanish. Instead of the rocky escarpments that usually depict Roland's last stand, there was a Spanish chapel, which had nothing to do with our quest into French history ... we were, after all, in Spain.)

My imagination really took flight, however, when I transitioned from history to French fiction. The giants who had kept me rapt during the dark days of the wars included Alexander Dumas and his *Count of Monte Cristo* and *The Three Musketeers*. But there was also science fiction. I recall spending many hours reading such tomes as Jules Verne's *20,000 Leagues Under the Sea* featuring the unforgettable Captain Nemo. These books were nothing short of addictive, and they were like candy to me. In contrast, so many of the American works of fiction, like those authored by Ernest Hemingway and J.D. Salinger, were required reading in American schools, subject to book reports and treated as an academic subject.

In the French school system, there was no such thing as an elective course. In America, subjects like home economics, music appreciation, physical education and other quasi-scholastic activities were available as a supplement to the required curriculum. American schools also devoted a lot of time to current events, business practices and even political issues. Civics was also considered an important part of the high school curriculum. I was particularly intrigued to find debating as an elective course. The idea of an activity involving the free and uninhibited give-and-take of arguments in an open forum was anathema to what the French or European political climate of the times could tolerate. Indeed, the last thing the Vichy government wanted was a frank discussion of current issues and events. Along the same lines, business philosophies such as *Laissez-Faire* or the economic theories promulgated by John Maynard Keynes and Malthus were strange and new to me when I came to America, since these concepts had remained totally unmentioned throughout my schooling in France. On the other hand, I was shocked at the extent to which American education was deficient in geography and world history. Even after all these years, I still use this superior knowledge, drilled into me in France at an early age, to my advantage during many social occasions. I am sure some people may even consider me pedantic!

Both in France and America, students were called upon to do some writing. In France, this usually meant long dissertations on obtuse subjects. In contrast, in the American system, a short essay or a simple book report would usually suffice. There seemed to be little emphasis in American high schools on grammatical analysis, sentence structure, classic literature or the study of the masters—except, perhaps, for Chaucer. With respect to that eminent poet, I had to wait until my junior year of college, at CCNY, my alma mater in America, where Professor Ousley, a scholar of medieval literature, was able to demystify the *Canterbury Tales* for me. In class, he always flourished his talents by reading, declaiming and interpreting the mellifluous blend of old French and old English languages that were spoken during the 13th and 14th centuries. Nobody could understand a word of what he was reading, but this was by far the most pleasant and easiest course of my American college education!

The difference between the French and the American systems was also very pronounced in mathematics. One of the better examples of this gulf was algebra. As an American student, all I needed to do was to apply a formula to solve quadratic equations. That's a lot easier than mastering the art of factoring as I had to do in France. Under the French system, formulas were never used; therefore the solution to quadratic equations had to be derived the long way. Similarly, in geometry, American schools provided formulas to prove theorems and solve problems. In France, the proof had to be painstakingly evolved, axiom by axiom, and then explained in writing in terms of a chain of logically interrelated propositions, beginning with the givens as stated in the problem, and ending with the ubiquitous "QED." The problems were presented to us in the form of a description dictated from the teacher's rostrum; we had to then derive graphic representations and proceed with the lengthy development and presentation of the "proof." The result was an inordinate amount of time and quandary, with hours upon hours of head scratching, pencil nibbling and all sorts of other anxiety-relieving habits employed while struggling to solve mathematical dilemmas. An American student would have been able to complete such an assignment in minutes by merely applying formulas, without having to look for any deeper meanings in the exercise.

In France, the deeds of the heroes and villains of French history dominated the study of what was considered "social science," and it was they who defined history. In contrast, American history tends to be shaped more by events, and it is more often than not those events that give rise to the historical personalities. I realize this distinction is somewhat moot. But one thing is clear—American history is driven more by current events, while French history can't get out of its past.

But nowhere were the differences more acute than in the area of student discipline. The workload was always heavy, and supervision was extremely strict. The sunup-to-lights-out routine was rigid, almost military in character. What the French teachers, proctors and school staff were allowed to do under the guise of discipline would have been incomprehensibly foreign to anyone involved in the education system in the United States. There was no taboo on corporal punishment and the study routines were draconian in terms of the amount of time during which we were effectively chained to our study hall desks. The degree of tenacity required for students to keep up was nothing less than an epic test of survival.

Which of the two systems is better? It's a question that remains debatable and totally subjective. In my view, I have always found the American system much more user-friendly; it was clearly less challenging and, in my opinion, far more in touch with the real world. On the other hand, I was set for life under the French system, which gave me a much deeper understanding of the fundamentals of the basic disciplines. That came in handy when I forgot a formula or encountered a problem where the solution had not yet been recycled into a formula. In the final analysis, I was really well served by both systems; in retrospect, I must admit that the pain was worth it.

The daily routine called for classes to start shortly after breakfast and last until noon. By 1:30, the midday meal was over and classes resumed until 4:00. We then had one and a half hours of free time and play, during which we could resume our marble tournaments and engage in whatever hobbies or activities we enjoyed. This was also the time when we were allowed to visit our food lockers where we kept whatever we brought on the school premises from home to supplement the school's limited diet. For me, this included the ubiquitous *foie gras*, salted ham and *saucissons* I brought from the château to share with my school friends. This always made me feel a little like Ragueneau, the purveyor of prepared meats in Edmond Rostand's *Cyrano de Bergerac*, who showed up on the battlefield to feed the heroic musketeers fighting for Gascony.

Before dinner, which was served a little after sunset, there was always a line in the quadrangle for attendance check and cleanliness inspection. Everybody was then admitted to assigned seats on wood benches in the large dining hall. All meals, including dinner, were reserved for boarders only, and served at tables by a small army of young servers recruited from the local population. The school had gone to great effort to distance itself from an institutional self-service cafeteria. This just would not have the requisite cachet; we were, after all, a private school ... even if the students were a bunch of spoiled brats! After dinner, we would amble into the large common study hall and stay out of trouble by doing homework until late at night. After returning to the dormitory in the evening, we were given about an hour of private time until lights out, which usually took place around 10:00.

To maintain this routine, boarding schools had created a supervisory cadre that relied on proctors for control and discipline. Proctors were a strange breed of men. Most were university students in their twenties who seemed to have ambitions limited to spending their lives as primary or secondary school teachers. Others were retired teachers who had found that the final result of their life's work was somewhat hollow. These accidental educators were charged with the unenviable task of maintaining discipline and close surveillance over us. They were easy butts of every trick and prank that we could dredge up, and we were nothing more to them than a bunch of privileged brats. They were called *pions*, which means pawns — the smallest piece in a game of chess. The *pions* had considerable power over us, and their frustration with their careers somehow translated into sadistic tendencies that showed in their enforcement of discipline and retaliation to our silly pranks. Much of our misbehavior occurred during the study period at the end of each day and the free-play session. A favorite trick was to align the legs of the proctor's desk in the study hall close to the edge of the dais so that, when he slammed the palm of his hand on the desk for order in the room, the entire desk, including papers, books, ink container and other paraphernalia, would fall over with a great crashing noise, all to the discomfiture of the proctor and to our unrestrained merriment.

Since fountain pens had not yet made their appearance, and would certainly not come within reach of students if they did, our writing was done with pen and ink. The ink was always found in a small ceramic well on our desks. This provided the opportunity for another kind of prank. We thought it great fun to empty our inkwells into the proctor's pockets as he walked between the aisles of the study hall. When he reached into his pocket, he would withdraw a horribly ink-stained hand, with the ink spreading along his pants leg, triggering uncontrollable, loud laughter by all in the study hall. (Now, so many years later, I feel regret about this as I recall that one poor man had a speech defect caused by mustard gas during his World War I service to France.)

In the dormitory, there were endless fights involving pillows and down comforters. On one occasion, such a fight broke out and the pillows and comforters burst. There were feathers all over, leaving every nook and cranny of the dorm, a long 150-foot gallery-like space lined with two rows of single wrought-iron beds, in a swirl of dust and assorted debris that made it look like it had been hit by a tornado. Mass punishment was promptly meted out but, since we felt deep down that we deserved it, we complied with the order to clean the place up and remain locked in detention interminably, with a minimum of grumbling.

Much of our impish behavior took place when the proctor left the room or was otherwise out of the line of sight. One such time occurred when we were assembled near our beds in the dormitory. The proctor exercised his territorial imperative by sleeping in the center of the gallery and separating himself from the students by creating a curtain of linen draped over a canopy frame around the bed, thus fabricating what he thought was a defense perimeter that provided an illusion of privacy. One night, we realized that this arrangement was an irresistible opportunity for mischief. While the proctor was fast asleep, we tied the sheets together, turning his enclosure into a shroud that became a virtual prison. He was doomed to discover this only after he woke up. Needless to say, his panic and the subsequent fury of his efforts to escape and unravel the knotted and twisted sheets were hilarious, and a fascinating spectacle that I will never forget.

"Ratting" was a common practice and subject only to the students' internal code of honor. It was not done, however, without the risk of retribution. The worst boarder-imposed punishment involved placing the "rat" in a *boite au caffards* (literally, a cockroach box). The *boite* was a manhole — part of the sewer system — located in the middle of the school's quadrangle. The latter, of course, served not only as the recreation and assembly yard, but also as the school's principal point of orientation. It was the crossroad to all destinations within the ivy-covered walls. The typical duration before rescue was about two days, as anything longer would have become a matter for the police to handle. Fellow boarders were taught from the outset of their life at the school to spit and discard all

Chapter 15

things unwanted and disgusting into the *boite*. This was done as a matter of habit, whether someone was in it or not. The message was clear — if you're going to be a rat, you might as well live like one.

The proctors had other means of dealing with insubordinate wards. The study hall was usually the principal arena. This was where some of us were doomed to write, for hours on end, such profound thoughts as, "I will not blah, blah, blah in class." This was also where various forms of corporal punishments were meted out, such as paddling or hitting finger tips with a heavy metal ruler — not quite as brutal as caning in Singapore, but pretty painful just the same. What made it more excruciating was that the punishment usually took place publicly, in full view of the students in the study hall. It was humiliating! The irony was that one would expect that rebellious behavior would lionize you in the eyes of your fellow students, yet when you are publicly punished for such actions, you emerged as nothing but a weakling and, therefore, a loser.

A different kind of punishment in this struggle between teachers and students was the dreaded report card. It was sent directly to the parent or guardian and contained both grades and unvarnished comments, delving into those things that students were least thrilled to have revealed about their performance and behavior. There was nothing to fear, of course, if you were a good boy, since this fact would be acknowledged in the report card as well. But, as with any Catch-22 situation, if indeed you were really a good boy, you would sooner or later acquire a "goody two-shoes" reputation with peers, and this might land you in the *boite au caffards*, since it was completely predictable that all good boys turn into rats.

The ultimate punishment, reserved for only the most egregious of misdeeds, was dismissal. The consequences of such action for the student, particularly for a boarder, were horrific. Acceptance in another private school would be difficult, and public school generally stopped at the elementary level. Moreover, French schools and parents communicated directly with each other, without the help of any intermediary such as a PTA. This empowered the individual teachers to deal in their own subjective way with all academic and disciplinary matters, effectively without recourse, as long as such actions were generally consistent with the system's overall policies. As such, teachers and even minor school functionaries commanded a level of authority that allowed no deflection from the focus of their primary mission: to drill knowledge and discipline into our heads.

For me, school in Revel was a mixed bag. As I have mentioned earlier, I liked being with my fellow boarders, we shared a lot of common values and there was a very comforting element of mutual trust in the relationships. The château was always within reach and the small allowance given to me by Tante Lily was sufficient for the bus ride between Revel and Auriac. The challenge was to get permission to leave the hallowed premises of the school. Sundays tended to be somewhat lonely in Revel and at the school. This was what led me to leave Revel for Auriac every two weeks, as soon as I was allowed to leave on Saturday afternoon. It should be noted that one of my essential missions during my Auriac visits was to replenish the stock of *foie gras* and other preserved delicacies that quickly ran low at the *Ecole de Garçons*. This was important, as I used them for bribes to get anything I needed within the school. This tactic was particularly effective because the cuisine at the school, though quite healthy, left a lot to be desired, and had none of the tantalizing tastes generated by Albertine's kitchen. But I really liked the school in Revel on many levels, and I performed fairly well there. What I wasn't so crazy about was the strict routine imposed upon all of us by the French educational establishment and the school regulations. But then again, I had always rebelled against authority.

Beyond the safety of the school walls, the war was winding down but still not over. The resistance had ratcheted up their activities. These now included generating confusion and disarray among the occupiers and a proliferation of direct violent acts of sabotage. In some instances, frontal armed attacks on German strategic targets were executed, and tensions ran high over the anticipation of bloody retaliation by the Germans. The French nation was imbued with a thirst for freedom and revenge. But I could only relish the moment vicariously because, until the liberation of France was complete, it was still deemed unsafe to return to the château for more than a brief visit. One still never knew who was a collaborator and what whispered information was being spread in the community.

In spite of this, life at the château was joyous that Christmas. The sense of anticipation that better times were just around the corner was everywhere. Tante Lily and Oncle Nino were like one-armed paperhangers, each continuing to do their part in the resistance. Tante Lily was busy

Chapter 15

with the safekeeping of all her wards, assuring that the Germans would not be able to indulge in the kinds of dastardly acts of revenge they were reputed to have done so often. She also continued with the management of the tenant farms. This in itself was a full-time job. Oncle Nino was absorbed in a flurry of FFI activities, mostly involving the resolution of policies relating to the postwar governance of a freed France. Among the most difficult of these issues was the struggle for dominance being played out throughout France between the French Communist party and the followers of *Le Grand Charles* (General Charles de Gaulle).

In preparation for the final Allied victory, there were many other concerns, such as the emotionally charged issue of what the fate of the reviled collaborators, the *Miliciens* and the German POWs would be. At the same time, there was the wrangling that prevailed relative to the development of policies for dealing with the postwar economy, the shortages and the distribution of scarce resources. Nino was working at the vortex of these efforts and was completely *au courant* (in the loop) on these matters.

As for me, I thoroughly enjoyed the holidays and looked forward to returning to the *Ecole de Garçons* for the second half of the year. I had done well thus far, and I did not see any clouds on the horizon. I had every expectation that life with my new family would continue without interruption.

Chapter 16

Reveling in Revel and the First Taste of PEACE

When I returned to Revel, in January 1945, the end of the war was clearly in sight. That winter, a sudden German counteroffensive threw back the Allied forces in the Ardennes, creating panic as panzers raced to cross the Meuse in a last ditch effort to save the Reich. For a few short weeks, history seemed to be repeating itself. But courageous units fought back and stopped the panzers one last time. General Patton, nicknamed "Old Blood and Guts," was a devotee of Guderian's rapid advance tactics. He had relieved the tenacious airborne troops at Bastogne by Christmas, and the Reich's quixotic last gasp — the Battle of the Bulge — failed. The way to Berlin was open and victory, at long last, seemed inevitable. Yet, the final defeat of Germany had acquired the characteristics of Zeno's paradox. While the distance between the Allies' invasion forces and Berlin kept getting shorter and shorter, being cut by half with every passing day, it seemed that the Allies would never get there.

In March 1945, after the coldest winter in 50 years, we learned that Patton's armored columns had crossed the Rhine and were plunging into the Nazi heartland. The liberators rolled across Europe in the wake of their victory at the Battle of the Bulge. They raced the Soviets, trying to be the first to reach and control Berlin. Their speed was such that they had to post thousands of maps throughout the villages and the countryside so that the convoys could get their bearings, lest their progress toward Berlin be impeded by having to ask for directions. Ultimately, the Americans and British reached Berlin at approximately the same time as the Soviets, thus the creation of East and West Berlin after the war.

But, at least, this was the end. On April 25, 1945, the Soviet forces linked up with the American forces in Torgau, on the Elbe River within

Chapter 16

the Berlin capital region. As Soviet forces neared his command bunker in central Berlin, Adolf Hitler committed suicide. Berlin surrendered to Soviet forces on May 2, followed shortly thereafter by the German armed forces in the West and those in the East. Victory Europe Day (V-E Day) was declared on May 8, 1945.

In the early afternoon, victory bells started to ring in Revel, joined by bells in every belfry throughout the land. It was, for most of us, a day of great jubilation and celebration. For others, however, like the collaborators and those with roles in the Vichy government, it was a day of fear and trepidation. The bells were proclaiming the long awaited victory, and I was stuck with my fellow boarders behind the tall walls that kept us inside the school. To say that we were bursting to get out and join the celebration does not begin to express our frustration.

That's how it came to be that, after dark on this happy day, a group of us scaled the school walls and landed in the streets to take part in the widespread celebration of the German defeat. The crowd in the streets had become an uncontrollable mob that was in danger of starting to riot. Later that night, these activities morphed into some pretty wild reveling, as the crowd lost all inhibitions and allowed their spirits to soar without any restraint. THE WAR WAS OVER!!! Drunk with happiness ... as well as other things ... one of my fellow boarders climbed the clock tower that topped the cupola above the Revel market place. From that vantage point, he waived the *Tricolore* (French flag) wildly. On his way down, in a state of complete inebriation, he slid down to the parapet of the covered market structure and tried to find a foothold midway down the cupola. There, struggling in the wind with the wildly flapping flag above him, he became entangled in the lines attached to the flag. What happened next was horrible. In front of the cheering crowd, he slipped on the slope of the cupola and, tragically, hung himself. The crowd's enthusiasm for the performance quickly turned to a shocked hush. Fortunately for our small contingent of escapees, we missed the event. Totally oblivious to this tragedy, we had rushed, full of malicious intentions, to the home of one of the proctors who had been our arch nemesis. This was a golden opportunity for revenge! We were in a fever to exorcise the demons of the war. We accomplished this by rampaging through the streets of Revel, throwing rocks at the proctor's house and breaking many of his windows. I really do not have a violent nature, but in the heat of the moment, having just tasted freedom from repression, we found it easy to surrender to the natural instincts that had welled up within us. We cast rational behavior aside and gave vent to our irresistible natural cravings to act out our anger and desire for revenge that we had kept bottled up for far too long. The poor proctor and his house just happened to be in the wrong place at the wrong time.

The next day, the proctor called me over as I was milling about in the quadrangle. He enlightened me to the fact that I was in a "serious situation." I, and I alone, had been seen and recognized the prior night. My options were extremely limited. I could rat on the others involved in the raid on his house and risk imprisonment in the Cockroach Box. Alternatively, I could clam up and face dismissal from school, never complete my education and face life-changing consequences too dire to think about, including my future with the de Bonnefoy family. What actually happened was kismet at work once again. In honor of V-E Day, the proctor dropped the matter. He decided that a formal admission of guilt, an apology and some yard work around his house would suffice. The end of the war was simply too momentous an event to be overtaken by mundane concerns over petty incidents.

As a fortuitous accident of synchronicity, the end of the war occurred at about the same time as the scholastic year was ending. I was anticipating another glorious summer of games and romping with friends in and around the village. For the first time, I would be able to move around without fear and anxieties. Thanks to Tante Lily, my summer vacation would turn out to be even better than I had hoped. Through her many wartime contacts, she had gotten me into a summer camp in Western Germany near the ancient Roman city of Trier. This was a rare privilege. The French government sponsored the camp for the benefit of children orphaned by the war, children of war heroes and other war victims. I spent three magic weeks at that camp enjoying long treks through the beautiful *Schwartzwaldt* (Black Forest), sometimes sleeping in tents, other times in imposing mansions and estates that graced that beautiful and picturesque region of Western Germany. It was a wonderful feeling to switch roles and act as the occupier for a change. Everyone treated us like guests of honor. We held an exalted position that fell just short of being considered martyrs.

Trier had suffered from Allied bombings and this was reflected in the conditions of its famous Roman ruins. Even though the wide avenues were

Chapter 16

cleared of the rubble that evidenced the recent fighting and destruction, the profusion of makeshift battlefield signs, the mix of military and civilian traffic and the many varieties of uniforms that swarmed in the streets, left no doubt that fierce armed conflict had occurred within months of our arrival in the city. I was particularly impressed by the massive stretch of *autobahn* (expressway) that, although now deserted and silent, still managed to communicate the awesome power the defeated Third Reich must have wielded.

After my bucolic interlude in the Black Forest, I had a chance to get to know Tante Lily's daughter, Marthou, a lot better. She was home from boarding school for the summer as well, and she had just passed her *Deuxieme Baccho* in her chosen specialty of philosophy. She was ready for a summer of fun, followed by either university or a career and a chance to bask in the glow of the war's end and the activities of her extraordinarily vital, popular and busy parents. Marriage was not even a blip on her radar screen, and neither were other responsibilities and entanglements. We became pals. I was a participant and co-conspirator in her romantic intrigues and expeditions as well as a convenient alibi when one was needed. We spent a lot of time at the St. Fereol reservoir near St. Girons, where I was able to demonstrate my newly acquired swimming talents and where Marthou could display all kinds of other talents. She was very beautiful, feminine, vivacious and flirtatious. In fact, she was a constant object of attention and, dare I say it, of desire from the male contingents in her age group. I played chaperone in situations where advances were rebuffed, and I knew to make myself scarce when they were encouraged. In such cases, I became her confidante. Ownership of a car was a major factor in determining the potential of prospective dalliances. A car meant the ability to participate in all of the regional events and visit nearby cities and places like St. Fereol that were out of easy bicycle reach.

Postwar shortages were worse than ever. To offset these hardships, we were anxious to test our newly acquired freedom of movement by traveling to the small principality of Andorra, in the middle of the Pyrenees. Its borders were open to both France and Spain and, with its economy based almost entirely on a prolific smuggling trade, everything was available for a price. The idea of the visit was Marthou's, but it sounded so enticing that Tante Lily wanted to come, too. I was, of course, indispensable, as was Marthou's boyfriend-du-jour, as he provided the transportation. Said car happened to be a Citroën *Traction Avant*. That particular car model, besides having faithfully served the French Resistance, was particularly well endowed for the mountains. It had an extremely powerful engine and exceptional road-holding capabilities. This was important because getting to Andorra involved almost exclusively mountain driving and some challenging grades.

Andorra is a tiny principality, sandwiched high in the Eastern Pyrenees, between the Languedoc region of France and the Catalan region of Spain. A country of less than 200 square miles, it was ruled by two co-princes — the president of France and the Spanish archbishop of *La Seu d'Urgell*. Charlemagne had given the country its independence and autonomy in the year 784, and Napoleon, with amused condescension, had let it stay as such. However, like Shangri-La, Andorra was, and still is, hard to reach. It involved negotiating a freezing and forbidding high pass, well above the tree line. The road required driving, generally without retaining walls, around hairpin turns that wound endlessly around the mountain. The challenge of the drive was aggravated by the fact that the turns had to be managed mostly by feel, since much of the drive was in the middle of the clouds, and visibility was zero. And then, the road itself was awful; badly paved, ill maintained, desolate, with virtually no markings. The view was a moonscape without respite, and just as comforting. By the time we made it to the top of the pass, we were anxious to reach any kind of sanctuary that would provide relief from the harsh mountainous environment. Then suddenly, just like Shangri-La, once on the other side of the pass, we descended from the deserted high point of the mountain into a sun-bathed magic valley that was warm, cozy, colorful and welcoming. We had arrived! We were in the beautiful valley that nestled Andorra-la-Vella, the principality's capital city. Once there, we wallowed in the warmth of the people and the environment, which made the hardships of the journey all worthwhile. A huge marketplace consumed the village-like city. Indeed, everything was available. No ersatz here! We found real coffee, not the substitute muddy brew, or *Pousse-café* that passed for coffee in France. Real sugar was available, not saccharine. Cigarettes with real tobacco, not sundried corn beards, as well as honest-to-goodness chocolates were plentiful. For me, however, it was the real pastries, with their delicious butter cream fillings, and ice cream that sent me into raptures. I don't think I have ever found anything that matched the pleasure of experiencing those great tastes after such a long period of deprivation.

Chapter 16

We had wonderful meals and, after eating, we went shopping for all kinds of goods that were impossible to find in France or were so drastically rationed that, for all practical purposes, they had to be considered unavailable. Marthou was in a buying frenzy and she bought silks and other cloths. Because liquor and silks would be prohibitively taxed on our return to France, she wrapped the material around herself in order to elude the duty on these goods. Tante Lily was more forthcoming, and simply paid the duty at the border on her purchases — bottles of anisette, a liqueur we could not find in France. Well, Marthou got caught at the border, and she had to unwrap all the wonderful material she had so painstakingly selected. She was escorted into a little private room and had to submit to a full body search. It was hugely humiliating and, worse than that, she had to surrender her purchases. She was mortified, inconsolable, in tears and furious with everyone and everything, but mostly with herself. We found out later that smuggling in and out of Andorra was the special province of a semi-clandestine organization that enjoyed an exclusive arrangement with the customs officials of France and Spain and a guild of professional smugglers in the region. No one else was privy to this long-standing relationship, so that ordinary civilians like Marthou never stood a chance of success in this nefarious enterprise.

While I was having the time of my life, the nation was still smarting from the pain and humiliation of the German occupation. Hatred, deep-seated white rage and wide-ranging expectations for revenge were in the air, and were prevalent throughout France. In stark contrast to the kindness which greeted me wherever I went, I witnessed with morbid fascination the reprisals meted out to collaborators and others with dubious wartime records. France unleashed its thirst for revenge, expressing its anger over seven years of brutal repression. It was a period characterized by hundreds of trials held throughout the nation, where acts of treachery and incidents of disloyalty were exposed and punishment meted out. Women faced the humiliation of having their heads shaved in public, in a circus-like atmosphere. The humiliation worsened later, as they had to wear makeshift scarves over their shorn heads like a badge of infamy. The fate of male collaborators varied with the nature and extent of their crimes and treasonous activities. Many had merely helped the Germans steal or deface French property; others were guilty of managing the ill-gotten gains from embezzlement schemes; still others committed more serious crimes like spying

Marthou de Bonnefoy and the Countess Alix de Bonnefoy (Tante Lily) (circa 1945).

Chapter 16

and denunciations. Punishments were brutal, obeying not the Geneva Convention but a code embraced by an ethic of retaliation. Executions were rare, but not unheard of. Incarceration and hate-driven beatings were common. Male or female, a new class of criminal emerged — the collaborator. Once labeled as one, the individual and his or her friends were instantly deemed untrustworthy. Collaborators were treated like society's pariahs. Like lepers, contact with them was carefully avoided. For those who had acted honorably, however, it was a period of vindication, restitution and entitlement.

V-E and V-J (Victory Japan) Days had occurred within a few months of one another and, by August of 1945, major readjustments were occurring in everybody's lives. Beyond seeking out and punishing collaborators, the last half of 1945 would see France preoccupied with overcoming the shortages which were actually far more severe after the war than during the occupation, and locating lost family members and friends. Everyone began to take stock of what they had — and what they had lost; they pondered who they were and what they had become. Without a doubt, everybody was keenly aware of the need to face the daunting task of fitting into a new world, one that was suddenly at peace.

For the de Bonnefoy family, this would mean a gradual but radical shift from an essentially rural life to an urban one. For me, the end of the war meant taking stock of the loss of everything I had possessed, not the least of which was my family. I had no information about the fate of my parents. The only information that Tante Lily was able to secure was that they had been interned in Drancy, a transit camp not far from Paris, from which they would most likely have been transferred to a concentration camp.

At the same time, I was bracing myself for my return to Revel to begin *La Quatrième* (fourth grade). And once again, I would be faced with a stark reminder that my fate was completely out of my control.

Chapter 17

The Courts Intervene

It was the fall of 1945, and I was back in Revel for *La Quatrième*. Having safely survived the difficult war years in the secure bosom of the de Bonnefoy family, I assumed that my destiny would be to live the rest of my life with them. It never occurred to me that the stability in my life would once again be jeopardized. Tante Lily and her family had become my family, my only family, in every conceivable sense. I had grown to love them, and wherever they lived was my home. Even as depleted as it was by the German occupation, Auriac was still viable enough to provide the basic needs of the family, and was still our home.

Tante Lily had spoken to me about adoption many times, and we assumed it would be a simple process. But the end of the war had brought out far too many people who were interested in what was to become of orphans like me. True to her word, Tante Lily began the process of formalizing my relationship with her family. The need for secrecy regarding my background was no longer necessary and, according to the best available information, my parents had perished in the camps, so we assumed that nothing would stand in the way of proceeding with my formal adoption. This was, after all, a private matter, purely between the de Bonnefoys and me. As it turned out, quite the opposite occurred.

I was now officially branded as a "Jewish War Orphan." This endowed the agencies formed to deal with the victims of the war with a stake in determining my future, and they had a very different concept of what my fate should be. Laudably, they were committed to meeting their mandate to reunite families scattered by the war. This was certainly a good thing for many war orphans ... but not for me! I was no longer an orphan — I had a new family and it was a close and happy relationship. I considered

Chapter 17

these social agencies to be interlopers in my private life. They, on the other hand, believed that it was their God-given mandate to reunite Jewish war orphans with their families or, failing that, at least with their religion and culture.

Once they established that my parents had been Jewish and the de Bonnefoy family was Catholic, they decreed that this was an untenable situation and that the plans for my future with the family would seriously interfere with their mission. As a consequence, the adoption process came to a screeching halt. To resolve the dispute, the parties at interest (excluding me, of course) agreed to convene a *Conseil de Famille* (Guardianship Conclave), to be held in front of a justice of the peace. The meeting was called for October 18, 1945, and would decide my fate. The *conseil* was a quasi-judicial body in which Tante Lily had little influence, and where I had no say at all.

While nobody was particularly happy about the outcome of the meeting, the results were actually not all bad. Adoption was no longer on the table; the matter was far too sensitive. Nevertheless, I would officially remain a ward of the de Bonnefoy family; they would continue the fight and I would be allowed to complete the *Quatrième* in Revel ... so far, so good. I could continue to live with my saviors, my new family, and that left some hope for adoption when everybody came to their senses. More immediately, I would be able to spend the upcoming holidays with the de Bonnefoys.

As always, my Christmas holiday with the de Bonnefoys was memorable. Tante Lily surprised us with a ski trip to Font-Romeu, a resort in the Pyrenees on the route to Andorra, perched at an elevation of over 7,000 feet. Our holiday lasted two weeks, and it was magic. Snow was a completely new experience for me. Except for the sleet I had encountered in Belgium and the light dusting of wet snow that had led to the ill-fated sled ride which had done its dirty work on my calf, I had never really seen snow, nor had I ever skied or experienced life at a resort. The adults, including Marthou and her girlfriend, stayed in the main lodge with Tante Lily. I stayed at a nearby boarding house or *pension* called *L'Hermitage*, which was part of the ski lodge's hospitality complex. It was superbly organized to relieve parents from having to deal with interfering children during their holiday, and kept the kids busy learning to ski and pursuing other activities. The *pension* provided lessons and equipment, indoor and outdoor games, races and special events. Meals could be taken there or with the adults at the main lodge. Most of the kids were between nine and 16 and all came from well-to-do families.

Chair lifts were unheard of in those days and rope tows were the preferred means up the slopes. The skis were wooden and heavy, and the concept of release-bindings had not yet emerged from the fertile minds of equipment designers. Boots were of stiff—in fact, very stiff—leather, and it took at least half an hour to lace them properly. The beginners' skiing experience consisted of sidestepping up a small hill, slipping two steps back for every step forward, until we reached the modest summit. We would then slide down, inevitably falling, and then jump up and repeat the process all over again! It was exhausting—even for my young legs. The real challenge was to manage a single turn, a maneuver that both the skis and my body seemed determined to resist. My will and motivation to master these fundamentals was so strong, however, that I managed to survive and was able to participate in a few of the resort's downhill activities— though not as gracefully as I imagined them in my dreams. There were a lot of bruises, of course. Luckily, the crude grooming of the slopes and the precarious condition of the equipment served to discourage hot-dogging and schuss booming at breakneck speeds down the slopes.

All of these perilous efforts to master the art of skiing paid off on Christmas Eve. We followed the instructor up the rope tow to the top of the mountain and, once there, attended midnight Mass in a small chapel. After the service, the instructor gracefully meandered down the slope, carving gentle turns, while holding a lit torch. Like ducklings, we followed suit as best we could. Despite some awkwardness in the execution of our turns, everyone managed to make it to the bottom. With the moon reflecting on the crystalline slopes and the utter stillness that surrounded us, the only sounds to be heard were those of the skis rhythmically crunching on the snow. It was an experience I will never forget. At the bottom, we rejoined the adults in the main lodge for an incredibly sumptuous formal dinner of roast goose with chestnut stuffing and lots of other treats to celebrate the birth of Jesus Christ.

(I was not to ski again until 1970, long after I reached the United States. Too many events would occur in the interim, deflecting me from this delightful pursuit. Eventually, in the late seventies, I became quite proficient in that sport. I even tried to master racing turns in the Snow

Chapter 17

Bowls of Vail, Colorado. Unfortunately, this earned me an excruciatingly painful broken tibia and kept me out of trouble for about 18 months.)

In January 1946, I returned to Revel to finish the *Quatrième*. A few short months later, the post-war Jewish do-gooders along with the Zionists and other well-meaning organizations prevailed on the authorities to reopen my case. They felt that there were too many loose ends in their control over my life. I must be taken from the clutches of these non–Jewish heathens as soon as possible. They felt that the war had robbed me of my cultural heritage and, with this rationale, they insisted on a path that would indoctrinate me into the Jewish religion and culture — something for which neither my parents nor I had any particular interest. To redress the injustice of having been deprived of a Jewish upbringing, an injustice I clearly did not feel, the agencies went back to the *Conseil de Famille* for control over my spiritual life, determined to teach me religion, whether I wanted it or not. In order to accomplish this, they believed they would need to lay claim to my body as well. Their plan was to extract me from the de Bonnefoy family and ship me off to Palestine, which, at that time, was on the verge of becoming an independent nation called *Israel*. Once there, I would live in a *kibbutz* (communal habitat) and fight the Arabs. Please excuse the understatement, but I was not thrilled with these prospects.

Tante Lily and I vociferously rebelled against these arrangements, and a legal *Gotterdammerung* between the parties ensued. There were endless meetings with haphazardly organized postwar governmental bureaus, loosely staffed with amateur social workers and legal mavens. They were aided and abetted by all kinds of social agencies with important names and fuzzy missions. The de Bonnefoy camp enlisted their friends and the participation of those in their circle of influence who could help counter this onslaught of misplaced concern.

When the smoke cleared in the spring of 1946, the decision of the *Conseil de Famille* from the prior October was amended. Nobody in authority could transcend the mountain of mass survivor guilt generated by the revelations of the Holocaust horrors. With this as its "Just Cause," the Jewish establishment prevailed, influencing the court decision in the matter. In honor of the six million Jews who had perished, I would be forced to remember my Jewish heritage. I would be placed in a ferociously Orthodox, Zionist-Jewish-French orphanage.

After the upcoming summer break, I would return to the *Ecole de*

Garçons in Revel for the first semester of the *Troisième* (third grade) while all the necessary arrangements were made. In January 1947, immediately following the Christmas break, I would begin my new life in an *OSE* orphanage. Tante Lily told me not to worry, as it was only a minor setback. She assured me she would continue to fight the court's decision, but for the time being, we would have to go along with their ruling.

Ironically, *OSE* or *Oeuvre de Secours aux Enfants* means "Mission for Rescuing Children." It was a French-Jewish humanitarian institution with a distinguished history of helping children during and after the war. The *OSE* had access to about a dozen old mansions or estates, which it used as orphanages to house the children that came under its care. For the summer, it had organized a camp in the beautiful Haute Savoie area of France, where its wards could be enriched in Jewish culture. That camp was to be my home for the all-too-soon-approaching summer break.

Alas, the term camp turned out to be a cruel euphemism for a series of squalid squatting areas where we would pitch our tents in the middle of agricultural fields. Really, the camping adventure was little more than a way for the *OSE* to save money. There were about 50 of us and five adult supervisors. The *OSE* provided tents, blankets, cooking and eating utensils and basic spices, such as salt and pepper. Other than that, we were to live off the land, digging potatoes, carrots and turnips directly from the fields and buying bread, milk and other staples from the farmers in the countryside.

The *OSE* Camp was, to say the least, a low-budget operation. What made it truly excruciating was that the spots where we deployed our tents were usually close to centers like Evian, where unimaginable wealth and glamour exacerbated our feeling that our own existence was hopelessly devoid of everything. We had nothing — no home, no family, and no money ... and if the Zionists had their way, no future, except as soldiers fighting in yet another war! We were homeless waifs wandering the countryside in search of sustenance. Our living conditions in the OSE camp were so poor that we barely managed to live off the land. The local farmers were also poor, providing another dramatic contrast with the opulence of the Evian glitterati.

In the evenings, we made open field fires, boiled potatoes, sang Zionist songs and stared wistfully at the lights of Montreux, Switzerland, just across Lake Geneva. We longed to be there in comfortable beds instead of

Chapter 17

shivering on a wet hillside on the shores of the great lake. Montreux seemed close, but enticingly unreachable. Yet it was suggestive of what we imagined "normal" life to be like, in a land of plenty, untouched by the war, amidst a bottomless supply of Toblerone and Nestlé chocolates, as well as other goodies that were unavailable in France.

We spent our days roaming the sloping hills, fields and villages. On a couple of occasions, we trooped through the city of Evian, looking like gritty ragamuffins. We watched the beautiful people, their Rolls-Royces and their other glitzy trappings displayed with nonchalance. The abundance of old wealth, which flowed in and out of the casinos for which Evian was so famous, was astonishing. Once, in the course of trekking through the hills, we came upon the Swiss border. What followed forever reinforced my disdain for the Swiss.

I had a little money that Tante Lily had given me. Beyond the closed barrier on the Swiss side of the border next to the guardhouse was a small gift store, not much larger than a kiosk. It was filled with chocolates and other sweets, clearly promoting this aspect of Swiss fame. As we had no food other than what we could gather in the fields, and as the money given to me by Tante Lily was eating a hole in my pocket, we saw no reason whatsoever why our yearnings should not be satisfied. We could almost taste the chocolate. Alas, the Swiss are the Swiss. The border guards did not demure; they simply would not let us cross the border to reach the chocolate-laden kiosk. The guards ignored our pleas. Even then, after the war was over and the Nazi threat was gone, the barrier to the Swiss border would not be raised, not even for a minute. And so, sadly, we turned back, vowing to take revenge on this heartless nation at the earliest opportunity.

To say that I was not a happy camper that summer would have been a monumental understatement! It was during this camping experience that I found myself suddenly overwhelmed, for no reason I could rationally identify, by an irresistible urge to cry. I had not cried in years. In fact, I was proud of the fact that nothing could bring tears to my eyes. Not in Belgium, not when my parents were captured, not when the Germans came to Auriac, not in Revel. To cry was, in my view, a sign of weakness and something that needed to be outgrown. Yet, in this one instance, it was like a dam bursting. I cried for two solid days, most likely making up for all the time that the tears had been held back. I wasn't feeling sorry for myself and I wasn't angry — that would come later — I just had this uncontrollable urge to cry, and I simply couldn't stop it. When the tears finally subsided, I wasn't feeling any better, although I did feel relieved at having been able to express some emotion about the events that had taken place since I lost my parents. I guess this is what is called a catharsis. If there was a bright side to the misery I endured during summer camp, it was that, for the first time, I was actually looking forward to returning to school in September. Revel wasn't a palatial estate, but it was safe and warm, and I was guaranteed three meals a day.

The legal battle over my custody had continued throughout the summer months. And all this great debate, of course, had taken place without either my presence or my input. By the time I returned to civilization, the court's prior decision had been reaffirmed. I would start the first semester of the *Troisième* in Revel, then be moved temporarily to an orphanage called *La Borie* (The Manor House) in the city of Limoges, France's famous porcelain capital, until I could be sent to Palestine. Because of what was always referred to as the "painful circumstances" that had brought me to the *OSE*, I would attend the *Lycée Gay Lussac*, a well-respected secondary school — and a *Lycée*, not some local trade school, thus continuing the academic course of professional study I had started in Revel, rather than switching to the kind of school that the *OSE* normally found preferable for its wards. Again, still trying to find a silver lining in all this misery, I would be allowed to visit the de Bonnefoys during all major holidays until the voyage to the Middle East took place.

Chapter 18

Life in the Orphanage

The first semester of the *Troisième* unfolded uneventfully, as did the Christmas holidays. Before I knew it, it was January 1947 and I had to face the reality of life in an orphanage and what remained of a tough school year. I had tried not to dwell on either my fate or the *OSE* that I hated with all my heart.

But, in all fairness, the *OSE* was really a well-established, respected and widely recognized organization, and there was no question that it did a great deal of good in areas where a tremendous amount of help was needed. Its actions were motivated by what it deemed best for the Jewish children who had been abandoned by the war. However, this required that they exercise a wide range of value judgments, many of which, in my opinion, took their actions far beyond their basic mission to feed, shelter and educate war orphans. Schooling and technical training for their wards would assure a useful and productive life and was clearly proper. On the other hand, I felt that their mandated training in the areas of religion and politics was an unwarranted and outrageous intrusion into my private life. The *OSE* went beyond what should have been a commendable

Peter at La Borie Orphanage (Limoges, France, circa 1947).

goal—assuring that their wards never forgot their Jewish heritage or the sacrifices others had made in the name of that heritage. Instead, they felt their mission was to force our immersion into Jewish culture. In order to accomplish this, all the orphanages were strictly Orthodox. This meant observing the Sabbath and a myriad of other holiday rites, maintaining dietary laws, spending endless hours in a synagogue, learning Hebrew and, most humiliating, wearing a *yarmulke* (skull cap).

On the political front, the *OSE* felt that part of its mission was to help populate Israel and to join the militant Zionist struggle for an independent Jewish State. Their wards were indoctrinated in that movement in preparation for their eventual participation in armed combat against the Arab coalition that had massed its forces to defeat the Jewish settlers once the United Nations officially declared Israel a state. Israel, we were told, was the Promised Land, not only biblically but politically as well. It was the only sanctuary Jews would have available to them, should there ever be another genocide like World War II. Israel would be the one place in the world where Jews could be safe, the only one they could call their own. They believed that it was the obligation of every able-bodied Jew to serve this cause and become a Zionist. Needless to say, my values were vastly different.

First, there was absolutely nothing in my background or culture to suggest the slightest interest in Jewish religion or rituals. I had been circumcised, of course, inadvertently putting my life at risk. But it had been done for sanitary, not religious or cultural reasons. My mother would never have guessed that circumcision would pose a far more serious risk than penile infection, something that, during the German occupation, would be akin to wearing the Star of David.

In contrast, my days as an altar boy in Auriac's little church had served me well as a cover during the Nazi occupation. But I can unequivocally affirm that there was never any kind of pressure on me to convert to Catholicism from the de Bonnefoys or the clergy. My religion was not and is not either Catholicism or Judaism. Even as a youth, I rejected the notion that evidence of being a good human being requires adherence to some ritual-driven "ism." Rather, I believe it is a highly personal—and private—inquiry into the mysteries of life; a quest for rational understanding of what we were meant to know, perceive or experience. The philosophy of Positivism, as explained by the French philosopher Auguste Comte,

Chapter 18

comes closest to reflecting my views on the subject. As such, I have always vehemently rejected the notion that there is no God. Instead, I eschew the question by averring the fact that it is far beyond me or other mere mortals to define what, if or who God might be.

Through the eyes of a child, I did not agree that Israel was the sole and unique sanctuary for all the Jews of the world. After all, but for the Nazi madness, I was living proof of this, having been accepted so warmly by the French in general and, of course, by the de Bonnefoy family in particular. Before the do-gooders from the Jewish establishment interfered, I had a perfectly happy existence with no need for a Middle Eastern sanctuary. I abhorred the notions that being Jewish should make me different, and that being Jewish should be considered more than a religion. I felt then (and I still feel now) that trying to raise any religion to the status of a nationality or, even worse, a race, is precisely the tactic that the Nazis had used so successfully to justify the persecution of Jews. Those views, in my opinion, have always served to segregate Jews from the mainstream of the population, thereby causing them to emerge as a convenient target for the placement of blame for all the problems of the world. No, I never considered Palestine my "Promised Land," nor Israel a sanctuary. I believed in assimilation. My country was never an abstract "Kingdom of Heaven" or a "Sacred Ancient Promised Land." It was any country that would have me as a citizen and treat me like everybody else, without any kind of hyphenation.

On the day I was to leave for the orphanage, Tante Lily arranged a meeting in Toulouse with a representative from the *OSE* in order to hand me over to them. After we said a very emotional goodbye, the *OSE* representative, a kindly looking middle-aged lady, stayed with me for the long train voyage from Toulouse to Limoges. In Limoges, we boarded a streetcar that brought us within view of the orphanage. From a distance, *La Borie* appeared to be a large, stately mansion with imposing wrought-iron gates, opulent landscaping and what seemed to be a vast manicured green expanse set up for croquet and other genteel lawn activities. Maybe life in an orphanage wouldn't be so bad —

Alas, that thought quickly evaporated, and the sad reality struck harshly as we approached the estate grounds. On closer examination, the

The only running water for bathing at La Borie Orphanage came from two faucets connected to wells in a courtyard (Limoges, France, circa 1947).

gates that had seemed so impressive actually didn't work; they were far too rusty. In fact, they were on their last legs. Any landscaping that may have existed was long gone. What seemed to be majestic front and back lawns were in reality over used soccer and athletic grounds where mud had replaced grass, completely erasing any illusion of the elegance that, at one time, might have graced the estate. The mansion itself showed its age and the ravages of complete neglect. As we walked inside, the evidence of this was appalling. The walls were dirty, with cracked plaster covered with graffiti. The place was generally bare, lacking any sign of personal care or homey touches that a sensitive staff might have created to make it feel less institutional; it looked forlorn and vandalized. We were met by a staff member who, once I was safely locked away and under the watchful eye of my new jailers, introduced me to my fellow waifs. The *OSE* lady who

Chapter 18

had escorted me from Toulouse disappeared, never to be seen again; her mission had been accomplished.

The orphanage housed about 40 children between the ages of ten and 18, a staff of four and the director, a Monsieur Levy, who looked a little like a foreshortened, Jewish, balding Ichabod Crane with very thick glasses and a very pronounced nose. He lived there with his family, exercising the full panoply of responsibilities that gave him dominion over the life, welfare and spiritual propensities of his charges. The orphanage was co-ed, but most of us were boys. We were divided into rooms containing four to six cots. For all practical purposes, there were no bathrooms. Indoor running water either wasn't working or did not exist. The supply of running water came from two faucets connected to wells in an open courtyard. Hot water was out of the question and, in the winter, the water was freezing. At least the toilets were indoors, and consisted of a few stalls, each equipped with a hole located strategically between two cement footprints stamped into the concreted floor. In the United States, this ingenious arrangement is known as a one-holer. Inside each stall there was a bucket of water, which needed to be refilled each time by the user. Of course, there was no toilet paper or anything like it.

The meeting and indoor recreational areas where we gathered as a group were generous, almost majestic in scale. Of particular importance to me was a large room that served as our dining room. We ate sitting at long tables of 16, arranged in a U-shape or, for special occasions, in a square. This enabled the room to serve as the general assembly area as well as a refectory. This was where ceremonies and religious rites were performed and where general discussions were held. Hebrew classes and religious education activities were conducted there as well. The room acquired a somewhat festive atmosphere every Friday night at the start of the Sabbath when the fare was a little better than on other days. Unfortunately, the Passover dinner, the Seder, was an endless, boring business, and the food was more symbolic than edible.

Zionist fervor was pervasive. We spent a lot of time singing Hebrew songs, the words to which we did not understand. They told of bold biblical deeds by bigger-than-life Israeli heroes. The tales of the fearsome Maccabaeus recurred over and over again, with their exploits sung in such fashion as to inspire a bunch of impressionable kids like us with the spirit to follow their example. Beyond the songs, we emulated life in a *kibbutz* by learning the traditional folk dances, including the *Hora*, Israel's traditional circle dance. I was being pulled into the vortex of a different kind of life — one with which I would never identify.

I was required to wear a *yarmulke* at all meals, and we observed the Jewish Orthodox dietary rules. These were strictly enforced, starting with the separation of milk-based food from meat-based. The meals were served on either dairy or meat plates and eaten with tableware approved by a rabbi. Of course, pork was completely prohibited and so was any meat from animals not slaughtered in the ritualistic manner prescribed by Jewish law. The irony of these dietary obsessions did not escape me. The postwar food situation in France was dire and, given the lack of meat and milk products that prevailed during those times, all these religious restrictions were academic and really quite laughable. Fortunately, lentils, garbanzo beans and rutabagas were not subject to any religious or dietary strictures and were plentiful; they became our main staples. Sinful stuff sent to me by Tante Lily like *foie gras*, goose *confit*, and other gourmet-like preserved meats that the Germans had failed to grab during their last moments at the château all violated some religious edict, so they were confiscated in the name of religious orthodoxy the moment they arrived.

Our one permissible meat was lung — really, really gross, not very tasty and certainly not appetizing — but nonetheless it was kosher, rabbi-approved and undeniably nourishing. Lung was also very heavy. Not inside the stomach (not that it was particularly digestible), but to carry. At least once a week, we would lug a large basket full of the weighty stuff from the slaughterhouse to the orphanage. The stronger boys took turns performing that chore, two boys at a time, with each boy holding one of the two coarse wicker handles of the basket used to carry the lungs. As I was among the stronger boys, I was one of the designated shleppers. I remember how painful this was. We had to cover a distance of about three miles. The handles of the basket bit into our hands, and when it was cold, our fingers cramped into a death grip around the handles. At the same time, the dead weight of the load seemed to increase with every step, causing blisters on top of the frostbite — and all for a comestible we had come to abhor.

Given the shortage of staff at the orphanage, we had to help alleviate the jobs involved with food preparation, cleaning and building repairs by doing much of the work ourselves. Thus, we helped in the kitchen, did all kinds of maintenance chores, tried (not too successfully) to grow fruits and vegetables in the garden areas, scrubbed and cleaned, repaired and did all things manual as best we could, to keep things in functioning condition. That left the management of the finances, the relationship with support organizations and any interactions with government and the public education system as the unique and predictable responsibilities of Monsieur Levy.

And, as if all this deprivation, misery and hardship weren't enough, one day the *OSE* had an epiphany: at the age of 16, I had never had a *Bar Mitzvah*. I was way past the age when a Jewish boy under goes the "coming of age rituals" and becomes responsible for obeying God's commandments in accordance with Jewish law. This usually occurs when one turns 13, and is marked by an elaborate ceremony where, on a Saturday morning in a synagogue, the boy about to become a man is called upon to participate in the reading of the Torah, preferably in Hebrew. He then must give a short speech to demonstrate his new maturity. Finally, even if his performance is a total embarrassment, he is congratulated, showered with gifts and, surrounded by family and friends, remains the star of the celebration throughout the afternoon and into the night. In the process, all present gorge on a sumptuous feast. In my case, however, I would make the transition to manhood in a manner not contemplated by these traditions or by the Old Testament.

To begin with, my rebellious spirit had made it impossible for me to memorize enough Hebrew to read from the Torah. I, therefore, would need to meet this element of the ceremony by reading a short passage from the Torah in French. As I refused to prepare a speech, I would have to skip that part of the rite altogether. Secondly, the ceremony would not occur in a synagogue, but in the refectory of the orphanage, and it would not be exclusively mine — I would have to share the event with two of three other hapless candidates for manhood. Of course, none of us had any relatives left alive who might attend the ceremony to cheer us on. After all, we were orphans. And as to the feast ... well, that would have to be lung and lentils.

As the day drew close, I was miserable and alone. To say the least, my heart was not in this. As an ultimate act of defiance, I decided to dump my *yarmulke* in the trashcan outside the refectory and, when it came time for me to perform, I put a dirty handkerchief on my head instead. My behavior achieved predictable results. When the formal ceremony was over, instead of lunch, I was sent to school, anchored to a desk and forced to study for five hours as punishment to expiate my disrespectful, sacrilegious behavior. I suspected that someday God would probably want to punish me for this also, but he would just have to wait — the *OSE* was doing just fine for now!

True to its commitment, the *OSE* had sent me to a *Lycée* and not a trade school. The *Lycée Gay-Lussac* was, predictably, not to my liking. In fact, given the circumstances, I doubt that there was a school on earth that I could ever have grown to like. I abhorred any establishment or institution that sought to control any aspect of my life against my will; I took out my unhappiness and frustrations with the *OSE* on everything. I resented the way the *OSE* had altered my life. I hated my courses, particularly Latin, and I wasn't up to the challenge of memorizing the French classics or the plays and poetry so prolific in French literature. But most of all, I despised the orphanage's strict religious training. My new life was even more miserable than I had expected and accordingly, so was my rebellious behavior. I was well on my way to becoming an incorrigible juvenile delinquent, and the *Bar Mitzvah* episode had only made it worse.

My next report card was an abomination, both academically and behaviorally. I was deemed insubordinate, uncooperative and generally a major problem. I did well in math, so-so in French, poorly in history and geography. I excelled in German, my second language, and in art classes, where I was considered a phenomenon. My greatest fear was that, should the *OSE* receive another one of these negative report cards, my grades might cause them to revisit the decision to send me to a *Lycée* instead of a trade school. Or worse, my behavior just might provoke them to speed up my dispatch to Israel in an effort to be rid of me.

To avoid this, instead of trying to improve my grades, I went to extraordinary efforts to intercept the delivery of the mail containing my latest report card. I then took the incriminating document and flushed it down the one-holer with a bucket of water. Next, I managed to steal a blank report card from the principal's office, and used it to create a new card, one that painted a vastly different, and much less damning, picture for Monsieur Levy to behold. In this connection, the forgery skills I had mastered with my parents during the war came in handy.

It wasn't long after that when I was summoned into the office of the

Chapter 18

Lycée's headmaster. It became immediately clear that this was not going to be a friendly chat. It seems that my report card-forging exploit had been discovered and the headmaster was livid. He was an imposing, heavyset presence, impeccably dressed, perfectly groomed and full of spit and polish. I recall that his shoes were particularly shiny and they squeaked quite noticeably on the glossy parquet floor. He was authority incarnate. I was appropriately intimidated. He approached me threateningly, balancing his heavy bulk on his narrow shiny shoes, all the while cursing at me loudly with shocking obscenities. His anger and outrage had reached a paroxysm and there was no doubt that he was ready to give me the beating of a lifetime.

As he reached me, he pulled his arm back to deliver the expected blow. I instinctively ducked, causing him to lose his balance on the slippery office floor. And there he lay, sprawled out in a most unflattering position, in front of his staff and the others who had been attracted by the commotion. An ominous silence settled into the room. There was actually something comical about this picture, but at the time, I was too scared to give in to my urge to break out in uncontrollable laughter. In fact, I was petrified, paralyzed with fear and apprehension. I was painfully aware that there would be consequences.

The room was cleared and the next day, after recovering his dignity, he advised me that I was not going to be expelled from *Le Lycée Gay Lussac*. He and Monsieur Levy had agreed that, because it was so close to the end of the school year and the "painful circumstances that had brought me under the *OSE's* care" ... yes, fortunately, there was always that ... there was a far easier solution available. I would be put on probation, finish out the school year in Limoges (assuming there were no new incidents), then I would be transferred to one of their other orphanages — far away from Limoges.

In spite of myself, once again kismet had allowed me to avoid any severe punishment and I would continue my education in a *Lycée*. I even had the summer with the de Bonnefoys to look forward to! Maybe things weren't so bad after all.

While I had been trying to adapt to my new life in the orphanage, all of the members of the de Bonnefoy family had begun to create their own new peacetime life. Oncle Nino, in recognition of his distinguished services for the resistance, had been appointed director of rationing for the Toulouse region. Tante Lily had become very active with many of the social agencies concerned with reuniting families broken up by the war. Concurrently, she struggled to save the progressively failing farms. Realizing the futility of this effort, she redoubled her efforts to assure the economic survival of the tenant farmers who had served the de Bonnefoy family for so many generations.

She sold many of the farms and helped place the farmers and their families in situations with opportunities for different kinds of employment. Needless to say, these opportunities required not only a recycling of working skills but, in most cases, relocation from farm life to an urban setting.

Since the family's immediate postwar activities emanated from Toulouse, they rented an ample and comfortable suburban villa on the Rue Ozenne within easy streetcar reach of the center city. Tante Lily, for the first time in her life, worked for a salary at the agencies she had been helping for so long as a volunteer. For the first time in centuries, the family left their ancestral Auriac estate behind in favor of life in a large urban center. There, in those fast-moving times, they could be at the nexus of everything that was happening, ready to be wrapped up in the flow of current events, trends and activities.

The de Bonnefoy family was not alone in this urban migration. The national mood was yearning to shift from rural to city life during the transition from war to peace. It was a process that was both exhilarating and traumatic. The newly acquired freedoms were bursting to break out, but the government was not yet stable or fully organized, the economy was uncertain and the shortages continued to subject everyone to severe rationing practices. To be in the know was critical for survival, and the best place to know what was going on was in the cities.

I was only dimly aware of Tante Lily and Oncle Nino's postwar activities, and the fact that the château had been virtually abandoned over those past six months had yet to dawn on me. I could not have imagined that extended visits to Toulouse would become more and more frequent for Oncle Nino and Tante Lily, and that visits to Paris would be considered even more alluring, holding a special cachet. The advent of peace and the exciting activities in the newly freed cities had gradually relegated the château in Auriac into the backwaters of everybody's interest and concerns. It represented an obsolete lifestyle and it was virtually in mothballs, rele-

Chapter 18

gated to be merely a holiday retreat. We would never again go back there to live.

The house the de Bonnefoys had rented in Toulouse was, of course, always available to Marthou and me, but we somehow never looked at it as a permanent home. It was more an interim convenience until a sense of permanence could be restored in the family. For me, there was no escaping the unenviable fact that I must live in a Jewish Orthodox orphanage. My life had changed and my attachments to the de Bonnefoy family had begun to ebb. Once again, I found myself on the threshold of a black hole of uncertainty. But the school year was over and summer with the family in Toulouse would allay some of my fears.

Prior to leaving Limoges, the decision had been made to send me to the *OSE* orphanage in Lyon, France's silk center. The agreement between the de Bonnefoys and the *OSE* had been that the de Bonnefoys would pay all expenses, including train fare and incidental expenses for the trip from Limoges to Toulouse, while the *OSE* would pay for my return trip from Toulouse to the orphanage in Lyon. The generosity of the de Bonnefoys was the reason I found myself luxuriating in the comforts of a roomy second-class compartment on the train to Toulouse that summer.

In the postwar era, trains were the principal means of transport between cities, taking on an importance comparable to that of today's airplane travel. It was a period when trains once again became fashionable, no longer serving as human cattle cars conveying soldiers or prisoners from one region, battle theater or internment camp, to another. As a result, a great deal of importance was attached to the quality of the accommodations onboard and the services available at the railway stations. The differences between third-class and second- or first-class travel were huge. Third-class meant no reserved seats. One was often doomed to sit on luggage in the crowded aisle, gawking into the third-class seating compartments and those lucky enough to have gotten a seat. Access to toilets was always a challenge. If one was lucky enough to have an assigned seat, it was in a compartment of eight, equipped with marginally upholstered banquettes behind sliding-glass doors. But to truly appreciate the hardship of third-class travel, a description of the lavishness and plush finishes of the second- and first-class accommodations is necessary. These luxurious compartments were impressively decorated with embroideries, antique prints and amenities consistent with the treatment of royalty. Instead of eight passengers per compartment, they accommodated only six in second-class and four in first. These journeys had a way of exacerbating the stark contrast between luxury and economy travel. The "have-nots" standing outside the overcrowded compartments gawking at the "haves" sprawled out on velvet banquettes always evoked a visceral sense of injustice for me. I never doubted that train travel must have helped fuel all kinds of political reform movements in Europe after the war.

Toulouse was a remarkably beautiful and compact city. The unique pink sandstone found in most of its buildings endowed it with the nickname "The Rose City." What really made it unique, however, was that it housed one of the oldest and largest universities in Europe, having been founded in the year 1229. Within the university, the *Ecole des Beaux Arts* was particularly famous and ranked with its rivals in Paris and Lyon. The center of the city was indeed its center of gravity. The huge square —*La Place du Capitole*— was named to honor the fact that the city had always been considered the capital of the Languedoc region. (More recently, of course, it has become the home base of Airbus and, as such, the center for the aerospace industry in Europe.)

While I was too young to take advantage of the many cafés that lined the wide sidewalks bordering the city's many parks and public squares, the shops were great and there were lots of movie theaters where I could spend my time. There was also a semi-permanent amusement park where, when I had a bit of spare change, I could get into a round of Bump'Em Cars, although I still don't know why that sport ever appealed to me! More importantly, I found the city aesthetically pleasing. I so enjoyed it that I would often take root in a spot that had a clear view of one of the dramatic city sights, and I would sketch or paint the image. Tante Lily would always proudly display my art in the living room of our Toulouse house.

Meanwhile, the impact of peace was being felt throughout France, necessitating a change in many behavior patterns and attitudes. Freedom of movement, open patriotism ... and chauvinism ... was widespread, and the focus of concern had shifted from security to economic welfare. Food, though generally more available, was still treated with a level of respect and appreciation that only an extended period of dire deprivation could have brought about. Throwing food away would be considered a mortal sin for a long time after the war. Leftovers were saved and served again.

Chapter 18

Unlike wartime, however, there was a silver lining. The belief in the sanctity of food raised the status of cooking from a matter of mere nourishment to that of haute cuisine.

The black market, which had put otherwise unavailable goods within our reach during wartime was still in vogue. While many of the goods were now available, they came at a steep price. There was a huge difference between "unavailable" and "in short supply," and the black-market was an indispensable institution in the case of the latter. Also indispensable was access to *influence*. It is no wonder, therefore, that the end of the war gave rise to a new class of amateurish entrepreneurs and would-be politicians. Everybody was, or needed, a broker. The networks of influence were extensive, crossed multiple fields and were present in most transactions — whether or not such influence was truly needed. I will always recall the day Oncle Nino surreptitiously slipped me a piece of paper with a name and address on it. The address led to a small Toulouse shop. The unique aspect of this shop was that it had underwear available. Now, said underwear was commonly available for about the same price without the intervention of someone with *influence*. However, the fact that *influence* was introduced into this transaction gave it a certain cachet that somehow made it feel special.

The Nazis were gone and Jews were no longer universal prey or readily available scapegoats, yet the subconscious would not release my inhibitions about urinating in public toilets. (Even now, over 60 years later, I am still hesitant to use public urinals when they do not screen most of my body from view. Recently, Joyce and I were on a holiday in Tibet, riding across a vast plateau on a tour bus filled with Germans. In the middle of the Himalayas, I was struck with a brief moment of panic when the driver called for an impromptu rest stop in the open. My first impulse was to panic — they were Germans, and they would see that I was circumcised and know that I was a Jew! While on an intellectual level I knew that this was no longer an issue, the conditioned response still remained.)

This brings to mind a hilarious film that came out in France, shortly after the end of the war. It featured Fernandel, the famous French comedian, and it was called *Clochemerle* after a small village not unlike Auriac. The movie became all the rage. But the principal star was not Fernandel; it was a very old, ordinary wall that had stood forever in the center of the village. What made the wall so special was the fact that, over the years, men had found it to be convenient to urinate against. As there were no windows until the third floor, this offered a private stand for the village's male population, and thus it became the official de-watering hole for the village. Various methods of urinating turned it into a sport, and it became a popular part of village life. The hilarious movie plot revolved around the antics of a bunch of feisty female church mice and other pious ladies who, by virtue of the strategic location of their abode, had windows directly above the third floor. They enjoyed front-seat views of everything happening at the wall, unbeknownst to the men below. It's no surprise that, with my phobia about urinating in public, my interest in the film was abstract and I had trouble identifying with this uniquely French sport. When I recall the movie, I realize that the fear of exposing my circumcision is the baggage I will alway carry from the war years.

Chapter 19

Lyon, and Light at the End of the Tunnel

The summer of 1947 passed quite agreeably, and I was ready for my next year of schooling. As if by intentional contrast, I found myself once again on the train, only this time in utter misery, standing in a crowded, oppressive third-class compartment on the trip to the orphanage in Lyon. The train was dragging me relentlessly deeper into a chasm of uncertainty: I had no familiarity with the city, the school or the orphanage where I was to live. To me, everything about this trip to Lyon was a textbook prelude to the orphanage. The trip to Toulouse in second-class had felt like an extension of the de Bonnefoy family and their life-style; the trip back to Lyon in third-class symbolized everything I hated about the orphanage. It was truly a Dickensian *Tale of Two Cities*.

The orphanage in Lyon was called *Les Hirondelles* (The Swallows) and it was located in the suburb of St. Genis Laval. It was a mansion comparable to *La Borie*, with roughly the same Spartan comforts and marginal facilities.

I would do *La Deuxième* (the second grade) at *Le Collège Des Minimes*. It sat high on a hillside above Old Lyon near the Basilica of Fourvière, overlooking the Saône River. To get there from the orphanage required all sorts of transfers. First, there was a bus ride, then a trolley bus. Like a regular bus, the trolley bus was free to navigate the streets, but it drew its power from a fixed overhead electric tract, which imposed the path of its route. The trolley brought me to the bottom of the steep hillside overlooking the Rhone and Saône rivers. There was a cable car there, known as *La Ficelle* (the string), which pulled passengers up the steep slope to the Fourvière Basilica.

Le Collège Des Minimes was oriented more towards science and technology rather than the classics and the arts. Assuming that I couldn't possibly do worse in Lyon than I had done in Limoges, I looked forward to turning the page and a new beginning. I would have the opportunity to work myself out of the nasty reputation I had acquired as a result of my insubordinate behavior in Limoges. I started *La Seconde* (second grade) with a vow to do better. I had calmed down. Life was a lot tamer. This was the last grade and the last school year before *La Premiere* (the first grade), at the end of which was the arduous baccalaureate. This had to be faced before I would graduate and begin a university-level program. I hoped to redeem myself and prove that I was worthy of this one last chance to join the educated French elite instead of the classless working masses.

I had a roommate at *Les Hirondelles* who became my confidant, best friend and partner in crime. His name was Didier. He had earned the honor of being accepted into Lyon's prestigious Silk College where he would pursue a career in the silk industry. I, on the other hand, was playing a lot of soccer, chess, ping-pong and other such heroic activities that had nothing to do with a career.

Food and clothing were still in short supply at the orphanage, but, fortunately for us, peace brought with it the compassion of the world community. Within our limited world, this translated into CARE (Cooperative for Assistance and Relief Everywhere) packages from the United States. CARE is a nonprofit, nonsectarian federation of agencies devoted to channeling relief and self-help to needy people in foreign countries. Founded in 1945, CARE represented some 22 leading cooperative, labor, relief, and refugee organizations. The CARE packages arrived about once every six months and always provided an excuse for a lot of fun and excitement at the orphanage.

They came in large wooden crates, ranging in size from three to six cubic feet. Some boxes contained mostly clothing items. Others were filled with various kinds of food products. A few toys were scattered among the boxes in no particular order. Beyond providing a great deal of levity, many of the goods were badly needed and most welcome. Moreover, the content of the crates allowed a vicarious glimpse of life in America, giving us hints as to what the American people wore, what they ate and how they spent their leisure time. Alas, the quest for answers only deepened the mysteries of this faraway land, as we were unable to account for some of the really bizarre items found in the containers.

The biggest mystery to us were the sweaters, jackets and sport shirts

Chapter 19

with gigantic, colorful letters sewn into the fabric in front, back, on the arms and the pants legs. No one could figure out what they meant, but we all agreed that they were very pretty. The boxes sometimes contained huge leather mittens with large holes where the thumb should be. We had seen comic strips showing kids using these strange gloves to play some sort of game, but the rules completely eluded us and we had no idea what their purpose was. All we knew was that they did not keep our hands very warm! It was always quite a spectacle to see a roomful of boys and girls prance around the refectory with gleeful abandon, rummaging in the boxes and coming out of the fray wearing trophies that made them look like a flock of colorful parrots. We had to face the fact that we just did not understand many aspects of American culture.

Whatever was included in the CARE packages in the way of food was, to say the least, interesting. Even more than the weird letters and numbers sewn into the clothes, the food packaging offered an even clearer mirror of life in America, further illustrating the cultural differences between the senders and the recipients. The big food puzzler for us was a Jell-O-like pink powder in a very pretty, colorful box. It was called Danish Dessert. When we were able to translate the English instructions on the box's label, it became eminently clear that we would never be able to enjoy the product the way it was meant to be eaten. Without stove or refrigerator, all we could do was simply eat the pink powder directly from the little cardboard box. But the box gave us a glimpse into what a typical middle-class American family looked like. Inspired by Hollywood, we could imagine how the pink sugary powder would be cooked, molded, and cooled into a sculptured jelly in a super-modern, antiseptic kitchen with a slick electric stove, a state-of-the-art refrigerator, and a broadly smiling Aunt Jemima in a white apron, triumphantly brandishing the finished dessert, artistically decorated with whipped cream, just like the colorful picture on the Danish Dessert box. Aunt Jemima's modern kitchen never looked so good, and the family scenes full of smiling faces and splendid surroundings all beckoned to a lifestyle we could only imagine in our dreams. Alas, we had no kitchen, no stove and certainly no refrigerator. Aunt Jemima was not to be seen, and whipped cream could not be further from the reality in which we lived. Maybe the next CARE package would supply all of that!

The packages contained very little chocolate, candy or other sweets that we were all craving, since the senders probably felt that we were as susceptible to tooth decay and weight gain as they were. Canned goods really dominated the contents. For us, however, the grand prize was always a can of sweetened condensed milk, a product most Americans do not consider particularly exotic, and whose availability is usually taken for granted. The thick, sweet, mellow, syrupy liquid in those cans required no preparation other than to punch two holes at one end of the can. What came out was ambrosia for the gods. There was nothing godly, however, about the scramble that ensued between the orphanage's denizens as they tried to grab the all-too-few-cans of sweetened condensed milk. The lucky few who wound up with them usually ran furtively, like leopards with their prey, for the cover and protection of their respective cots. Once safe, the objective was to punch two holes, suspend the open can from the ceiling with shoelaces, and lie on one's back on top of the cot. The position allowed the exquisite liquid to steadily drip into our wide-opened mouths. It was like experiencing a transfusion of unadulterated pleasure in an otherwise repulsive environment.

The first semester in Lyon passed without incident and I was looking forward to spending the Christmas holidays with the family for what might well be our last visit to the château. Oncle Nino had been called to Paris and had just moved there to become the chief of police for France's capital region. Tante Lily had moved from Toulouse to Paris as well, where she continued her work with child welfare organizations. She had found a lovely apartment in the suburban city of Neuilly-sur-Seine. Her transition from country squire to urban cosmopolite and her journey from Auriac to Paris via Toulouse would soon be complete. Most of the farms had been sold and, as the château was used less and less, they were planning to rent it to a wealthy doctor for a country retreat.

After a long, crowded train ride from Lyon, I arrived in Toulouse. As the train pulled into the *Gare Matabiau*, I was struck by a pang of nostalgia as the realization sank in that this was possibly the last time I would visit Auriac and the château. It was probably this mood that brought to mind the little village of Mane and the time I spent there with my parents and Robert Soula. I was expected in Toulouse that night, but my movements were, as usual, not monitored very closely. Detouring to Mane was not a dramatic escapade, just a short train ride on the local *Micheline*, a kind of

Chapter 19

diesel-powered train engine with passenger seats. I could easily reach the village in less than a couple of hours. I had plenty of time. I could walk around the place and see the little apartment building where I had last lived with my parents and where we had made butter and cheeses. If luck would have it, I might even find Robert Soula. Without another thought, I switched trains and headed to Mane. Wallowing in nostalgia, I had made a decision that would prove to be the turning point in my life, the most significant of all my encounters with kismet.

When I arrived in Mane, I got off the train on the village's main street, directly across from the post office. By some remarkable quirk of fate, the postmaster was taking some air at that very moment, and was standing in front of the building. Amazingly, he recognized me and called to me as I passed by. He asked if I was the son of the cheese maker he had known during the war. When I confirmed the fact that he was indeed correct, he ran inside and came out holding an old, mangled postcard. He told me that he had received it maybe a year or so before, and that he had been holding it in his desk, just in case someone might come by and claim it. I did not know what to make of the tattered post card. It was postmarked from the United States of America but was in German, actually German script, and, though I had studied this, I had no idea who had written it

Peter, in front of the post office where he found the postcard from his family in New York (Mane, France, 1996).

or what it said. I vaguely recalled my parents telling me that some of my father's relatives had escaped to America before the war, but that they had been searching for me was too much to hope for! The postmaster found someone who could decipher the postcard, which confirmed that there still existed a tiny remnant of my family, that they were alive and well in America, and best of all, that they were looking for me!

From that point on, my life changed in fundamental ways. I was no longer completely alone. Not only did I have a family, but it was an American family! With the enthusiastic help of the French postal service, it did not take long before I was in contact with my aunt and uncle — my father's sister, Lotte, and her husband, Al Werner.

Not surprisingly, they told the *OSE* of relatives on my mother's side who lived in Israel. This started yet another conflict over my future. Now everyone was in the fray. Communication was established between the *OSE,* the de Bonnefoys, my American family and my Israeli aunts. But at least the orphanage and a *kibbutz* were off the table and the choices for where I would live had been narrowed to family in either the United States or Israel. Moreover, I had a voice in the matter ... in fact, for a change, the decision was entirely mine to make!

It did not take me long to opt for the land of the Danish Dessert over a pioneering life in a Middle Eastern desert, where peace and security were still far from assured. Frankly, I was desperate for a normalized life, and I repudiated the idea of subordinating my existence to the ideals of saving the world and embracing world causes ... even if these involved the heroic participation in the creation of a new homeland for Jews. I felt that I was making the right decision for me, and that was enough. If this was perceived as a cowardly choice and branded me as a traitor to a yet-to-be-recognized Jewish state, so be it!

From that point on, my remaining time at the orphanage became easy. My guardians at the *OSE* were as sick of my antics as I was of their stifling, self-righteous attitude and their Jewish fundamentalism, and they offered no resistance to the process of getting me to the U.S. I began exchanging letters with my uncle and aunt.

Lotte and Al were the real pioneers, proud of the new roots they were able to establish in America and eager to conform to its ways. Aunt Lotte had become the matriarch of the American contingent of the family and she expected — no, she demanded — obeisance in all matters. She and Uncle

Chapter 19

Al lived on Long Island in New York and to me they represented the epitome of how immigrants should embrace this new land, its traditions, values and language. It was to Al and Lotte that I would always owe my presence in the United States and my sense of patriotism.

During the war, Lotte had volunteered as a WAC (Women's Army Corps), and her letters entertained me with tales of her epic KP (Kitchen Police) adventures involving scrubbing mammoth pots into which she would disappear for hours. She was now an executive secretary on Wall Street, the highly valued assistant to the chairman of the Hanseatic Corporation, a multi-national company, perhaps related to the Hanseatic League of old. Historically, the league was an important coalition of North German, Swedish, Danish and English "hansas," or guilds, whose ships roamed the Baltic and the North Sea in the middle of the 13th century to protect commerce and trade.

Al had Americanized his name from Werner Cohen to Albert C. Werner, thanks to the image-conscious Eastman Kodak Company, where he was employed as a research scientist. As was the case with much of corporate America at that time, Kodak felt that it simply could not be associated with anything Semitic and, as such, the name Cohen just would not do. Uncle Al was a near-genius. He had a German doctorate in chemistry, and had pioneered and advanced the state of the art in paint manufacturing. He was also a recognized Lincoln scholar, and had collected a voluminous anthology of that president's pronouncements.

To reinforce our growing relationship, they would send me a dollar bill in each letter. That was a thrill beyond all thrills. The dollar bill was totally different — French and European currencies were more ornate, larger, with sizes that varied with their denominations. The American money looked just like that usually displayed by movie gangsters like Edward G. Robinson and George Raft in Hollywood crime and detective films. This stimulated the imagination of everyone in the orphanage, as we passed my dollar bill from hand to hand. It was intently studied, even smelled, almost religiously as if this would transport us into a different world. Ironically, nobody cared what it was worth or what the exchange rate was! We wanted to become part of the world shown in the cinema. Holding on to this sliver of reality reinforced our enjoyment of living vicariously through the film noir characters that were then populating the big screen.

Passport used for immigration to the U.S.

Chapter 19

Passport used for immigration to the U.S.

The winter of 1948 turned into spring, and there was regular progress with respect to my future. My uncle and aunt in America had been able to find a properly endowed financial sponsor for my immigration: Jean Ulman, a tobacco heiress. As a proper sponsor, she enabled the immigration process to move forward without further delays. What remained was the thorny issue of which quota, German or French, I should hitch my identity to, given that I had no idea where my birth certificate was. Ironically, there was a lot more room under the German quota than the French, so it was decided that I would immigrate under the former.

The last days in Lyon were wonderful. The late spring weather was warm, a wonderful relief from the cold with which I had always associated the orphanage. The anxieties of the relentlessly approaching *Baccho* had vanished with the certain knowledge that I would never have to take this hideous exam. My education would be completed in America and all my misdeeds and bad behavior would be forever expunged, with no chance of them following me to the new continent. My future certainly looked promising.

It was with enormous relief that, just before the school year ended, I greeted the official, court-approved documents, signed by the *OSE*, my new family in the U.S. and the de Bonnefoys. Thus, the complexities of my immigration to America were finalized. Unlike the clandestine adventure via Spain and Casablanca contemplated by my parents during their desperate efforts to escape besieged France, my immigration to the U.S. the following month would be legal and sanctioned by all concerned.

Chapter 20

The Crossing and the Lady in New York Harbor

The ship was the SS *Mauretania*, one of the floating behemoths of the Cunard-White Star line. It had served as a troop transport during the war but had been recently restored into a luxurious passenger ship. I felt like a free man headed for the Promised Land — and not the one in the Middle East! I packed my little suitcase with one pair of underwear, a cotton shirt, a small jackknife, and a pair of socks. I was given an envelope of documents I would need at the other end of the Atlantic when I set foot on the new continent.

My voyage to America had started in Lyon, where I boarded a train to Paris. Tante Lily met me on the concourse of the Gare St. Lazare. There, we took the boat-train to Le Havre where I was to board the *Mauretania* for the Atlantic crossing to New York. Tante Lily and I embraced while tears ran down her cheeks. The drama of the event was deflected when, at the last moment, she took an inventory of all the papers involved in the immigration process. She went over all that I would have to deal with before embarking, and after landing on the other side of the world. Despite this distraction, the goodbyes were heart wrenching, as we were both well aware that the separation could well be permanent. We were spared some of the pain seen in movies, however, where the onset of the sea voyage usually shows the ever-widening gap between the dock and the ship as it ever-so-slowly yet relentlessly pulls away from the shore, producing an unbridgeable gulf between those who go and those who stay. In our case, the *Mauretania* was waiting at the dock, but its move away from the shore would not occur until quite a bit later, long after visitors had left.

It wasn't very long before I was cleared to go aboard the humongous ship. After the official document checks, I had no trouble finding my cabin;

Chapter 20

Cunard-White Star's Mauretania, *which brought Peter to the U.S. (The Open Agency, Ltd.).*

it was located at the lowest possible level of the ship, three decks down, without a porthole, a level sometimes called "steerage" in honor of the mechanical equipment and storage facilities that usually live in the cavernous spaces below the waterline. After leaving my suitcase in the cabin, I climbed back to the promenade deck where travelers and visitors were milling about. There, I met Tante Lily, who had gotten a visitor's pass. She introduced me to a portly gentleman in a wheelchair whom I had met years before and to his skinny but elegant wife. His name was Darius Milhaud; he was a polio victim and paralyzed from the waist down. Though I did not know it then, he was a world-famous composer and a great exponent of polytonal music, working alongside such cutting edge composers as Honegger and others in what was dawning as a new age for music. He was yet another soul Madame had protected during France's dark years. As they were traveling first class and I was in steerage, they agreed to watch over me during the crossing, enabling me to have access to those hallowed precincts on the ship the Brits had declared off limits to riff-raff like me. My passport to these areas would be my role as the family helper who would wheel Monsieur Milhaud around the ship. Needless to say, this arrangement was perfectly okay with me!

The actual departure was anticlimactic, because Tante Lily and I had exhausted our emotional reservoirs with the adieus that had taken place before we had boarded the ship. Once the ship left the harbor and made its way to open sea, I returned to my cabin. For the first time, I noticed what was in the room. There were two double-deck bunk beds and a sink. The commode was outside, to be shared with the other steerage class denizens, as were all bathing facilities. Without a porthole, we had no way to tell that we were below the water line, but the cabin felt claustrophobic nonetheless. It was badly lit and badly ventilated. But I didn't care — I was going to America!

My cabin mate, a large, heavy-boned African-American, didn't care either. He was gregarious, very cheerful and I could not understand a word he was saying. A short time later, I found out that the "King's English" I had learned in the French schools was not how one speaks in the United States. But by the end of the crossing, he and I would manage to communicate very well indeed.

That first evening, before the dinner service, he introduced me to something he called "scotch." He had a whole bottle of the stuff, and we proceeded to share it, slug for slug, until the bottle was empty. After that, the subjects of food, dinner or anything else became entirely academic. Communication was clearly no longer the problem! We were focused entirely on trying to stop the spinning of our heads and testing our capacity to expel the evil brew from our systems. Since I weighed less than my cabin mate and was nimbler as well as younger, I took the upper bunk. As there was tacit agreement between us on this matter, I climbed up and rolled into a fetal position. I thought that if I lay very, very still, there was a chance that the boat might stop rocking and the rest of me might settle down. Alas, neither the ship nor my body would heed my wishes. I somehow managed to reach the promenade deck, where I heaved my contribution to the English Channel, over and over again. I vowed that scotch would be an acquired taste which I would avoid diligently for the rest of my life! (In fact, I had no trouble staying true to that promise for better than 60 years, until I was persuaded to try a couple of single-malt scotches during a visit to Northern Scotland. Much as I hate to admit it, when I finally tried it, I loved the quaff ... it even reminded me of cognac, something any self-respecting Frenchman would consider sacrilegious.)

The next morning, with the turbulent English Channel behind us and the scotch finally ejected from my system, I managed to keep breakfast down. Indeed, I was totally intrigued by the crunchy stuff called "cereal" that was being served. I was amazed that this passed for food in such a luxurious setting, but I tried some with more than a little apprehension. Once I got used to the crunchy texture and I could see that everybody else emitted the same sounds, I decided that, as silly as this all was, I really liked the stuff. Ah, these Brits.

In the course of my first day at sea, I noticed that I was narrowly confined with my fellow steerage mates to a relatively small portion of the ship. There were doors or other kinds of barriers everywhere that told us, with very little subtlety, exactly where we did not belong. The British are really exquisitely and uniquely talented in making class distinctions, then driving the point home by hermetically sequestering people in the designated spaces where they belonged. Fortunately, I had an out — The Milhauds. They had not forgotten about me, and right after breakfast they managed to establish contact. They fished me out from the bottom of the ship and enabled me to come up to the upper decks where I could sense the ocean and partake in the pampering of cruising first class.

This was truly an elegant experience, one that lived up to all the wondrous imagery of glamorous transatlantic travel. Pushing the wheelchair around the decks, smiling non-stop while keeping Darius Milhaud and his wife company was indeed a small price to pay for this opportunity to taste the more genteel aspects of seaborne society. My cabin mate was fascinated by my experiences on the upper decks, and each night he insisted that I describe each moment to him so he could live vicariously through me. As enticement, he offered up another bottle of scotch but, as I was still under the spell of my last experience, I was able to successfully resist his entreaties. And so, the days on board flew by, punctuated by sumptuous meals and organized activities. I particularly enjoyed sloshing around the small swimming pool on the lowest deck of the big ship. The latter had assumed the movements of the ocean and this was as much fun as any amusement park ride.

I found high tea, on the other hand, very formal and unbearably boring. But after dinner, the traditional "horse racing" games, which passed for gambling, were fascinating. They were loud and brought out the enthusiasm and competitive spirit among the passengers. Uniformed ship stewards moved wooden horses along a cloth track stretched out in the ship's grand salon. The horses were moved in accordance with the outcome of rolls of the dice. It was usually in the middle of this activity that I was expected to disappear and descend into my dungeon. This was something I always did promptly and without arguments ... or even regrets. I was a very good boy; after all, I had to uphold the reputation and the decorum of both the Milhaud and the de Bonnefoy families.

I spent a lot of time at the stern of the great liner, below the promenade deck, watching its powerful screws inexorably carving a path through the ocean as the ship brought me closer and closer to my new life. In fact, the time at sea elapsed like an ephemeral mirage. It was not long before land was finally in sight and my arrival in New York City was imminent. This was the end of a journey that had started so long ago under the Brandenburg Gate.

The ship glided past the "Lady with the Torch" in New York Harbor. Like so many who have experienced this moment, it was exhilarating. It triggered an orgy of feelings that words could not express. While I could not read the verse on the pedestal of the gigantic statue, I had memorized the words long ago. Emma Lazarus's 1883 poem "The New Colossus," inspired by the ancient Greek statue, the Colossus of Rhodes, reads as follows:

> Not like the brazen giant of Greek fame,
> With conquering limbs astride from land to land;
> Here at our sea-washed, sunset gates shall stand
> A mighty woman with a torch, whose flame
> Is the imprisoned lightning, and her name
> Mother of Exiles. From her beacon-hand
> Glows world-wide welcome; her mild eyes command
> The air-bridged harbor that twin cities frame.
> "Keep ancient lands, your storied pomp!" cries she
> With silent lips. "Give me your tired, your poor,
> Your huddled masses yearning to breathe free,
> The wretched refuse of your teeming shore.
> Send these, the homeless, tempest-tost to me,
> I lift my lamp beside the golden door!"

Chapter 20

Statue of Liberty.

While my nearly adult eyes beheld the neo-classic monumental sculpture that the French had gifted to America as a mark of undying friendship, my still-childish mind's eye beheld the image of a cartoon strip that I could not extricate from the trivia in my mind. I saw Mickey Mouse, heroically rescuing a victim who had haplessly landed on the top of the statue.

Actually, the symbolism was perfect. I too had been rescued, and I had finally reached safety.

Epilogue

The *Mauretania* came to rest, docking in America at a debarkation pier jutting into the Hudson River on the West Side of Manhattan. Spring was gone and June gave a hint of what New York's stifling summer heat would be like. Once off the ship, I entered the enormous disembarkation hall, filled to capacity with thousands of confused yet jubilant immigrants like me. Unlike many, I had no trouble with customs, having left the old world with only one pair of underwear, a comb, a toothbrush, a pocket knife, a sweater and a couple of books — certainly no money, jewelry or alcohol. But I had been reborn in a vastly different world. This would be the slice of my life where I would learn a new language and bond with my new family. After what seemed like a long wait, Lotte and Al found me amidst the crowds. They would become the universal source of all the knowledge I would need as I entered the mainstream of American life.

We walked out of the large shed on the Cunard-White Star pier to where they had parked under the West Side Highway. They were driving a 1939 Pontiac station wagon, the kind with a wood-paneled body. They apologized for the age of the car, but to me it was glorious. It had a radio! Not only that, it also had an automatic transmission and was a pretty green color. And that was just the first of the many wonders to come.

We found our way across the Queensboro Bridge. I had never seen a bridge that big, nor so many buildings that high. Lines of cars, parkways feeding into boulevards, roads lined with billboards ... this was new and different, presenting a kaleidoscope of shapes and colors. These new experiences left me speechless and in a state of awe. While we drove, Lotte talked about the realities of life in the United States, about their financial condition, about each of our responsibilities, about the family and about

Epilogue

Reunion with the de Bonnefoy family — (left to right) Albertine Garrig, Marianne Kory, Marthou Roulet, Countess Alix de Bonnefoy and Peter (Paris, France, circa 1957).

what it meant to be an American. She talked about her job, her daily commute to Wall Street, Al's business and how I would fit into all this.

We emerged on Queens Boulevard, where we stopped for ice cream at a large Howard Johnsons, the kind that sold 28 flavors. What an experience! America indeed was the new world. It is difficult to imagine the impact of such an establishment on a waif who had journeyed so long and so far, coming from a continent where things like ice cream had become nearly extinct.

I would soon encounter many other exposures to American foods, all of which were wondrous temptations for anyone who had been deprived for so long. White Castle and White Tower burgers were particularly beguiling, both in terms of their taste and how they were served. This was, of course, the dawn of the fast food era. My special joy was to walk the streets of Manhattan and stop impulsively by one of the juice and hot dog stands that dotted the sidewalks, tasting what seemed to be a bottomless supply of food, all wrapped in sauerkraut and relish!

More importantly, I immersed myself in New York, learning English quickly and adding new skills to my development as an American. Yet my turbulent past was still there, and presented itself in the form of unexpected responses to perfectly unremarkable experiences. For example, the protective shield I had laboriously created during the war years to insulate me from troublesome emotions was shattered by my overreaction to the design of the New York bus windows. Their relatively small size was reminiscent more of an airplane than a tramway, and they felt claustrophobic. This struck me when I first arrived in New York City, and I couldn't help but compare them with the much wider and more generous French bus windows. Why should this matter to me? Well, it was through one of those large windows that I had last seen my parents, held captive by the Germans in the St. Girons town square. That memory will always remain a hostage of my psyche.

Yet there were more positive and equally powerful impressions on my unspoiled senses. The exuberant use of light and color, for example, was inescapable. Neon lights were like magic to me. Europe was still essentially drab after the war. Cars were mostly gray or black, signs were sparse and restrained and public lighting was, to say the least, subdued. The climax of this visual assault on the senses by neon signs, billboards and kinetic commercial advertising creations was Times Square. The gigantic displays that rose to the status of icons in the district were not only extremely exciting, but they inspired me, presaging my future passion with public architecture and urban design.

Lotte and Al lived in Laurelton/Rosedale, a Queens, New York, neighborhood. My new home was a modest, two-story Tudor-styled house on a typical, tree-lined street flanked with similarly English-styled homes. The house had a basement, and it was in that basement that they lived. I was to roost there in an alcove carved out of the living space. The rest of the house was rented to an English couple, and the rent helped pay the mortgage. Lotte was constantly upset about the couple's housekeeping habits, which she felt were disastrous in terms of the excruciating standards of cleanliness and neatness imposed by her German upbringing. Much as the Brits had been solid Allies during the war and the tenants exhibited

Epilogue

all of the values that had endeared that nation to us, Lotte could not stomach their slovenliness and the way they were treating her property. She was inconsolable, and lived for the day when she and Al could regain control of their entire home.

From day one, I made it my mission to comply with Lotte's agenda for my introduction to American life. I found out very quickly that, along with all the sweetness and honey, everybody in America worked. So I got a summer job as a sign painter. In effect, I learned a trade, I earned some money, I got to drink something called Pepsi and my language skills got a real boost. Every morning, my boss would ask me, "How d'you feel?"; I would dutifully give my forearm a squeeze and inform him that everything felt fine. The signs I painted taught me the meaning of "real estate," a term that was strange to me when translated literally … how could an estate be "unreal"?

The next item on the agenda was to prepare for citizenship. I began attending evening classes at Washington Irving High School in Manhattan three times a week to learn English, American history and the essentials of America's constitutional democracy. I also learned how to navigate New York City, both on foot and on the subway (above and below ground). Finally, I was indoctrinated in a variety of civic subjects, such as voting procedures, the education system, money management and the organization of government at all levels. To facilitate the familiarization process, I was introduced to a couple who lived in Greenwich Village and who were part of a volunteer organization dedicated to inuring new arrivals to life in America. They became, along with my family, trusted mentors and friends in my evolution to citizenship.

I had to learn English almost from scratch, as the "King's English" that I was taught in France was of very little help. It would take some time before I could communicate with ease. Though I did not appreciate it at the time, the fact that there was no one within my family or my circle of acquaintances who spoke French was ultimately a blessing … there was no option. I simply HAD to learn English!

It was decided that I would start high school in the fall of 1948, but at what school and, even trickier, in what grade? In terms of academic knowledge, I was closer to a college sophomore, but in terms of language

Epilogue

Peter (second row, center) on the Far Rockaway Swim Team (New York, circa 1948).

skills I was still in kindergarten. The Solomon-like solution was to have me start as a senior in the nearest high school, Far Rockaway High. The regents' examinations at the end of the year would then determine whether I would graduate and go on to college or spend more time in high school. Now, with a summer job secured, citizenship indoctrination under my belt and school decided on, I was ready for my new life to begin. I had new clothes, I had spent time with Jean Ulman, my sponsor, and struck an arrangement with her for a $75 per-month allowance, beginning the day I started school.

In school, I was more advanced than most in geometry, algebra, and physics; art was, as usual, a snap; strangely, English was not a problem, as I enjoyed learning from the poetry that made up a substantial portion of the course plan, but I had some problems with civics and history. I was able to overcome my inability to absorb the massive history text by purchasing Andre Maurois's encyclopedic *Histoire des Etats Unis* and doing my reading in French. Civics was even more difficult, as I came from a

Epilogue

culture where Malthusian theory and concepts like "diminishing returns," the teachings of John Maynard Keynes, and the whole field of economics were subjects not normally part of a European education curriculum.

I could not relate to American sports such as football, baseball and the like. For this reason, to avoid becoming an athletic wallflower, I tried out for the swimming team and was accepted ... entitling me to hours of practice and thousands of laps in the high school pool. This also earned me a new circle of friends. My circle was further broadened thanks to my best friend, Ted Strauss, who invited me to join something called a fraternity, another completely new experience for me.

Ted and I became inseparable. We both wanted to become architects, we lived in the same neighborhood and we shared in a small business that involved employing fellow students — usually high school juniors — to wash and Simonize cars. The enterprise was very successful — we had some 20 workers, all recruited from the lower grades in school, and we generated enough income to purchase a full range of equipment that let us dominate the neighborhood market. Alas, it all came to an end with the end of the school year and our graduation.

We had both passed our regent's exams. Ted's family could afford college, and he was accepted at Pratt Institute. He was on his way to a career in architecture. I had more of a struggle. Private college was simply unaffordable, and this level of help was not in my arrangement with Jean Ulman. Scholarships were out of the question as well ... I simply was not that good a student. With only one avenue left, I applied to the City of New York Public University System. Queens College rejected my application because I was not a U.S. citizen; Brooklyn College did not have that requirement, but in taking the entrance exam I inked in the wrong bubble on the test score sheet, thereby shifting all the answers by one hole. The consequence was predictable: I was not accepted. The leading school in the system was City College (CCNY). It had the most challenging and difficult entrance examination, but there was no citizenship requirement. My admission to the tuition-free institution was considered unlikely, as fewer than one third of the applicants were accepted and only a small percentage of those accepted survived the first two years. The system was designed to weed out all but the best, but I had no choice but to go for it. To my amazement, I scored sufficiently high on the marathon entrance exam and was accepted.

Epilogue

By that time, Aunt Lotte had turned into a blend of my mother and Tante Lily. There were, however, some notable differences. Lotte was just as obsessive as my mother had been about thrift and cleanliness and just as in charge of everything as Tante Lily, but I somehow always felt that I must have been a burden to her. She and her husband were empty nesters. Their only child, a daughter, was divorced and lived in a neighboring town. My arrival turned the clock back, as Lotte and Al were once again faced with the responsibilities of a new dependent ... and a teenager at that! The empty nest had acquired an unusual addition — a culturally incompatible war orphan not used to bathing regularly and unaccustomed to changing his underwear daily.

Adding to this was a long list of pressures that weighed on Lotte. Not only did the company where she worked on Wall Street require her to commute daily from Long Island into Manhattan on the Long Island Railroad, but the demands of her lofty position at the Hanseatic Corporation required impeccable business attire at all times. In addition, the management of the family's finances and the normal housekeeping chores all made life difficult for her, as she felt that too many of these burdens fell on her shoulders. She felt like a victim. It wasn't that Uncle Al didn't help. He did. He brought in his fair share of the family's income; it was just that he wasn't as focused as Lotte on the essential details. All this inevitably caused conflicts that made living in that household unpleasant.

On the one hand, Lottie was proud of the fact that she, more than anyone, had been responsible for rescuing me from the clutches of an overzealous Jewish establishment in Europe and saving me from the fate that awaited me there. On the other hand, my insertion into their life upset their well-ordered routines. They really disliked many of the friends I brought into the house and were extremely judgmental of their appearance. I, of course, liked everybody and everything, as I used life in postwar Europe as my standard of comparison.

Shortly after I arrived in the U.S., the house in Laurelton was sold, and a new, less expensive house in the neighboring community of Valley-Stream, outside New York City in Nassau County, was purchased. More affordable housing costs got rid of the pesky tenants, making it possible for me to graduate from an alcove in a basement to a real room all my own. I still felt that I was a burden on Lotte and Al — part of the problem, not the solution. This caused me to eagerly seek out space in the school's dormitory, Army Hall, when I started college. As an ultimate irony, Army Hall had originally served as an orphanage. I had come full circle!

CCNY did not have a school, nor even a department, of architecture at that time. But there was desire in the administration to evolve such a course of study. Three newcomers and I agreed to become guinea pigs, and the dean of students, Dean Gottschalk, went to work in implementing an ad-hoc curriculum. The degree was to be a Bachelor of Science in architecture, and it would not be accredited at first but it would shadow the course of study generally offered by schools of architecture throughout the United States. There would be great emphasis on engineering, with a selection of courses closely corresponding to those provided by City College for its civil engineering graduates.

In addition to my regular courses, my mentors at CCNY insisted that I get rid of my horrendous French accent. This meant that I would be committed, body and soul, into a speech clinic throughout my stay at City College — six supervised hours a week, matched by an equal number of hours of practice in front of a mirror. For hours on end, I practiced those difficult and uniquely American sounds so completely foreign to the French. The American "th" was difficult, but it was the "r" that qualified as the main culprit in frustrating the school's obsession to graduate only those who spoke perfect English. Thus, no foreign accents were tolerated and the prospects for graduation, even for some New Yorkers, was seriously compromised if they could not rid themselves of such local speech aberrations as the infamous "n-g" click from LON*GG* Island residents or the Brooklyn denizens who were unable to eliminate the "r" when pronouncing the word "oil," turning it into "earl" instead of the viscous substance we use on machinery!

In spite of all the challenges, I graduated from City College in 1953. Like a conditioned reflex, my 1-A classification in the Selective Service System reared its ugly head and I was drafted into the U.S. Army and sent for training in the deep South. To complicate things even more, I had fallen in love and married Marianne Greene, and life changed dramatically once again. We set up housekeeping in Enterprise, Alabama, which was near my Army post, Camp Rucker. Marianne employed her magna cum laude degree in philosophy to educate little kids at the local school, and I learned to kill enemy soldiers. Naturally, many hours of KP duty were part of my indoctrination, and I was called upon to scrub what may have

Epilogue

been the very same pots that had engulfed my Aunt Lotte when she had served as a WAC a dozen or so years earlier.

Although I had been drafted during the Korean conflict, kismet was still watching over me. The day my unit was scheduled to be flown to the Far East, a decision had finally been made regarding the shape of the negotiation table allowing the Communists to return to the talks, a cease-fire was declared and my trip was canceled. The politicians may have referred to Korea as a police action, but make no mistake, it was a war.

Three of my best friends from Auriac had been killed in the bloody battle of Dien Bien Phu in Vietnam. Elie, Albertine's son, Maurice Coret, the son of Auriac's grocer, and so many other boys I knew in school would disappear in Vietnam during the ill-fated attempt by France to reassert its domination over Indochina against Ho Chi Minh's strong urge for the colony's independence.

The fate of so many of my friends from the orphanages would not be any different. Israel became a state in May of 1948, and the *OSE* accelerated the time frame for their relocation to Israel, along with all the other able-bodied men under their control. Once there, my friends had indeed been made to join the army to fight yet another war, and I never heard from them again.

But I had been fortunate. Unlike so many of my childhood friends, I was safe and secure, completing my military obligation on U.S. soil until my honorable discharge in 1955. In the process, I would become an American citizen and change my name from Korytowski to Kory.

The years ... no, the decades ... would pass so quickly. I would have the opportunity to get to know many from my father's side of the family, but I would learn the fate of most from my mother's side only after they had passed away. My French family would stay in touch, but time and distance would take its toll. And, probably saddest of all, I would never have predicted the awful conflict that would irreparably chill my relationship with Lotte and Al.

The antipathy felt by many Jews against anything German is, of course, legend. But Lotte was an extreme example. She bore an unmitigated and obsessive hatred of anything German. Thus, no Volkswagens, Rhine wines, Zeilinger cutlery or anything else of German provenance was allowed in her home. I bore the brunt of this obsession when Marianne and I went to Europe for our honeymoon.

We had booked a transatlantic voyage on the cruise ship *Italia*. We had a lovely crossing; we enjoyed every moment of it, befriended our cabin steward, Herbert, and participated in all the silly games that pass the time at sea. I described all of that in letters to my aunt, naturally hoping she might vicariously share the experience with us. After we returned, an unusually long time passed with no answer to our letters, and calls went unreturned. Eventually, my uncle answered the phone only to inform me that Lotte did not want to talk to me. I had no idea what horrendous sin I had perpetrated to justify so drastic a reaction from her, but my uncle suggested that if I thought about it for a while, I would probably figure it out. He was right. I realized that, in my letters home, I had written lavishly about how nice the staff on the boat had been, completely overlooking the fact that they were German. How could I have been so insensitive!

I have never been able to understand the magnitude of Lotte's outrage, given that she and Al had left Germany and reached safety in the U.S. long before Hitler came to power. They had never suffered the pains of war and could only relate to the horrendous events in Europe through remote means of communication. Despite these aberrations, I will never forget that she was the one who brought me to America and showed me the ways of the new world.

Over the years, Lotte and Al continued to participate in the outward population shifts from the central city to the outer suburban rings as these areas reached their sociological tipping point toward a progressively Afro-American population. Their eastward trek on Long Island finally ended when they bought a post–Levittown split-level house in Massapequa.

Uncle Al eventually left the Kodak Company and its pristine corporate self-image to join a friend in expanding a small automotive ignition repair business. He died of a heart attack in 1967. After his death, Lotte returned to Rockville Center and lived there in relative seclusion until she died in her mid-eighties.

My father's twin sister, Lillie, married a Romanian Jew and had two boys, Bernie and Larry. The eldest, Bernie, was born in Romania, and Larry was born in Palestine, thus a true Sabra. Larry grew up in a kibbutz and served in the Israeli army. Eventually, the family left this pioneering land for the United States. On his way to U.S. citizenship, Bernie immersed

Epilogue

himself in a career with National Cash Register (NCR) in Dayton, Ohio. He did well there as a technical sales representative and retired successfully after more than 25 years of service. (It has now been more than 30 years since I last saw him.) Larry started his own business, a highly sought-after and respected auto-repair operation. Larry and Bernie had changed their names from Markowitz to Martin and, shortly after I arrived in the United States, Larry married my aunt Lotte's daughter — and his first cousin — Deena, who had recently divorced a California architect and was living with David, her five-year-old son from that marriage. The first child from her marriage to Larry was a daughter, Judith. In short order, two very good-looking brothers, Michael and Donald, followed. The fact that Larry and Deena were first cousins may have been the reason that Judy developed a rare blood disorder that manifested itself during her teens in the form of near blindness. Eventually, this led to her death in 1975, before her 30th birthday.

My father's sister, Lucy, became an indefatigable soldier in the quixotic battle for reparation payments from the German government. I recall seeing long letters she had sent to the maze of agencies charged with implementing the distribution of German reparation payments. She had even hired a German attorney in this effort. While she may have had some success in her efforts, I never saw, nor did I care to receive, one cent from these funds. In fact, I have always considered it to be blood money!

In spite of my uncle Fritz's playboy lifestyle as a young man, he eventually managed to marry a lady named Erna, who was extremely devoted to him and who, for some reason, found it entertaining to constantly pinch my buttocks, something I detested! They had no children, and when they immigrated to America they joined in the millenary store that Erna's family had opened some years earlier in Wilmington, Delaware. Fritz eventually developed a bad shoulder. It was an unremitting mystery ailment that was so painful that he became a virtual invalid and had to give up his participation in the business. He retired, and I eventually lost touch with that twig of the family tree.

I never knew my mother's family very well, as I was too young when the emigration out of Europe started. But, one evening a few years ago, when I had just begun to write these recollections of my childhood, I received a call from a stranger — Michal Frostig — asking if my name had once been Korytowski. I was delighted to learn that Michal was my second cousin, the daughter of Heine, who was the son of Kethe, one of my

Epilogue

mother's sisters. They had heard that I had made it out of Germany after the war, and asked Michal to try to find me when she and her husband, Gil, relocated from Israel to the U.S. They now live in California's Silicon Valley, where Gil is a senior executive with Intel. Since that first telephone conversation, we have spent many hours getting better acquainted, both on the telephone and through e-mails. Joyce and I visited with them in Sunnyvale, California, and we found this ex–Israeli twig of my family to be amazingly warm, welcoming and intelligent. Thanks to Michal, I now know what has happened to my mother's four sisters: Kethe, Magda, Gertrud and Rosel.

Sadly, Michal's grandmother Kethe never made it out of Europe, but her son Heine lived a full life in Israel and had two daughters, Michal and Ronit. By the time Michal found me, Heine was deathly ill and very weak. We were, however, able to speak by phone several times. A decade older than me, he had fond memories of the times we played together before the war tore our family apart. As a child, Heine's great passion was model trains. He passed this passion on to me, and trains, with all their accoutrements, rapidly gained a hallowed place in my own world of expectations. As I surely have mentioned before, I had always wanted a model train set full of passenger cars, freight cars, different kinds of locomotives and, of course, all the landscape features, and signaling devices. It had to be electric, not wind-up, with lots of tracks, switches, and control devices, just like Heine's set, which took up at least half a bedroom. Alas, all I ever got was the wind-up, spring-activated kind and a figure-eight track! While I will always feel a sense of deprivation for not having my very own train set, I am grateful for something far more important—I had an opportunity to have one last chat with Heine before he passed away. We did not talk about trains or toys; we were not about to squander Heine's limited energy on anything so trivial. We talked mostly about our respective families and we could not resist sharing our awe at being able to communicate over the enormous gulf between Miami, Florida, and Haifa, Israel, and the even greater gulf in time that we had covered, starting in the 1930s in Europe to now, well into the second millennium.

Magda survived the Second World War and immigrated to the United States, where she lived in New York until her death in 1968.

Trude was a spinster, so it fell on her to watch over the family's children. Quite remarkably, Trude lived in Israel for over 50 years without ever

Epilogue

learning a word of Hebrew. She spoke only German and spent all her time in a quintessentially German compound that was maintained like a colony.

Rose was killed during an Italian air raid on Tel Aviv in 1940. Her daughter, Aviva, still lives in Israel. She is diligently orthodox and strictly observant of Jewish religious rites and customs. Nearly 90, she has a remarkable grip on the history of our family. (She, and Michael's sister Ronit, who has an almost encyclopedic knowledge of the family, was of immeasurable help to me in piecing together this part of the tale.) Following gentle prodding from Michal to go to Israel and meet Aviva, I softened my *OSE*-induced prejudices about Israel and agreed to visit there. Our room during our stay in Jerusalem was at the stately King David Hotel. It was there, in the hotel's elaborate lobby, that I met Aviva, my first cousin.

As a show of appreciation for his services during the war, Oncle Nino had been placed in charge of rationing and food distribution for the Department de l'Haute Garonne, which includes the Toulouse region. Given the dire shortages that prevailed at that time, this was a position of considerable influence and importance. He was later appointed chief of police for the Paris region. I saw Oncle Nino one last time, around 1960. We had lunch in a Paris bistro. He was past his mid-seventies at that time, living with an Ethiopian mistress and dealing, on God knows what basis, with Muammar Qaddafi. At the end of lunch, he grudgingly conceded that, because of his advancing age, he was considering giving up skydiving!

During the same visit, Marianne and I visited Tante Lily, who was still working full-time for an agency in Paris dedicated to helping children. As soon as she heard we were coming, she organized everything. She provided us with a small car, a *Quatre Chevaux Renault*, to use during our stay. There were two stops I was hoping to make; one was to visit the château in Auriac, which we could not do, as it was abandoned and locked up; the other was to catch up with Marthou.

Marthou had married Guy Roullet, the scion of the Denis Mounier Cognac family, and they had a lovely daughter, Dominique, and an adopted son, Olivier. They lived in a large mansion in the center of the city of Cognac. The ancestral brew they distilled ranked with that of their intimate friends, the Martells, the Hennessys and the Remy Martins. We visited the distillery and were fascinated by the process that took place in

Epilogue

the traditional copper onion-shaped vats where unpurified grape marc was progressively turned into brandy, only to be further distilled so that the brew could ultimately emerge as three- and five-star VSOP Cognac.

To market their product, Guy had a long relationship with Carillon Frères, an international spirit importer and distributor. Shortly after our visit to France, the company organized a trip to New York for the Roullet family. It was glamorous, and I was part of it! They stayed in an outrageously luxurious suite at the St. Regis Hotel. They had most of their meals at the prestigious eateries showcased by the Restaurant Associates collection of epicurean masterpieces that were all the rage in New York at that time, and they got a good sample of the city's clubs and theatrical entertainment establishments.

But Marthou wanted one more kind of experience: a genuine American meal. She asked me to consult with the Carillon people on how to best satisfy this mandate. We agreed that Gallagher's Steak House in the middle of Times Square, famous for its huge slabs of beef seared over sizzling open flames, would be the ideal venue, best evoking how the cowboys ate in the American Old West. Rounding out the meal would be a lowly baked potato in its unpeeled state, corn on the cob (which no self-respecting Frenchman would serve, except as food for hogs), and vegetables like broccoli (unheard of in France). All of this made it a meal that was as foreign to the refined French culinary culture as it was common in the United States.

Guy was a hopelessly addicted anglophile, something that accounted for his dapper attire, his aristocratic demeanor and his leisure-time predilections. He loved English tweed and fast cars. Tragically, the latter passion eventually led to his death. He fatally crashed his Jaguar while speeding on a highway between Cognac and Paris. Marthou did not survive him by long. She died of cervical cancer.

The last time I saw Tante Lily was at a dinner in a Paris restaurant shortly before Marthou died. She had invited Albertine, who was thrilled to see me and meet Marianne. This was also an extraordinary outing for her, coming from the seclusion of her retirement in Toulouse.

All that is left now are the memories, which have become part of me and are permanently etched in my mind.

Epilogue

When I began writing this memoir, I felt the need to travel back to the places where I had lived as a child. I consider the re-creation of the memories of those times to be the ultimate manifestation of nostalgia, so visiting the neighborhoods of my childhood was an experience that I was looking forward to with great trepidation. Nonetheless, Joyce and I rented a car in Paris and drove to Brussels. We spent the night in a lovely, small, luxurious hotel in the center of the city, and the following morning we set out to find the neighborhood where I had lived so many years earlier. I remembered that the *Parc Josaphat* wrapped itself around much of the area where I had lived, and it turned out to be a handy landmark for finding Rue Des Coteaux. Number 323 was a narrow, two-story row house, just like all the others, on what seemed to be a predominantly blue-collar street. It was mid-morning of a grayish day, so common in Belgium. Nothing I saw seemed familiar. Nevertheless, having come this far, we proceeded to climb the four steps that created a stoop for the front door. With mixed feelings, I rang the bell. The door opened, and a somewhat disheveled man, who we must have awakened from a siesta, tried as best he could to make us feel welcome. His wife was not home, but he was fascinated to learn that I had lived in the house before the war and he invited us in. I clearly underestimated the extent of his interest, because by the time we had completed our survey of the living room, he had invited some neighbors over who remembered my parents. It was both a fascinating and intriguing peek into a past that no longer existed, and which I barely remembered.

The place felt very strange. It was the right house; the non-functional fireplace with its mantelpiece where my mother had left my father's Iron Cross was still in one corner of the living room. And that room still opened to the street, with the same balcony from which, to my parents' dismay, I gained popularity by giving my toys away. But the house on Rue Des Coteaux was dirty and ill-kept. This was something my mother would never have tolerated! The furnishings were totally incongruous with the architectural skills possessed by my father. The most astounding difference, however, was that the house had somehow shrunk by half— it was not the home I remembered, it was now just another blue-collar worker's home on a street of row houses. We eschewed a tour of the bedrooms, but I had to see the little backyard. It held such special meaning for me. It was there that I finally managed to reach the other end of the bridge that spanned the years since I had last seen the place. Miraculously, the little vegetable garden that had served to supplement our food rations was still there and so was the masonry wall that enclosed the yard. Even the barrel tiles that capped the wall were still there. I'll never forget how these tiles made it possible for me to lie on top of the wall like a lizard, and take advantage of the rare and precious moments when the sun deigned to make an appearance in this fundamentally gray environment. In fact, the sun was so scarce in Brussels and the rains so constant that the city was known indelicately as the "Piss-Pot of Europe." I recalled how, anytime the sun was shining, I would lie on top of that wall for as long as possible, pondering the nature of life and the world into which I had been born.

Yes, many of these aspects of our little house were still there, but they all seemed strangely small and a little foreign — different from the memory my mind had preserved all these years. It felt very cramped and ill-maintained compared to how I live today or, more importantly, how I thought I had lived in 1939. But this, I hasten to mention, was not supposed to be a scientific or forensic analysis into a long gone past. It was merely an exercise in nostalgia. I just wanted to see the extent to which memories could be recreated by revisiting familiar places.

I am sorry to say that this rarely works. It was not that the neighborhood had changed; it probably hadn't. No, the truth is that it was I who had changed and, as a result, the place looked and felt very different from the perceptions I had nurtured in my mind over so many years. Indeed, as Thomas Wolfe so wisely proclaimed, "You can't go home again." And, just in case I needed a further reminder, we headed to Auriac.

The château was in shambles — nearly unrecognizable. It looked deserted. We parked on the street beside the château, just off the village square. The large sycamores still stood in the back courtyard, but I couldn't bring myself to get out of the car. Another car pulled up and a man got out and started to unlock the back gate. Joyce insisted that I approach him and ask if he knew anything about the château's current ownership. When I began explaining that I had lived there during the war, he exclaimed, "*Pierrot?*" It was Olivier, Marthou's adopted son. Although we had never met, he had heard all the stories of the war years from his family.

He was clearly the "lord of the manor," using the name de Bonnefoy, and most anxious to show us around. At first glance, it appeared that he lived there alone, except for a threatening pack of a dozen enormous, ill-kept

Epilogue

howling dogs, evocative of Arthur Conan Doyle's "The Hound of the Baskervilles." The château was entirely devoid of the spirit, activity level and buzz that had prevailed during the war. Evidence of neglect was everywhere. The dirt and the extent of disarray defied description and viscerally offended my sensibilities. The fact that poor Olivier seemed totally oblivious to this added to my chagrin and filled me with regrets and an undefined sense of guilt. He invited us to spend the night, but thankfully, we had already made reservations at another château about 20 kilometers from there, and took our leave with a promise to return again on our next trip to France.

When we arrived at the Château de Garevaques, we met Marie-Christine Combes, who had turned her ancestral home into a charming boutique hotel. Her family had lived there since the 1500s and, like so many of today's French noble families, they found that they could only afford the upkeep on the family estate if it could produce revenue. Over dinner, I told her of my years in Auriac and, just like Olivier, she exclaimed, *"Pierrot?"* Also a postwar child, she was a distant cousin of the de Bonnefoys, and had heard the stories from her mother, who had been a close friend of Marthou (see photo on page 111).

Over the course of the next few days, we caught up on so much of what had happened in Auriac. Marie-Christine invited Dominique to join us for dinner, which was quite emotional for me, as I realized that she was the last of the de Bonnefoy family ... except, that is, for Olivier. He, as it turned out, was rumored to be Nino's love child from his union with his Ethiopian mistress, but no one really knew for sure.

I saw Marie-Christine and her family again on a subsequent trip to France. Joyce and I stayed in Paris at the Hotel du Pont, named after the famous 16th century bridge over the Seine. On that occasion, I hosted a mini-banquet at the hotel for Marie-Christine, her husband, Claude, and her mother, Dédé, who had traveled from the southwest of France to Paris to visit with us. Dédé was the star of the event. Her recollections of Marthou and the war years were fascinating. We recorded them so that, every now and again, we might resurrect the world and the times as she had experienced it.

Meeting Olivier came with an unexpected dividend. A few years after our visit, he received a phone call from my boyhood friend from Mane, Robert Soula, who was hoping to reconnect with people from his past. He gave Robert our phone number and, one evening out of the blue, I got a call from Robert. He had moved to Les Landes, near Biarritz, and had devoted his career to the preparation and marketing of duck *foie gras*. Without hesitation, Joyce and I planned another trip to France.

Some 60 years had elapsed since we had last seen each other. Robert was retired, my French had grown a little rusty, but it was such fun for our wives to meet and to meet Robert's family, including his daughter Catherine, her husband and his grandson. We had dinner at one of the charming *auberges* (country inn restaurants), which are so prevalent in the Beaune region of France. Robert's son-in-law displayed an uncommon level of wine knowledge and masterfully guided us through the complicated process of decanting the wine and judging, with a flourish, the consistency of the cork and the quality of the wine. Even more fun was recollecting some of the misadventures from when Robert and I were kids. Of course, my encounter with the sled came up, and he regaled us with many more stories of the times we had shared so long ago. One that I had forgotten was indeed hilarious; he told of the time we tried to roast potatoes in a pit over an open fire and my pants caught on fire. He had to rip them off me. Needless to say, the walk back home — with my bottom exposed — and the reaction of my mother, hysterical as usual, provided fodder for ridicule at my expense for years to come!

While we easily resumed our friendship over dinner and a few more visits, the gulf of time and the differences in our cultures took their toll. The kind of special bond that had existed during the war years was missing, despite our best intentions to maintain our friendship.

As for me, I've lived an amazing, full life — three wives, two children, four grandchildren, and a rewarding career replete with success and good health.

After my military service, Marianne and I moved to Cincinnati, where I started my career in the Slum Clearance Division of the city manager's office. It was a job that lasted for 17 years, during which I was responsible for slum clearance and administering the rebuilding of significant sections of Cincinnati. At Marianne's urging I was drawn to New York, where I resumed my efforts to improve cities by working for the state's Urban Development Corporation, a remarkable, innovative legislative creation

Epilogue

of Governor Nelson Rockefeller. This private-public benefit corporation produced vast quantities of mixed income housing and revitalized the downtowns of many of the cities in New York State. It was this taste of the private sector that morphed my love for cities into an edifice complex that also had the additional motivation of making money! I became a developer. It was in the course of this transformation that Marianne asked me to vacate the connubial premises, and I moved to a loft in trendy SoHo.

I soon met my second wife, Ruth Batchelor. She was a Hollywood maven, a well-known show-biz personality and a prolific songwriter. Ruth had two sons: Falcon had cystic fibrosis and required the steamy climate of the tropics, so he lived in Miami; Douglas was a preacher who lived in a Northern California wilderness. It was Falcon's desperate struggle with his disease that brought us to Miami and the decision to settle on Key Biscayne. Not many years after we moved, Falcon died. A few years later, in 1992, Ruth was diagnosed with multiple myeloma. She did not survive the year.

(A short time after that, I married my next-door neighbor, Joyce Indingaro, and we have now been married for nearly 20 years, but clearly that is another story.)

My marriage to Marianne proved to be fruitful. We had two children: Lisa and Erich, who are now, to say the least, fully grown, having both passed the age of 50!

Lisa is a graduate of Brown University, where she majored in linguistics, specializing in Chinese. After a tour in Malaysia with the Peace Corps, where she met her husband, Dallas Cooper, she returned to study computer science and started a long career in the field of information technology. She is currently employed in a very senior IT position by Green Mountain Coffee Roasters near her home in the Burlington region of Vermont. She has four children: Dana, who has graduated from college; twins Ari and Avery, and Ross.

Erich inherited more than his grandfather's name. He has made quite a name for himself as a cellist. He started playing at the age of seven and grew into adulthood with a cello as his constant companion. He concertizes throughout the world, spending a great deal of time on tour with Elizabeth Von Trapp. Between tours and busy performance schedules, he composes music and produces CDs, while at the same time growing garlic and raising livestock in the Quebec province of Canada, where he lives on a small

Epilogue

farm with his wife, AnnBruce, a ballet dancer. For me, his love of music has always mirrored that of my father's for the piano.

Delivering music is, unfortunately, something I never mastered; I cannot carry a tune, read music or play an instrument. But I do love to listen! Fortunately, with today's technology, Joyce, who is a techno-genius, has made sure that I have fingertip access to thousands of musical pieces and performances that bring the lifetime work of all the great composers and performers of our age to my ears, all reproduced in our home, in our car, on the beach, as if they emanate from a concert hall. But, as I consider myself to be only as sensitive as the next person, my appreciation of music is not really special. What *is* special is that this predilection toward music has continued to transcend generations. My grandson Avery plays the saxophone and has just started on the guitar. All this promises to materialize over time into the purchase of a huge amount of paraphernalia to preserve and reproduce all these sounds for friends and future generations. I am, of course, happy about this, and anxious to jump on the bandwagon to play Santa for the purchase of these toys.

My swimming obsession has also transcended the generations. My granddaughter, Dana, picked up this passion when she was in high school. She beat the best times I ever achieved by far. But for her career ambitions in the field of information technology, I like to think that she might have competed in the Olympics if she had continued with her swimming.

Ari has always been the jock of the family. He excels in soccer and baseball, but he also shares an interest in technology with Lisa, Avery and Dana. And then there is the last to arrive, Ross. He is really something special! He is frightfully precocious and adores gadgets of all kinds. He started at the tender age of six when, at his request, I bought him an altimeter-equipped watch. More recently, he sent me on a quest for an iPod-like gadget from Samsung, equipped with a GPS and Android apps. It is currently only marketed in Korea, and no one knows when it will come to the U.S. market. Ross is also enamored with explosives, and is always in the basement or backyard making things that blow up. We fervently hope that he does not follow Ted Kaczynski's example, but instead keeps focusing his experiments on homemade rockets, not lethal bombs.

Epilogue

And so, from the veranda of the quaint and unpretentious Key Biscayne Yacht Club, I now sit watching the sun set over Biscayne Bay. Arrays of large and small motor yachts and masts of sailing sloops loll in the foreground, with the Miami skyline in the background. It is the picture-perfect setting for me to muse over the trials and tribulations that brought me to this paradise. With the sun now nearing the end of its flawless descent beyond the horizon, I think about how unalterable its path has always been and, how very soon now, it will become a memory. While idly considering this, I am struck with the realization that, whether good or bad, the past cannot be resurrected; it must remain a memory, pristinely undisturbed, trapped in the private recesses of one's mind.

BIBLIOGRAPHY

Having experienced only a limited part of the Second World War as a civilian boy caught in occupied France, my interest in the subject led me to its deeper exploration. In the process, I have read, either in whole or in part, material from the following sources:

Asimov, Isaac. *Asimov's Chronology of the World*. New York: HarperCollins, 1991.
Fest, Joachim. *Speer: The Final Verdict*. New York: Harcourt, 1999.
Hart, B.H. Liddell. *History of the Second World War*. New York: Putnam, 1971.
Jackson, Julian. *France: The Dark Years, 1940–1944*. Oxford: Oxford University Press, 2001.
Kedward, H.R. *In Search of the Maquis*. New York: Oxford University Press, 1993.
Keegan, John. *The First World War*. New York: Alfred A. Knopf, 1999.
Keegan, John. *The Second World War*. New York: Penguin, 1989.
Macintyre, Ben. "Nietzsche and his Nazi Sister." *London Times*, March 28, 2008.
Massie, Robert K. *Dreadnought*. New York: Random House, 1991.
Roberts, Andrew. *The Storm of War*. New York: HarperCollins, 2011.
Shirer, William L. *The Rise and Fall of the Third Reich*. New York: Simon & Shuster, 1959.

I have also introduced quotations at appropriate points in the text to reinforce its meaning:

From A.J.P. Taylor in his book *Origins of The Second World War* (part of caption for photograph of father in World War I field uniform).
From an article by Ben Macintyre entitled "Nietzsche and his Nazi Sister" published in the *London Times* on March 28, 2008.
From the diary of a French soldier written May 5 to May 10, 1940 during the Blitzkrieg, from John Keegan's *The Second World War*.
From John Keegan's *The Second World War*.
A reference to Joseph Schmidt in a magazine advertisement. Name and date of publication not available.

In some cases, where sourcing was necessary and citations appropriate, they have been incorporated into the text for the convenience of the reader.

INDEX

Page numbers in *bold italics* indicate illustrations.

Abraham, Marcel 123
All Quiet on the Western Front, Erich Maria Remarque 9
Allied Forces 34, 44, 46–47, 49, 57, 62, 66, 77, 118, 120, 124, 131–133, 135–135, 149–150, 152, 197
Allies *see* Allied Forces
America 1, 14, 55, 67, 78, 83, 118, 133, 141, 142–143, 180–181, 183–184, 187, *187–188*, *189*, 190, 195–196, 198, 204, 206
American Jewish Joint Distribution Committee (JDC) 91
American Red Cross ix, 37, 58, 85, 116
Andorra 153–155, 159
Auriac-sur-Vendinelle, France 4, 92–93, 95–97, *98*, 99–112, 101, 103–105, 113–115, 117–118, 121–132, 134–138, 144, 148, 158, 163, 166, 170, 174, 177, 182, 203, 207, 210–211
Auschwitz ix, 15, 53, 85–87

Batchelor, Ruth 2, 213
Battle of Stalinrad 78, 133
Belgium 4, 12, 14, 28, 31–32, 34, *36*, 39, 42–47, 49, 51, 55, 60, 66, 117, 159, 163, 209
Berger, Stan x
Berlin, Germany 5, 8, 11–12, 14, 16, 18, 21–22, 51–52, 54, *55*, 150–151
Black Forest, Germany *see* Schwartzwaldt
Blitzkrieg 4, 35, 39, 40–45, 47–48, 53, 68, 73, 76, 93
Boivin, Pierre 1, 92
La Borie Orphanage, Limoges, France 164–164, *165*, 166–167, *168*, 169, 170–173, 175, 179
Brandenburg Gate 4–5, *6*, *7*, 93, 192
Breslau, Germany 52
Brown Shirts *see* Sturmabteilungen
Bruening, Heinrich 12

Brussels, Belgium 14, 19, *28*, 29–30, 36, *39*, 47, 49–51, 53–54, 56, 65, 85, 93, 209–210

Candide, François-Marie Arouet deVoltaire 4, 136, 141
Canet internment camp 60, 63–64
Canet-Plage, France 57, 60, 62–64
Cardenas, Sergio xi
CARE *see* Cooperative for Assistance and Relief Everywhere
Cassou, Jean 123
Catholic 31, 65, 92, 95, 113, 117, 123, 159, 166
"Chanson d'Automne," Paul Verlaine 125, 134
château *see* Auriac-sur-Vendinelle
Cincinnati 1, 27
City College of New York (CCNY) 2, 143, 200, 202
Cohen, Albert *see* Albert C. Werner
Cohen, Liselotte (Lotte) *see* Liselotte (Lotte) Werner
collaborators 11, 62, 65–66, 76–77, 80–81, 90, 93, 119–120, 123, 148–149, 151, 155, 157
Le College des Minimes 179
Combes, Claude 211
Combes, Marie-Christine 211
Comte, Auguste 113, 166–167
Conseil de Famille 159, 161
Cooper, Ari Kory ix, 213–214
Cooper, Avery Kory ix, 213–214
Cooper, Dallas 213
Cooper, Dana Kory ix, 213–214
Cooper, Ross Kory ix, 213–214
Cooperative for Assistance and Relief Everywhere (CARE) 180–181
Coret, Maurice 114, 203
Crowe, Bill xi
Crowe, Carol xi

Index

Cyrano de Bergerac, Edmond Rostand 144

D-Day 118, 120, 131, 134, 135
de Bonnefoy, Contesse Alix 54, 91–97, 99, 102, 105–106, 110–111, 123–124, 126, 128, 130–132, 136–137, 148, 152–153, 155, *156*, 157–159, 161–163, 167, 170, 174, 176, 182, 188–190, *196*, 201, 207
de Bonnefoy, Comte Antoine 92–93, 99–100, 105–107, 110–111, 118 119, 121–122, 124–126, 131–132, 134, 148–149, 173, 177, 182, 207, 211
de Bonnefoy, Marthou 105, 110, *111*, 153, 155–*156*, 159, 175, *196*, 207–208, 210–211
de Bonnefoy, Olivier 207, 210–211
de Bonnefoy family x, 91–93, 96, 101, 103–105, 110, 113, 115, 122, 128, 134, 152, 157–159, 161, 164, 166–167, 173–175, 179, 184, 187, 192, *196*, 211
de Gaulle, Charles 77, 107, 120, 132, 149
Denison, Nancy x
Descartes, René 6
Douai, France 56, 92
Dreadnaught, Robert K. Massey 17
Dreyfus Affair 18
Dubois, Monsieur and Madame 89–92

Ecole des Garçons, Revel, France 137–139, 148–149, 158–159, 161–162, 164–165
Engglenger, Pierre 1, 64, 68–69
Eschelbourne family 99, 110–111, 124, 128, 135
Evian, France 162–163

Flemish 28, 30–31
The Fog of War, Robert McNamara 3, 58
foie gras 75, 100–101, 108, 128, 144, 148, 170, 212
Forces Française de l'Interieur (FFI) *see* French Resistance
Fort Eben Emael 45
France 3–4, 8, 11–12, 14, 17, 34, 41–44, 46, 51, 53, 56–69, *70*, 62–63, 76–78, 80–81, 84–85, 91–92, 95, *98*, 106–107, 117–121, 123, 129, 131–134, 138, 140–143, 146, 148–149, 154–155, 157, 162–164, *165*, *168*, 170, 175–182, *183*, 187, 189, *196*, 198, 203, 208, 211–212
Franco, Generalissimo Francisco 67, 78
Free Zone (Zone Libre) *see* Vichy France
French Red Cross ix, 85

French Resistance 77, 93, 106–107, 117–125–126, 128, 131–134, 148–149, 154, 174, 184
Frostig, Michal Lublin ix, 205–207
der Füehrer *see* Hitler, Adolf

Gare d'Austerlitz, France 57–58
Garrig, Albertine xi, 100, 107–114, 117, 126–129, 148, *196*, 203
Garrig, Elie 100, 114, 203
German Army *see* Wehrmacht
Germany 4–9, 12–14, 16–20, *23*, 24–25, 39, 43–45, 47, 49, 51–53
Gestapo 66
Glassberg, Ronit Lublin ix, 206–207
Goebbels, Joseph 21, 66, 132
The Green Table, Kurt Jooss 19
Guardianship Conclave *see* Conseil de Famille
Guderian, Heinz Wilhelm 41–43, 45, 150
Guernica, Pablo Picasso 47–48
Gurs, France 53–54

Les Hirondelles Orphanage, Lyon, France 179–180, 182, 184–185, 187
History of the World, Isaac Asimov 8
Hitler, Adolf 4–5, 8–9, 11–13, 19, 34–35, 41–45, 47, 67, 68, 76–77, 118, 127, 130–131, 133–134, 151, 204

International Red Cross 57–58, 91
Iron Cross 24, 51, 63, 209
Israel *see* Palestine

Jew *see* Jewish
Jewish xi, 5–6, 8, 12–13, 18, 22, 32, 49, 52, 63–65, 67–68, 76–78, 85, 90–94, 123–124, 131, 133, 158–159, 166–162, 165–167, 169–171, 175, 177, 184, 201, 203–204, 207
Jews *see* Jewish

Key Biscayne, Florida *see* Miami
kismet xi, 1, 4, 49–50, 93, 105, 136, 152, 173, 183, 203
Klein, Danny xi
Klein, Joyce xi
Kory, AnnBruce 214
Kory, Erich ix, 2, 115, 213
Kory, Joyce Indingaro ix, xi, 2, 133, 141, 177, 206, 209–214
Kory, Lisa ix, 2, 115, 213–214
Kory, Marianne 2, *196*, 202, 204, 207–208, 212–213

220

Index

Korytow, Poland 54
Korytowski, Erich ix, x, 2–3, 7–16, 18–20, *21*, 22, *23*, 24, *25*, 26–27, *28*, 29–34, *36*, 37–39, 40, 49–52, 54–57, 60–64, 66–69, *70*, 71, 73–74, 78–80, 82–89, 92–94, 111, 116, 127, 130, 135, 157–159, 161, 163–164, 172, 182–184, 187, 193, 203–205, 209, 213–214
Korytowski, Fritz 54, *55*, 205
Korytowski, Lillie *see* Lillie Korytowski Markowitz
Korytowski, Lily Neustadt ix, x, 2–3, 5, 7–14, *15*, 16–22, *23*, 24–40, 49–52, *53*, *55*, 56–57, 60–64, 66–69, *70*, 71, 73–75, 78–80, 82–89, 92–94, 111, 127, 130, 135, 157–159, 161, 163–164, 166, 172, 182–184, 187, 193, 201, 203, 205–206, 209, 212
Korytowski, Liselotte (Lotte) *see* Liselotte (Lotte) Werner
Korytowski, Lucy 54–55, 205
Korytowski, Peter 1, 203, 205

La Bounce, Jules 89
La Bounce, Simone 89
Languedoc, France 57, 95, 102, 110, 119, 154, 176
Le Curé, Monsieur 93
Le Havre, France 4, 188
Leopold III 28, 45
Limoges, France 164, *165*, 167, *168*, 173, 175, 180
Lower Silesia, Poland 52
Lublin, Heinrich (Heine) 53–54, 205–206
Lublin, Kethe Neustadt *53*, 205–206
Luftwaffe 40
Lycée Gay Lussac 164, 172–173
Lyon, France 107, 175–176, 179–180, 182, 187–188

Mane, France x, 68–69, *70*, 73, 76, 78–80, 83, 85, 89, 182, *183*, 211
Maquis de la Montagne Noire *see* French Resistance
Maquisards *see* French Resistance
Markowitz (Martin), Bernie 205
Markowitz (Martin), Larry 205
Markowitz, Lillie Korytowski 54–55, 204
Martin, Deena Werner *see* Deena Werner
Matkov, Becky x
Matkov, Tom x

SS *Mauretania* 4, 188–189, 195
Mein Kampf see Hitler, Adolf
Meslin Leveque, Belgium 56
Miami, Florida 1–2, 206, 213, 215
Mila 18, Leon Uris 133
Milhaud, Darius 123, 189–192
Milice see collaborator
Miller Jones, Malcolm xi
Miller Jones, Ruth Ann xi
Montreux, Switzerland 162–163
Munich Beer Hall Putsch 8
Mussolini, Benito 8

National Socialism *see* Nazi
National Socialist German Worker's Party *see* Nazi
Nazi x, 6–7, 9–11–14, 18–19, 21, 30, 43, 49, 51, 55, 63–66, 68, 73, 76, 78, 83, 91, 94, 107, 118–119, 122, 124, 127, 132–132, 135, 150, 153, 163, 166–167, 177
Neustadt, Gertrud (Trude) 52, *53*, *55*, 206–207
Neustadt, Kethe *see* Kethe Neustadt Lublin
Neustadt, Leo *52*, *53*, 54
Neustadt, Magda 52, *53*, 206
Neustadt, Margareta *52*, *53*, 54
Neustadt, Rosel (Rosa) 52, *53*, 206–207
"The New Colossus," Emma Lazarus 192
New York City 1, 4, 48, 67, *183*, 185, 188, 192, 195, 197–198, *199*, 200–202, 206, 208, 212–213
Nietzsche, Elisabeth 9–10
Nietzsche, Friedrich 9–10
"Nietzsche and His Nazi Sister," Ben Macintyre 9–10
The Nightmare Years, William L. Shirer 13
Normandy Landing *see* D-Day

Oeuvre de Secours aux Enfants (OSE) 162, 164–169, 171–173, 175, 184, 187, 203, 207
Oncle Nino *see* Comte Antoine de Bonnefoy
orphanage 4, 161–162, 164, 202–203; *see also* La Borie; Les Hirondelles
OSE *see* Oeuvre de Secours aux Enfants
Ostend, Belgium *36*, 37, 116

Palestine ix, 14, 18, 52, 53, 55, 161, 164, 166–167, 169–170, 172, 184, 203–204, 206, 207
parents *see* Erich Korytowski; Lily Neustadt Korytowski

Index

Paris, France 57, 62, 107, 123, 141, 157, 174, 176, 188, **196**, 208–209, 211
partisans *see* French Resistance
Perpignan, France 57–58, 60
Petain, Maréchal Philippe 62–63, 76–77, 119
Pyrenees, France 53, 67–68, 78, 80, 84, 141, 153–154, 159

Reichstag 12–13
Resistance *see* French Resistance
Revel, France 92, 136–139, 148, 150–151, 157–164
The Rise and Fall of the Third Reich, William L. Shirer 13
Romania 14, 55, 204
Rotte de Neuville, Madame 91–92
Roullet, Dominique 207, 211
Roullet, Guy 207–208
Roullet, Marthou de Bonnefoy *see* Marthou de Bonnefoy
Russo-Finnish War 34

SA *see* Sturmabteilungen
St. Cyprien, France 57, 60
St. Girons, France 68, 80, 82–83, 114, 127, 153, 197
"Les sanglots longs des violons, ... Blessent mon coeur d'une langueur monotone" *see* "Chanson d'Automne"
Schmelzinger, Aviva ix, 52, 207
Schmidt, Joseph 20–21
Schutzstaffel 4, 14, 78, 85, 119, 127–128, 131
Schwartzwaldt, Germany 152–153
The Second World War, John Keegan 44, 46
SlaughterHouse-Five, Kurt Vonnegut 134
Soula, Robert x, 73–74, 182–183, 211–212
SS *see* Schutzstaffel
Statue of Liberty 4, 192, **193**
Stewart, John xi
Strauss, Ted 200
Sturmabteilungen 13

Tante Lily *see* Contesse Alix de Bonnefoy
Tantishe 105, 107, 110
Third Reich *see* Nazi
Three Penny Opera, Kurt Weil 9
Toulouse, France x, 57, 64–66–69, 76, 79–80, 89–92, 105, 135–137, 167, 169, 174–177, 179, 182, 207–208
Treaty of Versailles 8, 10, 12, 45

Ullmen, Jean 187, 199–200
United States of America *see* America
USA *see* America

V-E Day 151, 152, 157
V-J Day 157
Vendinelle River *see* Auriac-sur-Vendinelle
Vichy, France 58, 61–63, 64–66, 76–78, 90, 93, 118–119, 123, 133, 135, 137–138, 142, 151
von Hindenberg, Paul 9, 12
von Papen, Franz 12
von Schleicher, Kurt 12

Waffen SS *see* Schutzstaffel
Wannsee Conference 133
Waterloo, Belgium 36, 56
Wehrmacht 43–44, 47, 78, 83–85, 120
Weimar Republic 8, 14, 25
Werner, Albert C. (Cohen) **55**, 184–185, 195–197, 201, 203–204
Werner, Deena 205
Werner (Cohen), Liselotte (Lotte) Korytowski 54, **55**, 184–185, 195, 197–198, 201, 203–205
Wilhelm II, Kaiser 6, 13, 17
Witt, Malcolm xi
Witt, Marsha ix
World War I 7–8, 17, 19, 22–23, **25**, 34, 41–42, 44–45, 49, 52, 54, 62–63, 106, 121, 146
World War II x, 1–4, 28, 38, 44, 106, 133, 166, 206

Zionists 4, 18, 161–162, 166, 169

www.ingramcontent.com/pod-product-compliance
Ingram Content Group UK Ltd.
Pitfield, Milton Keynes, MK11 3LW, UK
UKHW041949140426
5217IPUK00014B/712